Food Purchasing and Preparation

Also available from Cassell

Doolan: *Applying Numbers and IT in Leisure and Tourism*
Jones and Merricks: *The Management of Foodservice Operations*
Jones and Newton: *Hospitality and Catering: A Closer Look*
Julyan: *Sales and Service for the Wine Professional*

Food Purchasing and Preparation

Roy Briggs

CASSELL

London and New York

Cassell

Wellington House
125 Strand
London WC2R 0BB

370 Lexington Avenue
New York
NY 10017-6550

First published 2000

British Library Cataloguing-in-Publication Data
A catalogue record for this book is available from the British Library.

ISBN 0-304-33866-4

Typeset by Hart McLeod, Cambridge

Printed and bound in Great Britain by Redwood Books, Trowbridge, Wiltshire

Contents

9 Salads   242

Single salads   242

Compound salads – Meat-based compound salads – Fruit-based
compound salads – Vegetable-based compound salads – Fish-based
compound salads – Salades chaudes/tièdes (hot/warm salads)
– Healthy eating: government guidelines

10 Buffets   255

Introduction – Room layout and arrangement – Assembly – Service

Buffet styles   257

Finger buffets – Fork or carved buffets – Fully-decorated buffets
– Costing and menu planning – Buffet centrepieces – Poultry and
game – Presentation of smaller cuts and entrées – Guidelines for the
decoration of cold buffets – Guidelines for glazing with aspic jelly
– Decorating cold buffets items – Colours and preparation
– Vegetarian buffet items

Index   275

Introduction

The larder section of a catering business – the area responsible for food purchasing and preparation – is known as the 'engine room' of the kitchen, and as the name implies, plays an essential role. The ordering and supplying of the correct items goes hand in hand with providing a consistent and high quality service which in turn means a profitable business. The aim of this book is to give chefs, managers, suppliers and students working in the hospitality and catering industry up-to-date information about what is required to run an efficient kitchen operation. The issue of food purchasing is covered in detail: guidelines are given as to the correct ordering of quantities/size of produce, as well as what to look for in terms of quality and freshness and how to store items correctly. In addition, throughout the book I have included recipes which will hopefully act as a guide to the best use of a range of food items. As well as the traditional menu fare – and in recognition of today's concerns with a healthier diet – vegetarian and healthy alternatives are also included.

There are many cookery books available, but very few go into detail about what is required prior to the actual cooking process: this book is an attempt to fill that gap. In *Food Purchasing and Preparation* I show how the key to maintaining quality, consistency and profitability in a catering establishment lies in the efficient purchasing, storage and preparation of food products. I outline specifically what the caterer/purchaser should expect from a supplier in terms of freshness and preparation of produce, as well as giving detailed information with regard to menu planning, and correct costing and budget control.

The 'GIGO' factor (garbage in, garbage out) can be the downfall of many businesses in the catering trade – both for suppliers and purchasers. This is often due to companies not taking the time to research and set purchasing specifications and to establish rules for the correct storage, safe handling and preparation of food items. And this is not helped by the fact that much of the information that is available is often out of date or unclear. To make matters worse, the technical terms that are used by suppliers are often different from those used by caterers, leading in some cases to confusion. This book explains and simplifies those terms so that both suppliers and caterers can be sure of supplying/receiving the right commodities. In addition, specific purchasing information for fish and shellfish, meat, poultry and game is given in Chapters 4, 5 and 6 – grouped under three main headings for easy reference. These are:

Specification – a clear description of what to expect in terms of quality; the different cuts and grades that are available; and the correct quantity or weight to order/provide.

Description – a user-friendly outline which gives a brief description of each commodity.

Uses – a guide to the cooking and menu planning of specific food items.

Also, where appropriate the percentages of losses during preparation are given as a way of helping to work out the correct quantities that are needed per portion, and thus avoid wastage.

The job of a catering professional involves far more than just food preparation and cooking. New regulations to do with health and safety, including food storage and hygiene and hot and cold holding, mean that caterers need to have strict working systems in place so as to ensure a safe, legal and successful business. An introduction to the health and safety regulations and how to implement them is outlined in Chapter 2; examples of the relevant documentation are also included. Chapter 3 covers all areas of food storage, including the relevant health and safety procedures, stock controlling, receipt and storage, and security.

The final section of the book, Chapters 6 to 10, is an invaluable reference guide which outlines the basic recipes and skills needed for preparations, hors-d'oeuvre, salads and buffet food and presentation. As a chef with almost forty years experience in the business, I have often wondered why it is that cookbooks – even those which are aimed at professional cooks – generally give amounts for only four people. Trying to multiply the recipes to suit larger numbers often leads to confusion and disappointing results. With this in mind, the recipes in these chapters, and throughout the book generally, are given in quantities more suited to the professional cook – and all have been thoroughly tested to remove any guesswork.

This book is written by someone who has first-hand knowledge of the industry and who understands the day-to-day problems faced by caterers and suppliers. It is hoped that *Food Purchasing and Preparation* will prove useful to students, caterers and suppliers alike, giving a comprehensive guide to an oft-overlooked area of the catering industry.

ONE

Controlling Resources

Introduction

All catering establishments are liable for the food and drink which is sold on their premises and must abide by various regulations such as the Food Safety Act 1990, Food Hygiene Regulations 1970, the Licensing Act 1964 and the Trades Description Act 1968. To run a successful catering enterprise means making quality and safety the main priority. Many catering outlets go bankrupt due to a lack of consistent quality, and one of the main causes lies in not having the foresight to keep up a good level of service with often non-standard ingredients (for example, different varieties of potato). Inexperienced supervisors or caterers often have difficulty balancing quality levels with the cost to the business. Purchasing specifications can contribute a great deal to achieving this aim, but it is only the start in a process which includes good health and safety practices, customer satisfaction and adherence to set budgets.

Many establishments in the catering industry sacrifice a part of their control circle, be it quality, health and safety or consistent standards, for a short-term fix. This can lead to such problems as the buying in of poor quality commodities and the under- or over-stocking of items. In turn, this can result in a situation whereby the business is forced to play 'catch up' and in order to meet one objective others are sacrificed, to the detriment of the business.

I have lost count of the number of catering outlets that have ruined what was a promising business by dismissing the importance of keeping rigidly to planned procedures or by not having the proper procedures in place. For instance, a lack of purchasing specifications will mean that a caterer is at the mercy of its suppliers, and may receive items that are profitable to the supplier rather than to the caterer; for example meat that has been cheaply or incorrectly produced, this includes meat that has been hung for too short a time or has come from animals reared on poor feed. Another thing to look out for is meat that requires a large amount of trimming. A favourite with unscrupulous butchers is to supply half fronts instead of correctly cut shoulders of lamb; these cheaper cuts include a large percentage of middle-neck, bone and scrag-end, for which the caterer pays the same price as a premium cut. Other common examples include the supply of stale fish, vegetables with a short shelf-life (due to poor or over-long storage) and substituted items, such as cheaper versions of frozen goods. Thus, portion control, hygiene and safety, menu planning, customer satisfaction, budget control and ultimately profits can be jeopardized because of what the supervisor accepts on delivery.

Quality

This can be defined as customer satisfaction, the carrying out of correct and consistent procedures, maintaining high standards, and attention to detail with regards to health and safety.

A professionally-run organization will adopt and monitor systems so as to ensure quality and more important, safety. Caterers are required by law to show 'due diligence'.

'Due diligence'

This means that an employer must keep a record of how procedures are implemented and monitored in order to prevent potentially harmful situations from occurring. These systems are often called company policies or house standards, and should clearly state:

What is the objective of the policy
Why the policy is in place
How it is to be achieved and monitored
Who is responsible for its implementation
Where the policy is to be implemented
When checks are to take place

It is the employer's statutory duty to provide evidence that all staff are aware of company policies, the standards that are required, and that the policies are implemented, monitored and supervised. A good example of one policy with which most caterers are familiar is the monitoring of refrigeration temperatures, but there are many more guidelines which need to be followed, starting with the receiving of goods. No matter how thorough in-house safety policies are, nothing can make up for goods that have not been checked and monitored on receipt (for more details on this procedure see Chapter 2, Critical Control Points, p. 27). In this respect, all staff should receive the proper training and this is often carried out in the form of an induction programme for new staff. This should be implemented immediately on their arrival, and monitored and recorded so as to be ready for inspection by environmental health officers.

Storage requirements

All deliveries should be checked to see that the correct amount has been supplied and the items are in good condition. This includes tinned foods which should be checked for any blown, dented, damaged or rusty tins: these should be rejected, as should ones with short or expired use-by dates. Careful attention should be paid to the food stores and to stock levels.

Food stores

Food stores should be well ventilated, have good lighting, be dry and cool and vermin proof. Above all, they should be cleaned regularly. As far as it is practical, packaging should be removed prior to storage. All food should be kept above floor level and away from heat and moisture, such as sunlight, hot water pipes and condensation. Any spillages must be cleaned up immediately.

Stock levels

I recommend always stipulating stock levels in all areas, the reason being that over-stocking can cause a variety of problems, including theft, loss due to stock going out of date, lack of space and cost of storage. Dry food stores, fridges and stock-holding areas such as cupboards, all benefit from having set levels of supplies. A chef or supervisor who lists the maximum levels at the start of the day will find that s/he has much more control over the monitoring of usage. And a check-list for each storage area which states what should be in place at the start of service will assist staff in their preparation and means that stock levels can be monitored.

The following points should be standard practice:

- The receiving area, times and correct temperatures should be specified and confirmed with suppliers.
- A nominated person should be responsible for accepting the delivery, for example the head chef, manager, supervisor or stores manager.
- The person who is to receive the delivery should be notified. Having two people available is often an advantage.
- Items should be checked against specification, the order book and the receipt.
- Check for temperatures, expiry dates (shelf-life), quality, damage, substitution of different types or brands of item.
- The delivery area should be safe, clean and contamination-free.
- Remove non-essential packaging, especially absorbent materials such as cardboard. Plastic wrap and vacuum-packed items benefit from being wiped over with a sanitizer.
- Transfer items to designated storage areas as soon as possible. Time limits should be set for transferring items to correct storage.
- From time to time safety checks should be made on delivery personnel and vehicles.
- No food should be accepted if any of the above criteria are not met.
- Fill in documentation on recorded temperatures, checks on vehicles and delivery personnel.
- All documentation should be kept for a minimum of three months for inspection by environmental health officers.

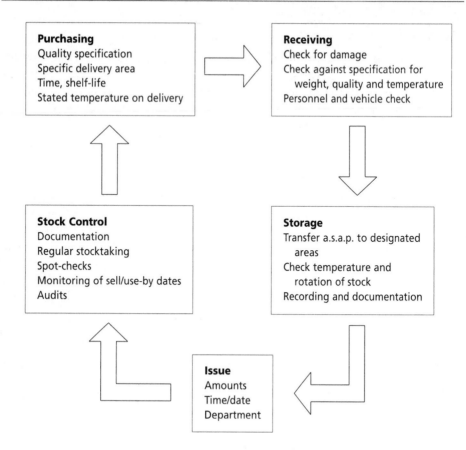

Figure 1.1 **A stock control flow chart**

Receiving areas and procedures

A number of important factors should be considered with regard to the receiving area. The following list is a general guide.

- ✓ The area should be clean and away from such items as chemicals and cleaning materials.
- ✓ It should be correctly equipped; ideally this should include a table, spring balance scales, a temperature probe, sterile wipes, a knife and storage containers.
- ✓ It should have the correct documentation; a list of suppliers' telephone numbers, copies of orders, a returns book, a folder containing purchasing specifications and acceptable substitute items/brands. In addition, there should be checklists for vehicle and delivery personnel, lists of acceptable temperatures on receipt and a goods inward book, which records what is delivered, any alterations, substitutions, or returned items, when, (date/time), what quantity, and who received the delivery. In a busy kitchen it is enough to confirm that the goods were received in good condition and other details such as cost, VAT, etc. can be dealt with in the control office.

Mark downs book

Occasionally, due to such factors as availability, weather conditions and so on, items which do not fully meet the desired standards may be accepted for a reduced price. This should be recorded in the mark downs book and passed to the control office to prevent the supplier from invoicing for the full amount, a confirmation signature from the person who made the delivery is also required. This should not include items that are the incorrect temperature, or anything else that may in any way compromise safety policies.

Food delivery, hygiene and temperature checklist								
Supplier............................								
Inspection carried out by.......................				Signature...........................				
Position..........................				Establishment........................				
Date	Time	Vehicle and Temperature	Personnel	Fresh meat, fish, poultry, etc: –2 – 2°C	Category A: 0 – 3°C or below.	Category B: 1 – 4°C or below.	Frozen food: –18 – –22°C or below.	Comments and action ✓ accept ✗ reject
Category A: All chilled foods, including cooked meat, bacon, dairy products, desserts, prepared salads								
Category B: Margarine/butter, prepared vegetables, prepared leaf salads, hard cheeses								

Figure 1.2 **Example of a food delivery, hygiene and temperature checklist**

Goods inward log

Below is an example of a goods inward log; this keeps track of all items entering the organization.

Day/time delivered	Supplier and items delivered	Total cost (VAT if applicable)	Returns	Credit note received	Checked by	Delivery note received/ amended

Figure 1.3 **A goods inward log**

Transportation of items to the storage areas

Moving items from the delivery to the storage areas should be completed within a set time and done so safely. A hazards analysis should be conducted to assess any risks, for example exposure to chemicals, the lifting of heavy items, the safe use of trolleys, lifts, etc. Potential hazards between areas can include: stairs, doors and shelves.

Problem-solving

The majority of problems can usually be settled at the time of delivery, and this is one reason for having a list of telephone numbers of suppliers readily available. A record should be kept of any discrepancies or deviations from set standards to allow for monitoring, and if these reoccur regularly then it may be necessary to alter your specifications to suit the changes made by the supplier.

Discrepancies

These include, the incorrect grade, quality or size of item; delivery of the wrong amount; incorrect prices; stale or damaged items. In the first instance, communication with your supplier should be sufficient to deal with the problem. But if the supplier fails to meet the required standards, alternatives should be investigated which may mean changing suppliers. It is always good practice to have two or three nominated suppliers in place should this be necessary. However, arbitrarily switching suppliers can often cause more problems than it resolves, so try to build a relationship with your supplier on an amicable and mutually beneficial basis. The supplier should be in no doubt, however, that you have the opportunity to change if necessary.

When a supplier fails to meet the required standards it is essential that problems are solved in a systematic way. First, check your own documentation, for example if and when the item was ordered, the amount/sizes ordered and the required specification. Then discuss the problem with your supplier; the problem may be beyond their control, for example bad weather can restrict the availability of fish or shellfish. Consider your alternatives, for example the supplier may suggest other options such as frozen items or you could use another supplier. If you are part of a larger group, it may be possible to borrow items from other units. Even if you are not part of a group, it is still good practice to be on friendly terms with other chefs/supervisors in your area as information can be exchanged to do with availability, quality, price, and so forth, and being able to borrow items in an emergency is mutually advantageous.

Record how you solved the problem and inform your supplier that you will be monitoring the situation. Also ask to be kept informed of any other changes that may occur, preferably in advance. Finally, as already mentioned, keep a list of suppliers' telephone numbers, along with the names of people to contact should it become necessary to resolve matters at a higher level.

Specialist security procedures

Staff should be made aware that there are policies and procedures in place within the company to prevent stealing. The following table gives a list of measures that will help deter staff from helping themselves.

Table 1.1 **Ways to deter staff from stealing**

Action	Result
Keep all unsupervised areas locked	Denied access means denied opportunity
Control access to essential areas	Limiting access shortens the list of suspects
Monitor the issue of keys	Can pinpoint culprits if items go missing by who has access to keys
Regularly check waste bins/bags	Deters staff from placing items in bins/bags for removal later
Allow only nominated people to be key holders and to have responsibility for stock levels	Highlights responsibility and encourages vigilance
Be vigilant	Acts as a deterrent
Do not allow personal items such as bags or shopping into secure areas	Prevents items from being hidden among personal items
Do not allow unauthorized people into secure areas	Often, people who are encouraged to 'help themselves' will do just that
Carry out regular spot checks on stock in fridges, freezers, etc.	Deters people stealing if checks are in place
Set maximum stock levels for all areas with notices explaining the penalties for theft	This makes it easier to check what should be left at the end of a shift
Keep staff lockers separate from changing areas. Place lockers in open view	Prevents items being slipped into lockers for retrieval at a later date
Train staff and make them use documentation, such as wastage books	Prevents excuses such as, 'The item was burnt so we threw it away'.
Make issuing and receiving of goods a two-person activity	Allows for cross-checking

The best way to prevent theft is to give the impression to staff, suppliers and delivery personnel that it would be impossible to breach procedures without getting caught.

Table 1.1 is based on four main strategies:

Prevention, deterrence, monitoring and detection

Prevention through not allowing the opportunity to steal. Trained staff should be responsible for receiving goods.

Deterrence by putting adequate systems in place and by encouraging a good attitude among staff.

Monitoring of systems, personnel and hardware such as keys, access, etc.

Detection by all the above plus random checks, stocktaking and supervision.

As head chef, I would often make a surprise visit on my usual day off to keep a check on procedures. I was always astounded by how many discrepancies I would discover, such as short weights and poor quality or stale items from suppliers who thought they could slip things through behind my back! But staff can also lapse, and returning early from a break can highlight such problems as:

- 'Staff feasts'. Staff taking advantage and bingeing on food which would normally be strictly controlled.
- Keys left with junior members of staff to lock up so that more senior staff can depart early.
- Sweet trolleys being decimated at the end of service.
- Excess items of food removed from the premises by employees.

Date	Type of stock wasted	Unit and number/ portions	Code or reason	Entered by	Confirmed by supervisor

Figure 1.4 **Example of a wastage book**

Codes

1. Damaged/display goods
2. Problems during cooking
3. Problems during preparation
4. Poor storage
5. Over-production
6. Theft
7. Freezer/fridge problems
8. Past use-by date
9. Cancellation or client shortage
10. Non-specified goods received
11. Staff meals/sell-offs
12. Hospitality
13. Client credited – poor quality
14. Client credited – poor service

* Other (please state)

Food safety alerts

It is important when a type, brand or particular batch of food is declared unsafe or contaminated, for example eggs or beef on the bone, that a notice is posted and all staff responsible are informed. Below is an example of a food safety alert record sheet.

FOOD SAFETY ALERT

Date: _____   Information received regarding: _____

Notification received from _____

The following is regarded as unsafe due to a:

Withdrawal by manufacturer/supplier   ☐

Food hazard warning   ☐

Emergency control order   ☐

Food /brand _____

Supplier /manufacturer /importer _____

Batch /code mark _____

Pack /size /weight _____

Reason for alert _____

No further orders, deliveries, or usage, of this product are
to be undertaken until this notice is cancelled.

Action to be taken if the above is already in stock _____

_____

For further information contact _____   Signed _____

Figure 1.5 **Example of a food safety alert record sheet**

Documentation

All invoices need to be checked against the goods inward book and the delivery note. Not doing this could result in paying the supplier twice – once from the delivery note and once from the invoice.

Credit notes

It is sometimes the case that a credit note is not received for returned goods within the time between stocktakes. This has the effect of depleting one period's value and enhancing the next. Provision must be made in the goods inward book for this credit to be included in the stocktake. The credit note should be matched against this provision when it arrives.

Display stock (see also Chapter 2, p. 26)

Display stock includes such things as fruit baskets, examples of dishes prepared for display to the customer or items used in self-service areas, for example breakfast counters. It should be established which display items are to be included in the stocktake. Stock which is not to be included should be entered in the wastage book and signed for by an authorized person.

Damaged stock

Stock that is damaged is included in the stocktake until it is off-set with a credit note from the supplier or written-off by means of the wastage book.

Forward orders

These are orders that have been placed but not yet delivered. Even if an invoice is received, these should not be included in the stocktake until they are entered in the goods inward book and a delivery note is received.

Internal transfers

Transfers between departments, such as liquor from the bar to the kitchen, must be recorded. The kitchen should treat the transfer requisition as a credit note and the bar should regard it as an invoice.

Requisition orders

A requisition order should be completed for all issued stock and should contain the following information:

A code or sequence number: All requisitions should be in duplicate form and numbered. The top copy is sent to the control office, or in the case of internal transfers, to the relevant department, then to the control office. The duplicate copy is kept by the department/person placing the order.

Department or unit/person ordering: In a large organization there may be more than one unit or department, such as the main kitchen, the larder department, the pastry kitchen, the staff canteen, and so on. Separate requisition orders means that usage can be monitored.

Date of issue: This should be the date when the stock is to be issued, not the date it was ordered.

Time: Recording the time of issue allows for more accurate monitoring of security.

Authorization: This may be the department head, or, for example when ordering several cases of champagne from the bar to the kitchen, a manager responsible. In either case, the authorizing person should know the reason for the requisition, the amounts which are usually needed, and the levels of stock normally held.

Brand/type: For example, 'strong bread flour', 'Hovis' or 'Moët et Chandon' champagne.

Unit and number of items: For example, ten x 20 kg sacks; one case (12 bottles).

Issued by/received by: This is essential for monitoring and security, and in the event of any questions which may arise.

Number _____		Time _____		
Dept _____		Date ordered _____		
Ordered by _____		Authorization _____		
Date issued _____				

Item	Brand/Type	Unit and no	Issued	Received

Figure 1.6 **Example of a requisition order**

Stocktaking

A stocktake is the counting and quantifying of all the commodities purchased by an organization that have not yet been used: this includes stock waiting to be returned to the supplier, display items, contents of cupboards, fridges, freezers and so on. The main purpose of a stocktake is to calculate the gross profit of a business by creating an opening stock level. This should give valuable information on such crucial matters as:

- The amount of money which is spent on commodities, i.e., the value of the stock in place.
- The demand for and use of individual items, thus enabling the monitoring of portion control, waste, popularity and security.
- The monitoring of stock levels and turnover, e.g., if an outlet is using only one case per week of a commodity that is available for delivery on a weekly basis, why, then, are there ten cases in stock? The majority of the stock should be acquired on a high turn-over basis so that capital is freed up for other uses, rather than lying dormant in the corner of the store. If over-stocking does occur, then the amounts and sell-by dates should be passed to the chef and/or supervisor so that menus or specials can be created to rectify the problem.

Organizing a store

It goes without saying that a store should be clean and tidy, but it is important to do more than just tidy up once in a while. All stock should have individual designated areas, with the same or similar items grouped together. As well, units of the same size should be stacked together, i.e., A5 tins together and not hidden behind A10s. Labels for example should be turned to face the front so as to avoid confusing one item with another, for example A5 tins of tomato puree for A5 tins of tomatoes. Stacking items in standard rows, such as A5s, A10s or A20s, can help with counting and makes it easy to spot when an item has been removed.

All opened packaging should be removed, and items stacked or amalgamated into full cases: In addition, the store should be arranged in a convenient order, e.g., alphabetical order and in a clockwise direction and with a guide to the layout. This will make stocktaking easier and help to ensure that items are not missed.

Stock rotation

This is vital to the running of a profitable organization as over-stocking can tie-up capital. Redundant stock due to expired sell-by dates or general deterioration is even worse as you have lost not just the item, but also the potential profit from that item. Even if a use can be found for stale items, such as staff meals, this can make-up for lost profits due to poor organization. The following points will help to ensure this does not happen:

- Last in last out – all new stock should be placed behind existing stock.
- Set average stock levels, e.g., the amount used in a regular month. Levels can be increased at certain periods, for example at Christmas.
- Coloured tabs are an effective and inexpensive way of differentiating between batches and for rotating batches of items, e.g. red for the oldest, then yellow, and blue for new stock.
- Regular spot checks help to ensure that systems are being followed; good staff training also helps.

Hazardous stock

Stock should be divided up into hazardous and non-hazardous items and staff should be trained to differentiate between the two. Designated areas should be set aside for hazardous items which comply with the instructions on the labels. Examples of hazardous stock include chemicals, bleach, pesticides and contaminated foods (see Chapter 2, COSHH, p. 32).

Stock recording

Stock is recorded on stock sheets which list the numbers and unit, for example litres, A10 tins, packets, etc. Bin cards which record the levels of individual stock items have largely been superceded by computerized systems as they are labour intensive and require regular manual updating.

Pricing policy

In order to establish a value on any stock which is held, an agreed pricing policy must be in place, this applies both to manual and to computerized systems. The price for the same item can vary over a period of time, so it is important to have a consistent pricing policy.

The three alternatives in general use are:

(i)   **Latest price** This would seem to be the most obvious choice, however prices can go down as well as up (due to special offers, promotions, etc.) and if items were purchased previously at the 'full price' then the value of your opening stock may be compromised.

(ii) **Average price** This is often the favoured option with computerized systems. To find the average, calculate the total cost of the number of items received then divide by the number of items.

(iii) **Standard price** It can be agreed with the supplier that over a given period items will be purchased at a 'standard' price. The alternative to an agreed price is to estimate the standard price per item, often building in a plus or minus variation.

As with all the alternatives, the key is to monitor the policy and if large variations occur then calculations must revert to the original price that was paid.

TWO

Health and Safety

Introduction

The implementation of health and safety procedures in the working environment is of the utmost importance to all. Everybody has a role to play, and the penalties for not taking health and safety seriously can be severe, including criminal prosecution and civil lawsuits which can result in costly claims for compensation, large fines and even imprisonment. Health and safety is a general term which also includes many legal responsibilities; both the employer and employees can be held responsible for neglecting the rules as set out under The Health and Safety at Work Act (HASAWA) 1974. Some regulations will be familiar such as: fire precautions, first aid and the control of substances hazardous to health (COSHH). But others may not be so familiar, including: the manual handling operations regulations, the prescribed dangerous machines order, the personal protective equipment at work regulations, and safety signs regulations. The list of legislation that applies to any given business depends on the individual workplace, but it is both the supervisors' and the staff members' responsibility to familiarize themselves with the relevant legislation and more important, to implement and adhere to the regulations.

In general, the catering industry in the UK has not had a good health and safety record and this is costly to all concerned, not least to the people who die each year and the thousands who are injured through accidents at work. The legislation is regularly updated, for example the Health and Safety (Young Persons) Regulations 1997. All individuals have a duty while working to take reasonable care not to threaten the safety of or harm anybody else including: other staff, customers, visitors, suppliers and contractors. This is called a 'duty of care' and is achieved by:

(a) denying access to dangerous situations or areas;
(b) warning of dangers by way of signs.

Food safety policy statement (Food Safety Act 1990)

Each unit within a catering establishment must have a policy statement similar to the example shown in Figure 2.1, this should be displayed prominently.

1. _____ (Unit title) will comply with the requirements of the Food Safety Act 1990 and with all its statutory provisions and with any regulations made under the provisions of the Act. All food handlers, contract caterers, supervisors and staff are required to assist in this.

2. Every food handler within this unit is required to ensure that their personal hygiene and working practices do not contravene the requirements of the Food Safety Act 1990.

3. It is a fundamental principle of this unit's food safety policy that personnel in charge of catering operations are responsible for ensuring that, as far as is practicable, hygienic conditions exist in their area of responsibility and that adequate precautions are taken to safeguard the health of the consumer.

4. _____ (Name or title) has overall responsibility for food safety in this unit. All staff are responsible for premises providing catering facilities and are to ensure that storage, preparation, cooking and service of drinks is carried out in accordance with food safety legislation. All personnel are expected to inform the manager responsible of any practice that may present a risk to health.

5. Statement will be brought to the attention of all food handlers working at this unit, and displayed prominently where food is prepared.

Figure 2.1 **Example of food safety policy statement**

External inspections

Most caterers are aware of inspections by environmental health officers with regard to hygiene, but are not familiar with the fact that the Fire Department and the Health and Safety Executive also have the right to inspect premises *at any time* to ensure that health and safety legislation is being strictly administered. All three agencies are entitled to be accompanied by a police officer or by an authorized person from another enforcing body. They may bring with them equipment or materials, take photographs, samples or recordings, and interview anybody they consider has information relevant to the case. They also have the right to inspect, remove or copy documentation.

Breaches of health and safety legislation can be dealt with in three ways, depending on the severity of the case.

1. They may give advice on improvement.
2. Issue an improvement notice, stating what is wrong, how it is to be put right and how long you have to rectify the situation.
3. Issue a prohibition notice. This means that a dangerous activity is stopped immediately and that work may not restart until the risk is removed.

Penalties

Failure to comply with an improvement or prohibition notice could result in a fine of up to £20,000 and six months in prison, and obstructing an inspection could cost the individual concerned up to £5,000.

Reporting procedures: 'RIDDOR'

The reporting of injuries, diseases and dangerous occurrences regulations (RIDDOR), places a duty on supervisors and other responsible members of staff to report the following to the Health and Safety Executive:

Fatal accidents
Major injuries
Dangerous occurrences
Accidents that result in someone taking more than three days off work
Certain diseases and conditions such as typhoid, paratyphoid, salmonella, dysentery, staphylococcal infections, septic cuts, burns, nose or throat infections.

The Health and Safety at Work Act 1974

Employers are obliged to:
- ensure the health, safety and welfare of all employees, contractors and visitors while on the premises
- provide and maintain safe equipment and premises
- ensure the safe use, handling, storage and transport of dangerous articles and substances
- provide information, training and supervision for employees to make sure they perform their jobs safely
- provide a working environment and facilities which ensures the welfare of employees

Employees are obliged to:
- ensure that their acts or omissions do not cause injury or damage
- co-operate with their employers to ensure safety in the workplace
- not intentionally interfere or misuse any equipment provided for safety reasons
- report any problems or dangers which could affect health and safety

Internal inspections

It is essential that safety procedure checks are in place and that these are carried out regularly. All departments should know which specific areas and items they are responsible for checking. Checks should follow a set schedule, an example of which is outlined below:

Items/areas to be checked	Frequency of checks	Person responsible	Action
Refrigeration temperature monitoring sheets	Three times a day; collate and review every week	Head chef	Report problems to management via maintenance report sheet
Delivery personnel and vehicles	Every month	Sous-chef	Complete checklist, report problems to suppliers via head chef

As well as checking individual areas, an overall safety audit should be carried out at regular intervals. This may highlight problems not picked up in the specific checks and acts as a second level of assurance. It should include checks on documentation such as maintenance records, staff training, notices, fire certificates, and so on. Finally, organizational policy and training should ensure that staff are fully aware of their responsibilities under health and safety regulations. Staff should be encouraged to report any discrepancies or problems and procedures should be in place for them to do so. A maintenance incident sheet is ideal for this purpose in which the following should be detailed:

1. Problem or fault identified
2. Date/time reported
3. Responsible person notified
4. Action taken/required
5. Time/date of next check

Staff training should include procedures outlining how to deal with emergencies such as fire, bomb threats, evacuation, and any breach of security; they should be taught the correct way to raise alarm, and administer first aid. Attention should be drawn to any important documentation such as instructions for the use of chemicals, and manufacturers' instructions on use, cleaning and maintenance of equipment, in particular, dangerous machinery.

Record keeping

The following records should be kept in a secure place, with copies and pro formas of operational records readily available in each area.

- Incident/accident books/sheets, fridge temperature monitoring sheets, risk assessments
- Manufacturers' guidelines for equipment use, maintenance records, maintenance request sheets, COSHH instructions, training records
- Fire certificates and safety notices
- Health and safety checklists

Department/unit/section					
Date Name			Signature		
	YES	**NO**		**YES**	**NO**
Entrance halls, staircases and passages			Are the floors in good condition, non-slip, clean and dry?		
Are fire doors in good condition, kept in operating position and unobstructed?			Is all equipment in good working order?		
Are all lights adequate and in working order?			Are there guards on dangerous machines?		
Are all escape routes free from obstruction and clearly identified?			Are all dangerous machines labelled?		
Are escape doors clearly marked and open easily?			Is the fire-fighting equipment in position, unobstructed and clearly identified?		
Are fire alarm points unobstructed?			Are notices on display, e.g., no smoking, fire, use of machinery, wash your hands?		
Is fire-fighting equipment in position, unobstructed and without visible damage?			Is rubbish stored in suitable bins with well-fitting lids? Are they emptied regularly?		
Are all floors in good condition and kept clean and dry?			Are knives stored correctly?		
Are all electric flexes, leads, plugs, switches and sockets without visible damage and in proper working order?			Do all staff wear suitable protective clothing?		
Toilets			Are all materials stored in such a way as to be safe?		
Are all appliances clean and undamaged?			Is food stored correctly?		
Are all doors, locks and catches in sound working order?			Is refrigeration temperature monitoring in place?		
Is there a supply of soap (or equivalent) and nail brushes?			Is any food exposed or left standing?		
Are hand-drying facilities in place, clean and working properly?			Are all surfaces, clean, undamaged, free from grease/food debris?		
Are all lights in order?			Is there any grease build-up on cooking equipment?		
Are bins of used paper towels emptied regularly?			Is there any evidence of vermin or insects?		
			Are fly screens in place on open windows?		
Are notices in place?			Are staff adequately trained and supervised in the use of dangerous equipment?		
Kitchens			Are chemical agents correctly labelled and stored properly in a lockable cupboard?		
Is the lighting adequate?			Are cleaning and manufacturers' instructions in place?		
Is the ventilation adequate?			Is HACCP in place? (see p. 27)		
Is the water supply adequate?					
Are there separate hand-washing facilities?			Is there anything that could present a tripping hazard?		

Figure 2.2 **Example of a safety audit checklist**

	YES	NO		YES	NO
Are these areas regularly cleaned and disinfected?			Are COSHH records kept?		
Is there anything that could present a tripping hazard?			Are pest control records kept?		
Are these areas regularly cleaned and disinfected?			Are accidents/incidents recorded?		
Are these areas regularly checked for vermin and insect infestation?			Are fire drills held regularly and recorded?		
Is access to and egress from the building unobstructed?			**People and practices**		
Offices			Do all staff wear safe and suitable shoes?		
Are electrical sockets overloaded?			Do staff wear jewellery?		
Do telephone, computer or equipment cables trail and present a tripping hazard?			Do staff mop up or ignore spills?		
Are shelves and cupboards stacked so that they will not tip over?			Do staff lift objects in a safe manner?		
Is all electrically-powered equipment in safe working order?			Do staff reach for objects above head height in a safe manner?		
Is first aid equipment available? Are stocks checked regularly?			Do staff leave objects where they may cause a tripping hazard?		
Are first aid instructions displayed?			Are cables trailed across walkways?		
External – Including outbuildings, car parks, grounds, etc.			Are safety guards removed from moving machinery?		
Are lights adequate, clean and in working order?			Do staff know the correct cooking and storage temperatures?		
Are lights well sited to safeguard employees and public?			Do staff know how to measure correct temperatures?		
Are manhole covers, pavements or lights broken, or gully grates missing?			Does the unit have a policy statement on health and safety?		
Are any drains or gullies choked?			Is on-going training/instruction made available to staff?		
Is there any accumulation or obstruction by combustible rubbish?			Are staff aware of emergency procedures?		
Are adequate steel bins with lids provided to contain rubbish until it can be disposed of?			Is a qualified first-aider on site and identified?		
Record keeping					
Are service records kept on all equipment?					

Remarks/recommendations

Action required	Date reported By When
Remedial action taken	Time/date. Checked by: Name
	Signature

Maintenance/defect report card				
Date	Location			
Does fault affect health or safety?	Yes	No		Reported by _____
Description of fault and action taken (e.g. isolated defective item, 'do not use!' notice in place)				
Received by _____ Date received			Item to be repaired or replaced?	
Repair to start on			Replacement ordered on	
To be completed on			In place by	
Approved by			Inspected by	
Request for new equipment or utensils, please fill in reason for request above. Ordered on				

Figure 2.3 **Example of a maintenance request or defect report card**

Health and Safety (Young Persons) Regulations 1997

A young person is defined in law as someone who has not reached the age of eighteen, as opposed to a child who is someone who has not yet reached the minimum school-leaving age. The Health and Safety (Young Persons) Regulations were introduced to reduce the incidence of accidents and ill health in young persons within the workplace. The regulations require employers to complete risk assessments prior to the employment of young persons and retrospectively for those already in their employment. The following needs to be taken into account when completing risk assessments:

- The immaturity and lack of awareness to risk of young persons
- The fitting-out and layout of the workplace
- The nature, degree and duration of exposure to physical, biological and chemical agents
- The forms, range and use of work equipment and the way in which it is handled
- The organization of processes and activities
- The extent of the health and safety training provided or to be provided to young people

It should be noted that there is no new requirement for employers to provide written risk assessments where previously there were none, i.e., businesses with less than five employees, and the assessments should be completed prior to employment or the provision of work experience for each young person.

Dangerous machines

The Dangerous Machines Order 1964 states that:

> No person shall work at any machine unless he/she has been fully instructed as to the dangers with it and the precautions to be observed, and has received sufficient training in work or at the machine: or is under adequate supervision by a person who has thorough knowledge and experience of the machine.

The following is an example of the types of dangerous machines in a kitchen environment and how training can be monitored and recorded:

Date	Equipment	Trainer	Signatures	
			Candidate	Trainer
	Waste disposal unit			
	Small food mixer			
	Hobart food mixer			
	Gravity feed slicer			
	Rotary bowl chopper			
	Food processor (robot coupe)			
	Liquidizer (base mounted)			
	Liquidizer (hand held)			
	Potato rumbler			
	High-pressure steamer			
	Food mincer (small)			
	Food mincer (Hobart)			

General safety rules

- Do not use machines for which you have not been trained.
- Never use defective machinery.
- Never use machinery with defective leads or plugs.
- Do not allow water to come in contact with an electrical appliance.
- Do not distract other workers while using equipment.
- Recognize possible causes of accidents within your own area of work.
- Be aware of accident prevention.
- Know what to do should an accident occur.
- Wear protective clothing.
- Follow the manufacturers' instructions on the use and cleaning of equipment.
- Know where the mains cut-off switches are situated for gas and electricity.
- Know where the fire appliances are situated, and know how to use them.
- Know the procedures in the case of fire, bomb alert, etc. and practice evacuation procedures.
- Know how and where to raise the alarm in case of fire, etc.

Risk assessment

Risk assessment is not as complicated a process as it sounds; it simply means that you have to examine your workplace to see what could potentially be harmful to people. A hazard is anything that may cause harm, such as mechanical equipment, chemicals and so on. A risk is the chance, large or small, that someone may be harmed by the hazard. The following is a brief guide for risk assessment:

✓ Spot the hazard, e.g., slippery surfaces, fire hazards, dangerous machinery, chemicals, lifting of heavy items, etc.
✓ List the people who are most likely to be harmed: staff, customers, cleaners, etc.
✓ Check controls: are controls adequate and legal and do they reduce the risk as far as is practicable?
✓ Further action: is the risk removed or can it be reduced by the use of protective equipment and better training?
✓ Record the result and inform staff of the appropriate documentation, for example company rules, manuals, manufacturers' instructions, etc.
✓ Review and revise in line with changes to the working environment.

In the next section, I have given examples of risk assessment on three typical items of kitchen equipment. Employers/supervisors should undertake to provide similar assessments and instructions for items of equipment in their own unit. Ideally this should be in the form of an induction handbook with space to record any training given to staff. It should also state the controls already in place, such as induction courses, any training/supervision which is needed, COSHH, manuals, safety policy statement, and indicate to the operative where further information is available, for example the manufacturers' instructions.

Examples of risk assessment: instructions for use and cleaning of catering equipment

1. Gas range

> **Relevant to:** kitchen staff and cleaners
> **Potential risks:** burns, scalds, fire, explosions, chemicals

Operating instructions

Lighting the open flame burners
1. Hold gas igniter or lit wax taper to the appropriate burner.
2. Turn burner tap anti-clockwise to full on position (large flame symbol).
3. If a low flame is required, turn tap beyond the full on position to the stop position (small flame symbol).
4. To turn off: turn the tap clockwise to the off position.

Lighting the gas oven
1. Open oven door.
2. Turn thermostat knob to the pilot position.
3. Press and hold red button, at the same time press the spark ignition button to light pilot flame.
4. Keep red button pressed for approximately 20 seconds to ensure that the pilot flame is lit, then release button slowly and set the temperature; close the oven door gently.
5. If the pilot does not stay lit, turn off the thermostat and wait for approximately 3 minutes then repeat stages 2, 3 and 4.
6. If the oven fails to light after repeated attempts, inform a supervisor who should fill out a maintenance report and take the oven out of service. Place a 'do not use' notice on the oven.

Minimizing the dangers:
   – Always use a clean, dry oven cloth
   – Do not use an apron as an oven cloth
   – Do not pull shelves out too far
   – Do not overload the oven
   – Never tip a drip tray towards you to observe its contents.

Cleaning

Note: prior to cleaning always switch off the electrical supply at the isolating switch.

Daily cleaning
Boiling top:
1. Allow to cool thoroughly, wipe pan supports clean using a detergent solution.
2. Remove hot-plate drip trays by pulling the stainless steel handle below the front panel.
3. Wash the drip tray in a detergent solution and dry before replacing.
Note: The drip tray must be cleaned immediately after something has boiled over on to it!

Weekly cleaning
1. Soak pan supports in detergent solution. Wash and dry.
2. Remove burner caps, main burner casting and burner trays, wash in a detergent solution, dry thoroughly before replacing.

Oven (inside):
1. Remove oven shelves, shelf hangers and drip trays for cleaning, wash in a detergent solution and dry thoroughly.
2. Remove side hangers, wash and dry.
3. Wipe out any spillages from around the burner, taking care not to dislodge any wires or probes.
4. Replace oven fittings in reverse order.

Oven (outside):
   Clean the outside with a mild detergent and hot water;
   do not use scourers or scouring powder!

2. Deep-fat fryers

Relevant to: kitchen staff and cleaners
Potential risks: fat burns, fire burns, fire

Minimizing the dangers:
- Always check that the thermostat is set to the correct temperature in accordance with the food that is to be cooked. To prevent oil foaming and running over the sides, never overfill with oil or food.
- Always use clean/good quality oil or an alternative frying medium. Strain/filter oil on a daily basis, or after each service if in heavy use.
- Never have rolled-up sleeves.
- Ensure that the floor space immediately in front of the fryer is free from grease.
- Don't use wet food when using the fryer.

Cleaning
1. Heat oil until warm, then switch off.
2. Strain/filter oil into a clean, dry receptacle that is of a suitable size.
3. Close the drain cock.
4. Fill to oil level with solution of hot water and detergent; turn on and allow to boil for 10–15 minutes.
5. Drain off and dispose of soiled water.
6. Wipe out and dry with clean cloth.
7. Clean fryer bodywork with solution of hot detergent water, and wipe dry.
8. Ensure that drain cock is completely closed and that the frying pan is completely dry.
9. Gently pour back fresh or strained oil, and top up to level as marked inside pan.

3. Kitchen knives

Relevant to: kitchen staff and porters.
Potential risks: cuts

Minimizing the dangers:
- Carelessness with knives causes accidents.
- All blades must be kept sharp: never use a dull or blunt knife.
- Only use knives for their intended purpose. Do not use knives for opening tins or cans.
- Knives should be kept in a rack or case when not in use. They should not be left loose in drawers or left lying around, for example in dirty pots or in sinks.
- Never cut directly onto stainless steel or Formica surfaces; always use a secure cutting board. Any knives that have defects in the handle or blade should be reported to a supervisor and discarded.
- Never use knives with greasy hands or handles.
- Do not carry knives in your pocket. A knife should be carried with the tip facing directly to the floor.
- If you drop a knife, never attempt to catch it.

Cleaning
1. Always wash knives one at a time, and as a separate function from the general washing up duties.
2. Wash in very hot water containing detergent solution.
3. Rinse off in hot, clean water.
4. Using a clean dry cloth, dry with the blade facing away from your hand.
5. Return to receptacle.

Temperature control

The food hygiene regulations state the necessary safe temperatures for the handling, storage and service of food items and this is an integral part of the Hazard Analysis and Critical Control Points (HACCP) procedure, which we will outline in more detail in the following section (see p. 27).

Storage temperatures

HACCP guidelines recommend 8°C or below as the optimum storage temperature for cold or chilled foods. Here, however, I recommend 5°C or below since this is the UK industry standard and ensures compliance with the regulations.

Cold/chilled foods	5°C or below
Frozen foods	−18°C or below; ice cream fridges should be between −5 and −10°C
Hot foods	Cooking: minimum 75°C
	Holding: 63°C or above

Safe range = below 5°C or above 75°C

Some cold/chilled fresh foods are best stored at cooler temperatures, such as meat, fish and other types of seafood, and should be kept in a 'chiller' with a temperature range of 0°C to −2°C. Temperature monitoring commences with delivery and all suppliers should be aware of the required minimum delivery temperatures; these must be checked on delivery (see Figure 2.4 for an example of a temperature monitoring sheet). No food should be accepted that is not within the specified temperature range. Food items should be transported to the correct storage area as soon as possible.

Exemptions

There are several exemptions to the above requirements. These include:

(i) During food preparation there may be times when the food is subject to temperatures outside the 'safe' range, however, work practices should be organized in such a way as to keep this period to a minimum.

(ii) Food which is to be sold within a short time of preparation: hot food does not have to achieve a precise minimum, e.g. the centre of rare beef, provided it is served within four hours.

(iii) Food which has been processed, preserved or packaged to prevent the growth of organisms.

(iv)   Baked goods to be sold on the day of production or the next day provided nothing has been added, for example cream.

(v)   Raw food which is intended for further processing which will make it safe for consumption, e.g. fresh meat and fish. This does not include items which are to be served raw, such as steak tartare, sushi, etc.

(vi)   Foods which must be ripened or matured at room temperature; however, once ripe or mature they must be stored below 5°C.

(vii) Foods that are to be served cold may be kept outside the safe zone for one period of up to four hours, after which time they must be discarded or chilled until used.

(viii) Hot food may be kept for service or display for one period up to two hours, after which time it must be discarded or rapidly cooled, it may then be reheated for final sale.

(ix)   Display foods: food can be on display for up to four hours, e.g. hot meat on carveries, sweet trolleys, buffets, salad bars and cheese boards, provided it is eaten within the designated four hours. Left-over hot foods (e.g. roast joints) can be chilled quickly after display and served cold at the next service; left-over cold food, however, must be discarded.

High-risk foods

This refers to food items which will readily support the growth of food poisoning organisms and should not therefore receive further cooking prior to service, for example:

- Cooked fish
- Cooked meats
- Pâté
- Cooked egg dishes
- Pre-prepared dairy products that may only be reheated.

Some food poisoning bacteria can form spores which may survive the cooking process. If cooling is delayed or takes a long time, these may grow or produce toxins (poisons). After cooking food should be cooled quickly to prevent or reduce the possibility of this happening.

Below is an example of a temperature monitoring sheet; readings are taken at the end of cooking time, the start of the holding period and at the end of the holding period.

Food item	Cooking			Holding		Initials
	Date	Start time	Start temperature core	Finish time	Finish temperature core	

Figure 2.4 **Example of a temperature monitoring sheet**

Hazard Analysis and Critical Control Points (HACCP)

HACCP is a system for assessing potential hazards in food outlets and deciding which are critical to the safety of consumers. It was first developed for NASA in conjunction with the Pillsbury company and the US Army Research Laboratory as a means of ensuring that food could be safely reheated and eaten in space without having to check each individual meal. The system was adopted first by the food manufacturing industry and then in a simplified form by the catering industry. It is often referred to as 'assured safe catering'.

Under the revisions to the Food Safety Act 1990, more stringent hygiene controls were introduced which outlined a system for identifying hazards and assessing their risk to the public. The Food Safety Act requires the following measures:

- Compulsory food hygiene training/supervision commensurate with the job.
- Requirement for hazard analysis of the food business and identification of steps critical to controlling food safety.
- Documentation to show proof of 'due diligence'.

It remains the job of the environmental health officers to enforce the regulations, but LACOTS (Local Authority Coordinating Body on Food and Trading Standards), has the overall responsibility of ensuring standards are applied consistently on a national basis.

A major advantage of the HACCP system is that it involves all members of staff, thus making them aware of their responsibilities and promoting food safety.

The setting-up and implementation of HACCP

In the first instance, establish a team; this should include management, supervisors, operatives and support personnel such as porters. The following is a guide to the implementing of HACCP:

1. **Explain HACCP** This includes the legal requirements, how problems can be highlighted and solved.

2. **Choose the area to be covered by HACCP** Identify hazards, preventative measures and critical control points (CCP) using the HACCP decision tree (see p. 27). Produce a flow chart and guidelines, design checklists, decide on controls or eliminate hazards.

3. **Introduce HACCP** Involve all staff, allocate individual responsibilities and establish levels and tolerances for each control point, introduce a monitoring system for each CCP and decide on the appropriate documentation.

4. **Staff to attend induction courses** Train staff and monitor record-keeping.

5. **Review and monitor the system** Allocate time for checks, state who is to apply the system, what they are to do and how they should do it, e.g. all chilled foods to be probed in the centre for temperature checks on delivery by the sous-chef or deputy. Maintain and collate records, hold regular reviews at team meetings, update and modify the system.

The main aim of critical control points is to break the food poisoning chain.

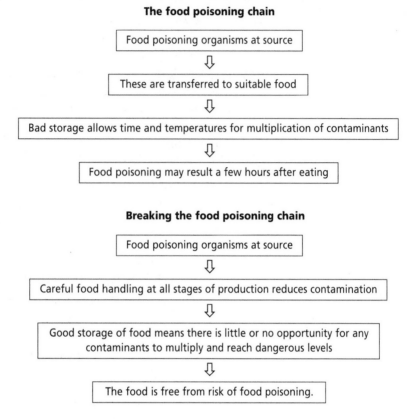

The food poisoning chain

Food poisoning organisms at source
⇩
These are transferred to suitable food
⇩
Bad storage allows time and temperatures for multiplication of contaminants
⇩
Food poisoning may result a few hours after eating

Breaking the food poisoning chain

Food poisoning organisms at source
⇩
Careful food handling at all stages of production reduces contamination
⇩
Good storage of food means there is little or no opportunity for any contaminants to multiply and reach dangerous levels
⇩
The food is free from risk of food poisoning.

Hazards, risks and critical operations

The following table lists the hazards, risks and types of critical operations to be found in a catering establishment.

Source of hazard	Risk if not controlled	Types of critical operations
Ingredients and commodities	Bacterial contamination and growth	Purchase Inspection Receipt Storage Stock rotation Transport
Intermediary stages of production and products	Contamination, growth and survival	Preparation Cooking Hot or cold holding Transport
Plant and equipment (e.g. holding equipment)	Contamination and growth	Cleaning Disinfection Maintenance Pest control Monitoring

Source of hazard	Risk if not controlled	Types of critical operations
Premises and environment	Contamination	Cleaning Disinfection Maintenance Pest control Ventilation/air supply

A food safety hazard is the potential from pathogenic bacteria, organisms, chemicals and foreign matter to cause harm.

A food safety risk is the likelihood of such harm occurring, taking into account the preventative measures in place. The equation for risk/hazard likelihood is as follows:

Risk = Hazard severity: $\times$ *Likelihood of occurrence:*
                      3 = may cause food poisoning.   3 = extremely likely.
                      2 = may cause contamination.   2 = possibly.
                      1 = not serious.   1 = unlikely.

HACCP decision tree

Once the hazard has been identified, the following system of criteria should be applied:

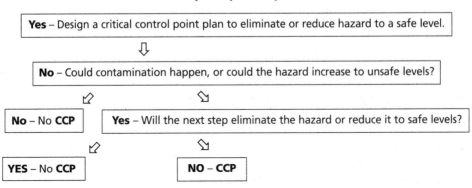

Could measures be put in place to prevent the hazard?

Yes – Design a critical control point plan to eliminate or reduce hazard to a safe level.

⇩

No – Could contamination happen, or could the hazard increase to unsafe levels?

No – No **CCP**   **Yes** – Will the next step eliminate the hazard or reduce it to safe levels?

YES – No **CCP**   **NO** – **CCP**

Stage	Hazard	CCPs	Action and recording
Receipt	Bacteria present Contamination	Inspect suppliers and delivery vehicles State required temperature on receipt Inspect packaging	Temperature check on delivery 5°C or below Refuse if packaging is damaged
Storage	Bacterial growth Contamination	Safe storage Stock rotation Date/day stickers	Regular fridge temperature checks Never exceed safe storage times
Preparation	Bacterial growth Contamination	Limit holding times and time at ambient temperatures Safe storage temperatures Personal hygiene	Keep below 5°C or above 63°C

Stage	Hazard	CCPs	Action and recording
Use	Contamination	Staff hygiene practices Clean equipment Correct storage and handling	Specify safe procedures Monitor cleaning rotas
Service	Hot holding Cold display	Staff training Temperature checks Time limits	Record times Apply minimum and maximum temperatures Allocate responsibilities and recording systems

Note: Fridge temperatures should be monitored by placing a gel pack or small container filled with coloured water, labelled and sealed with cling film, in the fridge. The temperature should be taken with a probe pushed through the cling film. Do not rely on fridge temperature displays. Gel packs should have day demarcation labels.

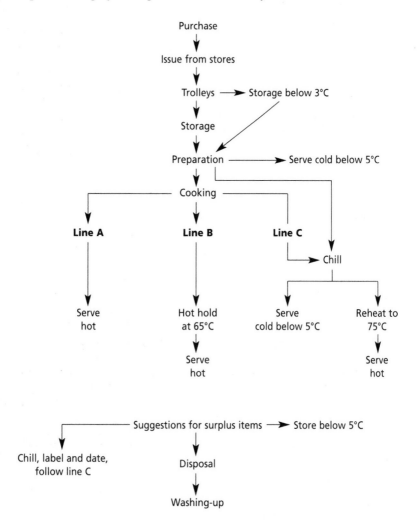

Figure 2.5 **Critical control point stages**

The table below represents the critical control point stages and the appropriate measures to counteract any potential dangers.

	Step	Hazard	Action
1.	Purchase	High-risk food (ready to eat foods) contaminated with food poisoning bacteria or toxins.	Buy from reputable supplier. Specify temperature at delivery. Store within fifteen minutes.
2.	Receipt of food	High-risk food (ready to eat foods) contaminated with food poisoning bacteria or toxins.	Quality and packaging check, visual/sensory check, temperature/vehicle check.
3.	Storage	Growth of food poisoning bacteria or toxins on high-risk foods means further contamination.	Store high-risk foods wrapped and at safe temperatures. Date and label high-risk foods. Rotate stock and check recommended use-by dates. Check and monitor storage areas.
4.	Preparation	Contamination of high-risk foods. Growth of pathogenic bacteria.	Limit exposure to ambient temperatures during preparation. Prepare with clean equipment used for high-risk (ready to eat) foods only. Separate cooked and raw foods. Wash hands before and between handling foods.
5.	Cooking	Survival of pathogenic bacteria.	Cook rolled joints, chicken and reformed meats, e.g. burgers, to at least 75°C in the thickest part. Sear the outside of other meats (e.g. joints of beef, steaks) before cooking.
6.	Cooling	Growth of any surviving spores or pathogens. Toxin production and contamination with pathogenic bacteria.	Cool foods as quickly as possible. Do not leave out at room temperature to cool unless cooling period is short (e.g. place stews, rice, etc. in shallow trays and quickly cool to chill temperatures.
7.	Hot holding	Growth of pathogenic bacteria and toxin production.	Keep food hot: above 63°C.
8.	Reheating	Survival of pathogenic bacteria.	Reheat to above 75°C.
9.	Chilled storage	Growth of pathogenic bacteria.	Temperature control (regular checks). Date code high-risk foods. Use in strict rotation and always check shelf-life.
10.	Service	Growth of pathogens bacteria and toxin production. Contamination.	Cold service: serve high-risk foods as soon as possible after removing from refrigerated storage. Hot foods: serve high-risk foods quickly.

Hygiene and cleaning procedures

Employers have a legal duty to ensure that food premises, equipment and utensils are kept clean and well maintained. Cleaning should be carried out in a systematic way, this means establishing cleaning schedules, training staff in the appropriate procedures and standards, providing suitable equipment and materials and establishing monitoring procedures. The most effective approach is to work with the suppliers of cleaning materials. Cleaning procedures and the use of materials are covered by COSHH (Control of Substances Hazardous to Health) regulations. Reputable suppliers of cleaning materials will have standard COSHH assessments in place, and this can simplify the setting-up of a cleaning system. The law requires that an assessment be made of the hazard presented by the use of a substance, for example if breathed in, ingested, allowed to come in contact with skin, eyes, etc. Risk is defined as the likelihood that a substance will cause harm during use; the risk will depend on:

- The hazard presented by the substance, usually a chemical.
- How the substance is used.
- How exposure is controlled.
- How much of the substance people are exposed to.
- How long people are exposed to a hazardous substance.
- If people are particularly vulnerable to a substance.
- The manner of an employee's occupation, e.g. the jobs undertaken, etc.

Complying with COSHH regulations involves:
- ✓ Assessing the risks involved in the work undertaken.
- ✓ Deciding on the necessary precautions.
- ✓ Preventing or controlling the risks.
- ✓ Ensuring that the measures are implemented and maintained.
- ✓ Monitoring exposure of workers to hazardous substances.
- ✓ Informing, training and instructing employees of the risks and precautions required.
- ✓ Reviewing assessments regularly (less than five-year intervals) when procedures or working practices change.

COSHH (Control of Substances Hazardous to Health)

Suppliers of cleaning materials are required to provide safety information on labels and hazard data sheets for each substance. This can greatly assist in COSHH assessments as they contain essential information such as any risk to health or of fire, guidance on safe storage, transport, the safe handling and disposal of chemicals, and who to contact for advice or in an emergency. In addition employers have a duty to inform and train their staff in the following:
- Control measures, their purpose and how to use them.
- Protective clothing, equipment and how to use it.
- Results of monitoring and health implications due to exposure.
- Emergency procedures.

Further information and advice on COSHH is available from your local environmental health officer and the Health and Safety Executive.

Cleaning systems

Systematic cleaning procedures ensure that cleaning is carried out regularly, safely and efficiently. The following criteria should be used to organize cleaning routines:

Who is to clean?
What is to be cleaned?
When it is to be cleaned?
How is the item/area to be cleaned?
Which equipment/materials should be used?
What should be the outcome of cleaning (free from grease, deposits, etc.)?
Who should monitor the system?
When is maintenance to be carried out?
Where is information located (hazard data sheets), including procedure and safety considerations?

The working environment

Management of the Health and Safety at Work 1992 regulations cover four main areas:

- **Maintenance**. All equipment, ventilation, lighting, etc. must be maintained in good working order, including regular monitoring and maintenance systems.
- **Environment**. This includes ventilation, lighting and cleanliness.
- **Conditions**. This covers space, working area, condition of floors, prevention of accidents such as slips.
- **Facilities**. Includes toilets, washing facilities, drinking water, changing facilities.

First aid (See also Reporting procedures, p. 16)

It is an employer's duty under health and safety legislation to provide first aid. Notices should inform employees of the location of facilities and who the trained personnel are. On average there should be one first aider for every fifty employees and one should be available at all times. All first aid boxes must be clearly labelled and contain general first aid instructions, and at a minimum, the following:

Six sterile dressings (four medium, two large)
Four cotton wool packs
Two eye pads with attachments
20 waterproof blue plasters (various sizes)
Sterile water
Blunt-ended sterile scissors
Two triangular bandages
Tweezers, plastic gloves, twelve safety pins, plastic disposal bags
Instructions on who to contact in case of an emergency

No drugs or painkillers should be stored in a first aid box, and a nominated person should be responsible for regular monitoring of the use-by dates, and restocking.

Safety signs

These should be clearly displayed in a prominent place in the relevant areas. The four categories are:

Red	Prohibition signs	Round with a red border and red crossbar, e.g. 'no smoking', 'no running'.
Yellow	Warning signs	Triangular with a yellow background, e.g. 'hazardous, toxic'.
Blue	Mandatory signs	Round with a blue background and white symbol, e.g. 'safety goggles must be worn'.
Green	Emergency signs	Square or rectangular with a white symbol on a green background, e.g. escape routes, first aid.

Fire precautions and emergency procedures

Local authority fire officers must check all premises before a fire certificate can be issued.

Specialists are required to check fire-fighting equipment, alarms and emergency systems like lighting on a regular basis. These checks and procedures must be recorded and kept ready for inspection by the local authority.

All work premises must have procedures in place to deal with such emergencies as fire or bomb threats. The premises, fire-fighting and monitoring equipment and staff training must be checked regularly. In-house checks should make sure that routes are clear from obstruction, equipment is available and in good working order, and staff are trained in what action to take in an emergency, including the location of fire-fighting equipment, how to raise the alarm and evacuation routes. Regular drills should be scheduled to monitor these procedures.

The various types of fire extinguishers are listed below:

Colour	Type	For use on	Should not to be used on
Red	Water	Wood, paper, fabrics	Fat or electrical fires
Cream	Foam	Fat, oil	Live electrical equipment
Black	Carbon dioxide	Inflammable liquids, live electrical equipment	Paper or fat fires
Blue	Dry powder	Fat, oils, live electrical equipment	Fires involving metals, e.g. magnesium
Green	Halon – a liquid that vaporizes on contact with air, creating a non-conducting gas	Inflammable liquids, gases, live electrical equipment	Fires in enclosed spaces: gas should not be inhaled Fires involving metals, e.g. magnesium
Various	Fire blanket	Fat, oil, people (wrap around to smother fire)	Any other type of fire

Security equipment

There are many systems available which protect premises, equipment, personnel and members of the public. Some examples include:

- Alarm systems, electronic tags to prevent theft or removal of items
- Swipe cards for staff access; electronic keys for customers and hotel guests
- Electronic-coded keypads for entry
- Passwords (for example, for computer systems)
- Video cameras
- Security lights, personal alarms
- Computer security cages
- Security shutters
- Identity cards for staff, visitors, contractors
- Security marking of equipment to confirm ownership
- Door/entrance alarms to alert staff of people entering a building or area

Staff should be aware of security and receive training in the systems and procedures applicable to their work area.

THREE

Food Storage, Refrigeration and Hygiene

Introduction

Everyone who is involved in the preparation of food should be aware of the rules for food handling, and the causes and spread of infection due to improper procedures. The government recommendation that all food handlers should be properly trained and/or possess a qualification in food hygiene has been a huge step in the right direction. It has meant that a great number of caterers have been made more aware of the risks involved and their responsibilities. Most of the basic food hygiene and handling rules should by now be second nature to those working in the catering industry, so in this chapter we will look at the broader issues to do with the larder section.

Many foods are placed side by side in the larder as it is used for both storage and preparation. The larder frequently produces items that are to be served uncooked, this means that the highest levels of hygiene are necessary if contamination and cross-infection are not to take place. It is often used for the cooling of food and thus should be air conditioned or refrigerated to obtain a consistent temperature of less than 8°C. Preparing foods in a cool room (a cooled/refrigerated preparation area as opposed to a cold room, which is in essence a large refrigerator) greatly lessens the risk of bacteria multiplying to dangerous levels. A cool room will also save on undue wear and tear of fridges.

High-risk foods

The need for adequate refrigerated storage space and the correct methods for storing foods cannot be stressed enough. It is vital that food is held at the correct temperatures and that these temperatures are monitored constantly. Foods which can be easily contaminated include:

- Stocks, soups, sauces and gravies
- Meat and meat products (e.g. pies)
- Milk and dairy products
- Eggs and egg products (e.g. quiches)
- Fish and shellfish

- Foods that require preparation (i.e. handling)
- Foods that are reheated

All the above require extra care during storage and preparation

Ten most common causes of food poisoning

1. Food prepared too far in advance.
2. Food stored at the wrong temperature, i.e. at room temperature, not refrigerated.
3. Slow cooling of food prior to refrigeration.
4. Insufficiently high temperatures when reheating food which means that bacteria is not destroyed.
5. Using cooked food that is already contaminated with bacteria.
6. Undercooking meat and meat products.
7. Not thawing frozen meat or poultry for sufficient time.
8. Cross-contamination from raw to cooked foods.
9. Holding hot food below 63°C.
10. Infected food handlers.

Refrigeration

A common problem is often a lack of space in both fridges and freezers so that food is often crammed together, allowing little or no circulation of air and, in the case of fridges, providing an ideal environment for cross-contamination. A cool room helps overcome this problem. As a general rule, the temperature should not exceed 4°C; 2 – 3°C is ideal for a general purpose fridge or cold room. Freezers should be − 18°C or below. The temperature levels should be monitored and recorded on a regular basis, this will highlight any problems. The time a fridge takes to recover to its recommended temperature should also be checked. The temperature reading should not be taken until after the fridge has had time to recover to its correct temperature – approximately ten minutes after the door was last opened.

Rules for general purpose refrigeration

1. Ensure that the correct temperature is maintained, 1 – 5°C.
2. Do not overload fridges, as cooling air cannot circulate.
3. Place fridges and freezers in a cool well-ventilated area.
4. Segregate different types of food, especially raw and cooked food.
5. Cover food.
6. Rotate stock regularly.
7. Use non-corrosive containers. Do not leave food in opened cans.
8. Do not place hot foods in fridges.
9. Keep fridges, curtains and the surrounding areas clean.
10. Defrost fridges regularly.
11. Regularly check fridge seals and remember to keep the door shut.

Holding cabinets

These can be fridges or freezers and are solely for the storage of food that is already at or very near to the required storage temperature. The small refrigeration plant used in holding cabinets is only adequate for keeping already cold items cold and is very poor at recovering its temperature; this means that if the door is continually opened and closed, the temperature will be raised to an unacceptable level for lengthy periods. The same is true if warm food is placed in it, or if frozen food at too high a temperature is placed inside a freezer cabinet.

Temperatures

Foods should ideally be segregated into separate refrigerated areas, for example:

Fish and shellfish: fish fridge, 0°C to −2°C.
Meat and poultry: chiller, 0°C to −2°C.
Raw food: general purpose fridge/cold room, 2°C to 3°C.
Cooked food: general-purpose fridge/cold room, 2°C to 3°C.
Defrosting food: separate cabinet at up to 10°C.
Freezer: −18°C minimum.
Blast freezer (freezing): −40°C or below.

The chiller is a useful piece of equipment, as not only can food be kept safely for longer periods, but it allows the chef to substitute chilled items for frozen, which means better quality and a decrease in processing time (defrosting). A chiller can also be used to chill buffet items prior to glazing.

Fish and shellfish

If possible fish and shellfish should be stored in a separate chiller at a temperature of 0°C to −2°C to prevent any smells or juices contaminating other foods. Prior to preparation and cooking, the fish can be stored in a general purpose fridge at 2°C – 3°C. It should be covered with plastic film and placed underneath cooked foods.

Meat and poultry

This is best stored separately in a chiller at 0°C to−2°C. Meat and poultry will keep well for long periods at this temperature (up to ten days for beef). Also, as with fish, it may be removed to a general purpose fridge for short periods.

Cold room/general purpose refrigerator

Cold rooms and refrigerators are used for the short-term storage of food prior to cooking or preparation and for foods that can be stored at higher temperatures, such as fruit, cheese, dairy products, fats, salads, cooked meats/charcuterie, pies and sandwiches. These items have a tendency to deteriorate or freeze at lower temperatures, as is the case with lettuce which is ruined if this happens.

Chill room

A cold room that is at a temperature of 0°C to −2°C is known as a chiller or chill room and is used for the large-scale storage of fish and shellfish, meat, poultry and game.

Defrosting cabinet

The thawing of small items can quite adequately be achieved in the general purpose refrigerator. However, large roasting joints, turkeys etc. will often take too long to defrost in an ordinary refrigerator set at the correct temperature. If large frozen items are regularly defrosted then it is advisable to have an engineer set the cabinet at a higher temperature. Once defrosted the item should be used immediately or transferred to a cooler fridge and cooked within 24 hours. A thawing cabinet should be set at 6°C – 8°C, on no account should the temperature rise above 8°C.

Thawing items outside the fridge in warm conditions is a bit like playing Russian roulette, as is defrosting in hot water. In fact, cold water is a far more efficient way to defrost. If it is not possible to buy chilled items instead of frozen, then the best policy, apart from the above, is to use a microwave big enough for the purpose and to cook the item immediately.

Freezers

Freezers should be set at −18°C to −20°C and must not be overcrowded as the cooling air needs to circulate. When items are delivered they should be checked to ensure that they are still frozen; if they have started to defrost they should be refused and returned. Such items as frozen vegetables should be removed from their cardboard containers, as these may have been contaminated during transport.

Blast freezers

These work on a similar principle to fan convection ovens; but whereas a fan oven blows hot air to cook the food, a blast freezer circulates freezing cold air around the items so that they can be quickly frozen. There are various advantages to a blast freezer; in an ordinary freezer food can take a long time to freeze; this is particularly the case with larger items where the centre of the food takes even longer to become cold, never mind freeze. This method also produces large ice crystals which impair the texture of the food. Ordinary freezers can be inefficient as placing items in them will cause the temperature to rise and hence raise the temperature of the other already frozen items. An ordinary freezer with large amounts of food may take ages to recover its correct temperature. In contrast, a blast freezer quickly cools the food to a temperature of about −40°C. Since it is not used to store food, there is no problem with the items to be frozen raising the temperature of those around them. Once frozen, items should be transferred to an ordinary freezer for storage.

Table-top/small fridges

A recent and welcome addition to the range of refrigeration, small free-standing fridges and table-top fridges are ideal for storing foods during preparation or prepared foods (*mise en place*) prior to cooking, especially in a busy *à la carte* operation. Refrigerated drawers are also an advantage in a busy operation for the storage of prepared foods prior to cooking/service.

Fridge curtains

Plastic curtains on walk-in fridges can be a dangerous source of contamination. They are used to restrict the air flow in and out of cold rooms, but they can quickly become contaminated via food that has been carried through them. Therefore, they should be highlighted for regular cleaning, i.e. daily.

Refrigerated display and food service units

These are intended to be used at the front of house to display foods to the customer at strictly controlled temperatures. They are suited for the presentation of wrapped items such as sandwiches, salads, dairy produce and sweets. The temperature is thermostatically controlled and is usually set at between 4°C – 6°C. Cold air circulation is an advantage with these units, as is an automatic defrost cycle. A recent development is the refrigerated salad counter which keeps salads at a temperature of 4°C – 7°C. All display cabinets should be fitted with a 'sneeze guard' to prevent contamination by the customer.

Hygienic organization of refrigerators

As has already been stated, it is recommended that different foods are kept separate, but if this is not possible then the various foods in the fridge should be arranged in such a way so as to minimize the risk. Raw foods must always be placed towards the bottom of the fridge to prevent liquid dripping onto other foods and contaminating them. Foods should be covered with plastic film to stop cross-contamination, to retain moisture and to prevent any strong odours from being released which could spoil other foods. All items should be labelled and date coded.

Cooling of foods prior to refrigeration

Cooked foods should be cooled as rapidly as possible prior to being refrigerated. No more than 90 minutes should elapse between foods being cooked and placed in the fridge. The temperature of cooked foods should fall to 15°C within a maximum of 90 minutes. Environmental health officers are particularly vigilant about the correct procedures for the cooling of food. Gone are the days when the chef could leave items to cool overnight or all afternoon before placing them in the fridge.

Listed below are a few guidelines which will assist in the safe cooling of food and help maintain a good relationship with the environmental health officer.

- Always remove hot food from the cooking vessel and place in a cold, shallow, wide tray.
- Place a wire cooling rack under the food to allow air to circulate underneath, this speeds up the cooling process.
- A note of the time when cooling commenced should be placed adjacent to the food, or better still, use a food timer.
- The food should be kept covered while cooling; however, plastic film or tin foil placed directly over the food will inhibit the cooling process. To avoid this, put a wire cooling rack over the food and cover, this will allow air to circulate over the top of the food.
- Place the food in the coldest part of the kitchen or cool room; alternatively, place it in an empty blast freezer/chiller and monitor the internal temperature with a probe. Transfer to a refrigerator once cooled.

Maintenance, defrosting and cleaning of refrigeration

Most modern refrigeration has an 'automatic defrost' function, but if this is not fitted a fridge should be defrosted regularly; preferably once a week for efficient operation, and immediately if the monitoring of temperatures demonstrates a slow recovery time or a consistent rise in temperature. Freezers should be defrosted if any build up of ice is noticed or according to the manufacturer's recommendation.

The contents of the fridge/freezer should be removed to alternative cold storage, the machine turned off and defrosted, the shelves/trays removed, washed and sanitized, the inside of the fridge/freezer should be cleaned with hot water and detergent, paying special attention to behind the rubber or plastic seals. Finally, it should be sprayed with a sanitizer and wiped dry with a sterile cloth. The cabinet then needs to be left to return to its required temperature before re-stocking.

Fridges and freezers require regular monitoring and maintenance by a qualified engineer, and the best way to do this is to place the equipment under a regular contract. Records should be kept of any maintenance that is carried out.

Temperature range for storing and holding of foods

The recommended range of temperatures requires that *all* cold food should be kept below a maximum of 5°C. Hot food should never (apart from being cooled) drop below a minimum of 63°C.

Equipment cleaning

All equipment, boards, work surfaces, sinks, taps and so on should be cleaned and disinfected after coming into contact with raw food, especially meat and poultry. Separate colour-coded boards and tools can also help to avoid contamination, as will colour-coding storage areas, for example fridges.

It is also a good idea for the chef to change any clothing that may have come in contact with raw meat. A butcher's apron or plastic apron will protect the chef's uniform from contamination, and this can be swapped for a clean one once preparation is complete.

Protective measures against insects

An electronic insect electrocuter is an essential piece of equipment in the summer months, especially in areas where raw meat and fish are prepared. It must be remembered that the bulb needs to be changed annually. Fly-screens should be fitted to windows and open doorways.

Storage of dry foods

Food items not requiring refrigeration should be kept in a well-ventilated, dry, cool store. The store should also be well lit and all items placed above floor level. Fresh fruit and vegetables should be stored in a separate area. Remove plastic film or wrapping as this can lead to condensation which encourages mould and other fungal growth.

Free-standing shelving away from the walls should be used to allow good air circulation and to prevent pests crawling up the walls onto the food.

Security (See also Chapter 2, p. 35)

All storage areas should be able to be locked, this includes rooms, cabinets, fridges and freezers. Checklists can be used to detail the daily contents of each area, this enables a mini-stockcheck to be made at the start of each day and the levels to be replenished with issued items. Checklists also give a good indication of levels of consumption, highlighting excessive usage or pilfering.

Ordering and receipt of goods

In Chapter 2, a range of example specification forms are given which can be easily adapted for individual house standards. Specification forms will greatly assist the person responsible for ordering goods, as well as making clear to the supplier exactly what is required. They also help in identifying any discrepancies when goods are received and ensure correct portion control and costing.

A specific area should be designated for the receipt of goods, and their weight, temperature, quantity, size and quality should be checked by an experienced person against the order specification and the delivery note. Any discrepancies should be dealt with at the time of delivery, and any item which is sub-standard should be returned. The temperature of foods that require refrigeration should be checked and suppliers notified if the goods have not been transported according to the regulations, i.e. below 5°C for long-distance deliveries and below 8°C for local deliveries. A record must be kept of any returned or damaged goods, or goods which are accepted for a credit against the original price.

Issuing of stock items

All issued stock items need to be recorded, preferably on a standard requisition form; this may be a duplicate book or a standard self-duplicating triplicate book. This book should include the following information:

- The date
- Number of items
- Weight of items or amount in the case of liquids
- Department to which they are to be issued
- Authorized signature of person ordering/receiving goods
- Signature of person issuing goods

When using a triplicate book the top copy should be kept in the stores as a record and to assess consumption and assist future ordering; the second copy should go to the control office or the person responsible for control, for example the food and beverage manager; the third copy is kept by the head chef or kitchen supervisor.

All documentation should be cross-checked at set periods following a general stocktake.

FOUR

Fish and Shellfish

Fish

Fish are cold-blooded animals that live in the water and have a vertebra, gills and fins. We are fortunate in the UK to be surrounded by sea and to have an abundance of rivers and lakes which give us access to a large variety of fish and seafood. Fish is a delicate and nutritious alternative to meat and a good source of protein. Great skill is required in the selection, preparation and cooking of fish as it deteriorates very quickly. It must be purchased very fresh, prepared immediately and cooked delicately if it is to be enjoyed at the peak of its condition. Although a lot of customers may not be able to tell one fish from another, poor quality or badly prepared or cooked fish is something which will be immediately obvious to the diner, especially to the devotees of fish who are prepared to pay for what is often an expensive dish.

Food value

Including fish in our diet, especially oily fish, is encouraged by nutritionists and dieticians. Fish is high in protein, second only to meat, contains essential minerals and is rich in vitamins A and D. Eating fish bones, for example those of sardines, whitebait and tinned salmon, provides calcium and phosphorus.

Oily fish is believed to help prevent heart disease; evidence for this comes from the Japanese who eat large amounts of it, usually raw as sashimi, and who have a very low rate of heart attacks compared to the West.

White fish has concentrated amounts of vitamins A and D in the liver (hence the importance of cod liver oil) and is easily digested, making it particularly suitable for sick people or people with delicate stomachs. Oily fish, however, is not easily digested and benefits from the addition of citrus-flavoured sauces and astringent herbs.

Types of fish and modern farming methods

The availability of fish has to some extent changed due to the rapid expansion of fish farming. Fish farming of salmon and trout is not a new phenomenon: many private rivers and lakes have been stocked with fish for many years. However, this practice is different to the modern, intensively-reared methods of farming. Fish which are raised 'naturally', i.e. non-intensively, are for the most part not confined except by the natural boundaries of the river or lake; occasionally their food may be supplemented and their habitat improved, but in general they are allowed to live as they have always done, that is 'in the wild'.

In contrast, intensive farming means that large quantities of fish, for instance trout, are kept in ponds or tanks in much closer proximity to each other than they would otherwise be in the wild; and instead of a 'natural' diet they are usually fed on proprietary fish pellets. Due to the confined spaces, disease and parasites can be a major problem. As with battery hens or cereal-fed cattle, the variety of the feed directly relates to the depth of flavour. Salmon gains a lot of its flavour, and indeed colour, from its diet; modern farming means that artificial alternatives have to be used, and there has been some concern expressed about the safety of some of these feeds.

Fish can be classified into three groups:

1. **White fish**
   (a) Round Fish e.g. cod, whiting, hake, haddock, bream, bass
   (b) Flat Fish e.g. plaice, sole (lemon and Dover), turbot, halibut, brill, skate

2. **Oily fish**
   All oily fish are round in shape e.g. herring, mackerel, trout, salmon

3. **Shellfish** (see the following section, p. 68)

For the purposes of purchasing, fish can be divided into two categories:

Fished Naturally-reared and caught fish
Farmed Artificially-reared, farmed fish

It has to be said that the big increase in farmed fish has provided several advantages for the caterer in that farmed fish is:

Readily available
Reasonably priced
Very fresh
Consistent in size (this means less waste and good portion control)

Fish can also be classified by:

(a) The method of preservation, e.g. smoked, frozen, pickled
(b) The size/weight and type of cut, e.g. darnes, cross-cut/quarter-cut fillets
(c) Saltwater or freshwater: freshwater fish include trout, salmon, salmon trout, and eel

Quality

Flesh The flesh should be firm and resilient to the touch, this means that when pressed it regains its shape quickly. There should be no signs of damage such as bruising.
Eyes The eyes quickly dry out and become dull and sunken once a fish is killed, so look for full, rounded bright eyes.

Gills The gills, like the eyes, become dry and lose their colour very quickly once killed; they should be bright red and still moist.

Scales The scales should be moist and cover the whole fish; a fish begins to lose its scales when it has been out of the water for too long.

Skin The skin of a fresh fish is covered with a coating of 'slime', this aids it in its passage through the water, and is another indication of freshness.

Smell Even if all the above indicators are satisfactory, the smell should be the ultimate deciding factor. If a fish looks good and smells fresh then it should be safe to eat; if there is any doubt *do not* purchase it. The consequences of food poisoning from fish can be serious, and no amount of disguising can put right the crumbly texture and offensive smell of cooked stale fish.

Purchasing

The buying of fish can at times be more problematic than almost any other commodity. Many factors beyond the chef's control will influence the availability, price and quality of fish. These include:

Location

Access to a wholesale fish market is a real advantage as the chef can select the best of the catches prior to compiling a menu. He/she should look to purchase fish of the best quality, the most economical size and then to negotiate the best price.

Quantity

The quantity of fish purchased will affect both quality and price. Fish sold at wholesale markets are normally quoted at a price per stone (6 kg). Wholesalers purchase the best fish in large quantities, so it pays to buy from a wholesaler if possible.

If this is not possible, the alternative is to use a fishmonger. However, the small fishmonger usually does not understand the demands of the catering trade: they cannot compete with the buying power of a wholesaler and therefore buy in small quantities what is left after the wholesaler has made their choice. Sometimes the fishmonger may have to purchase from a wholesaler, adding his or her premium onto the price. This can make it very expensive for the chef to buy from a fishmonger.

Weather

The weather, for example storms at sea, can mean that types of fish are sometimes in short supply or expensive. This problem can be avoided by visiting a wholesaler to see what is available and at what price and compiling a menu to suit. A chef that can use the services of a major wholesaler is at an advantage as in times of shortage the markets usually supply the bulk purchasers as a priority; large wholesalers also have access to several markets both in the UK and abroad. The small fishmonger may be left with little or nothing or is forced to purchase fish at a price which is prohibitive.

Seasons

Although frozen fish is available all year round and most wholesalers can supply imported fish quite consistently, there are certain seasons when some types of fish are at their best, most plentiful and therefore most economically priced. Even a chef who cannot visit the market can take advantage of these times by always questioning the supplier as to what is in season.

Fresh fish should always be delivered in insulated boxes and covered in a layer of crushed ice. Fish may be purchased:

(a) **Whole** on the bone by number and weight
(b) **As fillets or cuts** by number and weight/size/cross- or quarter-cut (fillets)

Medium-sized fish are superior in both taste and texture; small fish can lack flavour and large fish may have a course texture.

Portion control

There will always be a certain amount of wastage when preparing fish; this will vary according to the type of fish and the manner in which it is prepared.

Whole fish to be served on the bone

Loss can be between 10–15 per cent depending on whether the head is removed or not. It is important to order the correct size of whole fish for cutting into darnes, troncons, and so on as not stating the individual fish size could leave you with undersized cuts and mean that a high percentage of the fish is lost due to the removal of the head, guts, fins etc. A good guide when ordering whole fish – such as turbot and salmon – for portioning is to allow approximately 300 g (12 oz) per portion on the bone.

Whole flat fish

Loss from gutting, trimming, and filleting is approximately 50 per cent.

Whole round fish

Loss from gutting, trimming and filleting is approximately 60 per cent.

Pre-prepared fillets (for grilling)

Fillets for grilling, i.e. with the skin left on, will have a minimum of weight loss unless previously frozen.

Pre-prepared fillets (for poaching)

These may lose up to 25 g (1 oz) per fillet due to skinning and trimming.

Frozen fish

Frozen fish is often coated with an 'ice glaze' – this means that individual fillets or pieces of fish are covered in a layer of ice to keep them separated. It is important that the chef is aware of whether or not the stated portion size is inclusive or exclusive of ice glaze as 30–50 per cent of each individual portion may be lost when thawed. If frozen fish is purchased *inclusive* of ice glaze, it is vital that the price per kilogram/portion and the number of portions required should be calculated on the basis of its thawed weight.

Average portion sizes

Small cuts, e.g. fillets, suprêmes and goujons

85 g (3 oz)	Fish Course = 2 × 85 g
113 g (4 oz)	Set main course = 2 × 113 g
141 g (5 oz)	*à la Carte* main = 2 × 141 g
170 g (6 oz)	Grilled fillet = 1 × 170 g or more

Cuts on the bone, e.g. troncons and darnes

113 g (4 oz) – 141 g (5 oz)	Fish course = 1 × 141 g
170 g (6 oz)	Set main course = 1 × 170 g
226 g (8 oz)	*à la Carte* main = 1 × 226 g

Whole fish, e.g. herring, mackerel, trout, Dover sole

113 g (4 oz) – 141 g (5 oz)	Fish course = 1 × 141 g
170 g (6 oz)	Set main course = 1 × 170 g
226 g (8 oz) – 340 g (10 oz)	*à la Carte* main = 1 × 340 g

Storage

Fish deteriorates at a faster rate than almost any other food. The ideal situation is for fish to be used on the day of purchase; however, this is not always possible. The next best alternative is to store fish in a purpose-built fish refrigerator where the temperature is held just above freezing point, i.e. 1 – 2°C. The fish should be washed, covered in crushed ice (to prevent drying out) and kept separate from other foods. Frozen fish should always have a coating of ice glaze and be stored at a minimum temperature of –18°C. It should be kept covered with plastic film to prevent freezer burn and used in strict rotation. Smoked fish should be kept in a sealed container to stop strong odours tainting other items of food.

Seasons for fish

The following list gives the seasons when types of fish are at their best or most available; exact dates will vary, so it is advisable to check with your local fish market, wholesaler or fishmonger.

All year round – cod, plaice, whiting, brill, halibut, bream, turbot, tuna, coley, sole, haddock, sardine, farmed salmon and trout.
Spring – whitebait, mackerel, salmon, conger eel.
Summer – salmon, mullet, salmon trout, herring, skate, whitebait.
Autumn – skate, dogfish, eel, red mullet, haddock.
Winter – skate, mackerel, whiting, haddock, flounder.

Varieties, specifications and uses

Note: All weights are for standard portion sizes, depending on the type of course offered.

Cod

Specification: Order by number and weight or by fillet weight. Cod for cutting on the bone will be between 3 – 4¹/₂ kg (6 – 10 lb). Fillets/suprêmes will be taken from a cod weighing no more than 5 kg (10 lb). They will have a minimum amount of excess skin and bone.

Darnes will be cut from a cod weighing between 3 – 4¹/₂ kg (6 – 10 lb). The darne will be cut from the middle part of the cod and should be an even size and thickness; the flaps of skin and bone at the edges of the belly will be trimmed square, any congealed blood will be removed from the inside of the backbone.

Weights: 170 g (6 oz); 198 g (7 oz); 226 g (8 oz).

Description: A large round white fish with a clean fresh flavour; the texture consists of large white flakes. Cod can grow up to five-feet long; small cod are called 'codling' and are superior because their flesh is more compact and they have a sweeter flavour.

It is available fresh or frozen, but is best between October – February. Cod is particularly suitable for luncheon menus.

Uses:
Poach: as darnes or flaked and used in various dishes such as fish cakes, pies, cod au gratin.
Grill: as darnes, maître d'hôtel, etc.
Fry: as fillets (or parts of), shallow- or deep-fry, coat in breadcrumbs or batter.
En papillote: as suprêmes with butter garlic and parsley.

Plaice

Specification: Order by number and weight or by fillet weight. Plaice ordered for filleting will be between 1¹/₂ – 2 kg (3 – 4 lb); for serving whole between 340 – 453 g (12 – 16 oz). Fillets will be taken from a fish weighing between 1¹/₂ – 2 kg. Cross- or quarter-cut, as specified in recipe. All traces of bone will be removed; undersized fillets or those with excess roe are not acceptable.

Weights: 113 g (4 oz); 141 g (5 oz); 170 g (6 oz).

Description: A medium-sized white flat fish, with brown skin and red spots. The spots are an instant sign of freshness as they are bright red when fresh but rapidly become dull when stale. The flesh has a good flavour with a soft texture. Plaice is available fresh or frozen.

Plaice is often substituted for sole in recipes due to its more economical price; although this may be acceptable for luncheon/banquette service, no other flat fish can replace the firmness and excellent flavour of Dover sole.

Uses: Grill, shallow- or deep-fry, poach.

Whiting

Specification: Order by number and weight or by fillet weight. Whiting ordered for filleting will be between 396–500 g (14–18 oz); for serving whole, 283–396 g (10–14 oz). Fillets, will be taken from a fish weighing between 396–500 g (14–18 oz). All the main bones will have been removed.

Weights: 113 g (4 oz); 141 g (5 oz); 170 g (6 oz).

Description: Medium-sized round white fish related to the cod family and with a similar flaky texture. Best time is from December to February. The most well-known dish specific to whiting is merlan *en colère*, commonly called 'curled whiting' (the literal translation is 'angry whiting', as it is made to appear that the fish is biting its own tail).

Uses: Deep- or shallow-fry, poach, bake; the flesh may be used in forcemeats.

Brill

Specification: Order by number and weight or by fillet weight. Brill ordered for filleting will be between 3–4 kg (6–8 lb). Fillets/suprêmes/medallions will be taken from a brill weighing no more than 4 kg (9 lb). They will have a minimum of excess skin and bone.

Troncons will be cut from a fish weighing 3–4¹/₂ kg (6–10 lb). The troncons are cut from the middle part of the brill and should be an even size and thickness; the flaps of skin and bone at the edges of the belly will be trimmed square. All congealed blood etc. will be removed from the inside of the backbone.

Weights: 170 g (6 oz); 198 g (7 oz); 226 g (8 oz).

Description: A large flat fish similar to turbot but darker in colour, mottled brown on one side and white on the other. Brill is often used as a less expensive alternative to turbot, but the flavour is not as good and the colour of the flesh is greyer. It is sometimes confused with turbot, but brill has a smooth skin as opposed to turbot's warty skin and a yellowish-white underside.

Uses: Poach, braise, grill, shallow-fry.

Hake

Specification: Order by number and weight or by fillet weight. Hake ordered for filleting will be between 1–1¹/₂ kg (2–3 lb). Fillets will be taken from a fish weighing between 1–2 kg (2–3 lb). All the main bones will have been removed.

Weights: 170 g (6 oz); 198 g (7 oz); 226 g (8 oz).

Description: A member of the cod family, hake is similar to cod in texture.

Uses: Suitable for all methods of cooking.

Sea bass

Specification: Order by number and weight or by fillet weight. Sea bass ordered for filleting will be between $1^1/2 - 2$ kg (3 – 4 lb).

Weights: 170 g (6 oz); 198 g (7 oz); 226 g (8 oz).

Description: A firm white fish that has lately gained in popularity. The fashion is to bake, grill or sauté the fish with the skin on as the crisped skin is a major part of its appeal. Once filleted, the fish is normally cut into suprêmes or diamonds and presented skin-side up.

Uses: Bake, grill, sauté.

Halibut

Specification: Order by number and weight or by fillet weight. Halibut ordered for cutting on the bone will be between 4 – 5 kg (8 – 11 lb). Fillets/suprêmes will be taken from a halibut weighing no more than 5 kg (11 lb). They will have a minimum of excess skin and bone. Available fresh or frozen.

Troncons will be cut from a halibut weighing 4 – 5kg (8 – 11 lb). The troncons are cut from the middle part of the halibut, and should be an even size and thickness; the flaps of skin and bone at the edges of the belly will be trimmed square. All congealed blood will be removed from the inside of the backbone.

Weights: 170 g (6 oz); 198 g (7 oz); 226 g (8 oz).

Description: A large white flat fish. Similar to turbot and available fresh all year round except in May and June; best time is from August to April. A small halibut is called a 'chicken halibut', it has firm flesh with a flaky texture and good flavour.

Uses: Poach, grill, shallow- or deep-fry.

Sea bream

Specification: Order by number and weight or by fillet weight. Bream for braising whole will weigh between $1/2 - 1$ kg (1 – 2 lb). Fillets will be taken from a fish weighing between $1^1/2 - 2$ kg (3 – 4 lb), they will have a minimum of excess skin and bone.

Weights: 170 g (6 oz); 198 g (7 oz); 226 g (8 oz).

Description: A round white fish, available throughout the year but best from February to October. Bream has grey-white flesh with a flaky texture and a moderate flavour. It is usually found on inexpensive luncheon menus or as an ingredient in fish cakes.

Uses: Shallow- or deep-fry, braise or stuff and bake whole.

Turbot

Specification: Order by number and weight or by fillet weight. Fillets / suprêmes / medallions will be taken from a fish weighing between 4 – 5 kg (8 – 11 lb), they will have a minimum of excess skin and bone.

Troncons will be cut from a turbot weighing 4 – 5 kg (8 – 11 lb). The troncons are cut from the middle part of the turbot and should be an even size and thickness; the flaps of skin and bone at the edges of the belly will be trimmed square. All congealed blood will be removed from the inside of the backbone.

Weights: 170 g (6oz); 198 g (7 oz); 226 g (8 oz).

Description: A large white flat fish, in season for most of the year, but best from March to August. It is greyish-brown in colour with warts, known as tubercules, on the dark side and white underneath. It has no scales, a firm, flaky texture, and an excellent flavour. Small turbot under 3 kg are called 'chicken turbot' or 'turbotin'.

Turbot is prized by chefs along with Dover sole and salmon. Turbot is normally used for the most prestigious of menus which is reflected in its high price.

Uses: Poach, grill, boil/long-poach whole, shallow-fry.

Note: Turbot is gutted very carefully through a small hole just under the head.

Tuna (tunny)

Specification: Sections/steaks of Albacore tuna.

Weights: (Steaks) 170 g (6 oz); 198 g (7 oz); 226 g (8 oz).

Description: Tuna has been available for many years tinned and preserved in oil, but fresh tuna has grown in popularity. It is also available frozen. Albacore tuna is the most prized type, the others – bluefin and bonita or longfin – tend to be drier in texture and darker in colour.

Tuna has a dry texture which is made worse by baking or grilling. This can be improved by marinating in a mixture of olive oil, lemon juice, parsley and seasoning; cooking en papillote will also help.

Uses: Tinned, for use in salads and hors-d'œuvres. Steaks: grill, bake or braise (Provençal-style).

Coley (saithe, pollock)

Specification: Order by fillet weight. Fillets will be taken from a fish weighing between 3 – 4 kg (6 – 8 lb), they will have a minimum of excess skin and bone.

Weights: 170 g (6 oz); 198 g (7 oz); 226 g (8 oz).

Description: Coley is a round white fish, its course grey flesh turns white when cooked. It has a mediocre flavour and was little known in hotels and restaurants prior to the 'cod war' when it was then used as a substitute for cod (which at the time was unavailable or expensive). It is at its best from June to December.

Uses: Found usually on inexpensive luncheon menus, or as an ingredient in fish cakes, fish stews, etc. Coley can be poached, shallow- or deep-fried.

Sole (Dover)

Specification: Order by number and weight or by fillet weight. Sole ordered for filleting will be between 600 – 700 g (1^1/4 – 1^1/2 lb); for serving whole, 340 – 453 g (12 – 16 oz). All bones will be removed; undersized fillets or those with excess roe are not acceptable. Fish weighing less than 250 g (9 oz) are designated 'slip soles', and the price should be adjusted accordingly.

Description: A flat, oval-shaped white fish with a dark upper skin and white underneath. Available all year round, but at its best when half-roed – June –January.

Dover sole is the most prized fish of all. Its firm texture and excellent flavour make it the ideal first choice for classic poached fish dishes and many other methods of cooking. Although there is no real substitute for Dover sole, its sometimes exorbitant price means that it is mainly seen only on *à la carte* menus and those of the more exclusive hotels and restaurants; for table d'hôte menus and other less prestigious outlets, plaice and lemon sole are often offered instead.

Uses: Poach, shallow- or deep-fry (Colbert), grill, cold buffets, forcemeats. An ideal fish for all classic cooking.

Sole (lemon)

Specification: Order by number and weight or by fillet weight. Sole ordered for filleting will be between 800 g – 1 kg (2 – 2^1/2 lb). Fillets will be taken from fish weighing between a minimum of 800 g up to 1kg (2 – 2^1/4 lb). Cross- or quarter-cut, as specified in recipe. All traces of bone will be removed; any undersized fillets or those with excess roe are not acceptable. Available fresh or frozen.

Description: Broad, white flat fish, with a brownish-yellow upper skin and white underneath. The flesh has a softer texture and less flavour than its cousin the Dover sole. At its best between July – March.

Uses: Poach, grill, shallow- or deep-fry.

Haddock

Specification: Order by number and weight or by fillet weight. Fillets/suprêmes will be taken from a haddock weighing no more than 2^1/2 – 3kg (5 – 6lb). They will have a minimum of excess skin and bone.

Weights: 170 g (6 oz); 198 g (7 oz); 226 g (8 oz).

Description: A round white fish similar to cod, with a flaky texture and good flavour, and, in my opinion, superior to cod. Haddock is generally more expensive than cod and care must be taken to make sure it is identified correctly: this is easily done by looking for two dark patches found on each side of the neck, just below the head. Legend has it that these are the fingerprints of God who once picked up a haddock and since then the fish has borne these marks. Apart from cod, haddock is the biggest catch in the UK. Its best time is from November to February. Available fresh, frozen and smoked (see smoked/finnan haddock)

Uses: Poach, bake, deep- or shallow-fry.

Smoked / finnan haddock

Specification: As for haddock. Finnan haddock is naturally smoked and contains no artificial colours. Available as a split whole fish or in fillets.

Description: A great deal of haddock is smoked but the most famous is finnan haddock which is named after the village of Findon near Aberdeen in Scotland. The traditional method of producing finnan haddock is for a medium-sized haddock to be split and cleaned and the head removed. The fish is then salted, dried and finally smoked.

Care must be taken when purchasing smoked haddock to ensure that it has been produced in the traditional manner. Modern-day producers often substitute an inferior version that has been coloured and flavoured to resemble finnan haddock. It has a bright yellow surface with white interior flesh; the surface is more moist than the traditionally-prepared version but the flavour is vastly inferior.

Uses: Poach, kedgeree, haddock Monte Carlo, savouries.

Sardine

Specification: Order by weight. Size will vary, but on average the best size is 10 – 14 cm (4 – 5^1/$_2$ in).

Description: A very small oily fish related to the Pilchard family, with silver-coloured skin and dark flesh; a strong, good flavour when fresh. Care must be taken when purchasing and serving fresh sardines as they deteriorate rapidly and the flesh soon becomes pasty and the flavour over-strong. Available fresh, frozen and tinned.

Uses: Fresh: grill, shallow-fry. Tinned: cold buffets, canapés, savouries and sandwiches.

Salmon

Specification: Order by number and weight or by fillet weight. Salmon ordered for serving whole or for cutting on the bone will weigh between 3 – 5^1/$_2$ kg (6 – 12 lb). Fillets/suprêmes will be taken from a salmon weighing no more than 5^1/$_2$ kg (12 lb). They will have a minimum of excess skin and bone.

Darnes will be cut from a salmon weighing 3 – 5^1/$_2$ kg (6 – 12 lb). The darne is cut from the middle part of the salmon and should be an even size and thickness; the flaps of skin and bone at the edges of the belly will be trimmed square. All congealed blood will be removed from the inside of the backbone.

Weights: 170 g (6 oz); 198 g (7 oz); 226 g (8 oz).

Description: Large round oily fish with a light blue back and silver skin on the belly. Firm pink to red coloured flesh with a flaky texture. Excellent flavour when 'fished' less so when 'farmed'. Available all year round but best when fished June to August. Available fresh (farmed or fished) or frozen, whole or in portions, tinned and smoked.

Uses: Poach, grill, shallow-fry. Cold presentation – gravlax; salads; salmon mayonnaise; Cooked, decorated and presented whole on cold buffets; sandwiches; hors-d'œuvre.

Salmon trout (aka sea trout)

Specification: Order by number and weight or by fillet weight. Salmon trout ordered for serving whole or for filleting will be between 2 – 4 kg (4 – 8 lb). Fillets will be taken from a salmon trout weighing no more than 4 kg (8 lb). They will have a minimum of excess skin and bone.

Weights: As for salmon.

Description: Similar to a salmon but smaller and the skin is darker in colour. The flesh is a similar colour to salmon with a firm flaky texture and a milder flavour. Salmon trout should not be confused with 'salmon smelts' which are undersized salmon. Salmon trout are thicker at the tail and not as streamlined in shape as salmon. Available March to August, but at its best during May.

Uses: Poach, grill, braise, shallow-fry.

Trout

Specification: Order by number and weight.

Weights: 113 g (4 oz); 141 g (5 oz); 170 g (6 oz); 198 g (7 oz); 226 g (8 oz); 283 g (10 oz).

Description: A round oily fish, there are several varieties: brown trout is caught in lakes and rivers and has a pinkish-coloured flesh, it is in season from March to September; rainbow trout is also caught in rivers and lakes but is mainly farmed. The flesh of a rainbow trout is similar to that of the brown but does not have such a good flavour and is darker in colour. Rainbow trout is at its best from February to September.

Trout is available fresh (fished or farmed) or frozen, smoked, whole or in fillets.

Uses: Grill, shallow-fry, poach, cold presentation.

Whitebait

Specification: Order by weight. The length of the fish will not exceed 5 – 6cm (1 – 2¹/₂ in). Available fresh or frozen.

Description: Very small silver-coloured oily fish. Whitebait are the fry or young of herrings and sprats and are at their best from March to August. They can be deep-fried and eaten whole in which case they should have a crisp, crunchy texture and an excellent flavour.

It is important to keep whitebait cool during preparation, otherwise they have a tendency to break up and the oil to leak out of the flesh; iced water will assist in keeping the fish firm and intact.

Uses: Deep-fried and served as hot hors-d'œuvre, fish course, or as part of a selection of fried fish (fritto misto).

Mackerel

Specification: Order by number and weight. Mackerel ordered for serving whole will be between 226 – 283 g (8 – 10 oz). Mackerel for filleting will weigh between 340 – 453 g (12 – 16 oz).

Description: A medium-sized, round, oily fish, with a silver/green-coloured skin with black bands. Available all year but best from October to March. Mackerel has a soft textured dark-coloured flesh with a distinctive flavour. The texture and flavour of mackerel deteriorate rapidly, so it must be purchased and served as fresh as possible.

Mackerel is also available smoked as fillets.

Uses: Whole: bake, grill. Filleted: poach, shallow-fry. Smoked: hors-d'œuvre, pâté, cold buffets, canapés, sandwiches.

Eel (freshwater)

Specification: Medium-sized eels are usually 50 – 70 cm (1^1/2 – 2^1/2 ft) long and should be purchased live to ensure freshness. It can also be bought smoked.

Description: Snake-like shape, dark green/grey colour, firm, oily textured flesh. Buying live eels will guarantee freshness and a good texture, as they quickly become tough once killed. Good all year round apart from May. Smoked eel, although often difficult to come by is highly recommended, especially when served hot.

Preparation: Kill the eel by a firm blow to the head, the skin is removed by cutting just behind the head and pulling the skin off in one go. Cut along the underside and remove the guts, then wash well to remove any blood; remove the fins, then fillet or cut into sections.

Uses: Jellied eels, stewed eels, poach, deep-fry. Smoked: hors-d'œuvre, pâté.

Eel (conger)

Specification: Medium-sized eels will be 1^1/2 – 2 m (4 – 6 ft) long and should be as fresh as possible.

Description: A large, dark grey-coloured oily sea fish that can grow up to 3 m (10 ft) in length, it has white flesh and is useful in fish soups and stews because of its gelatinous texture. Conger may be smoked and used to make pâté.

Uses: Fish soups and stews, and as for freshwater eel.

Mullet (red)

Specification: Order whole by number and weight. It will weigh between 198 – 453 g (7 – 16 oz), and should be as fresh as possible – old or emaciated fish should not be accepted.

Description: A round white fish measuring approximately 30 cm (12 in) long, with a red back and silver-pink belly. Its flesh is firm with a flaky texture and excellent flavour. Red mullet is at its best between April and September. Mullet, particularly red mullet is considered a great delicacy and is often called the woodcock of the sea because, like woodcock, it doesn't need to be gutted (neither mullet nor woodcock has a gall bladder). However, the gills and scales need to be removed and the vent cleaned. The entrails, especially the liver, is considered by aficionados to enhance the flavour.

Uses: Grill, bake, *en papillote*.

Mullet (grey)

Specification: Order by number and weight, between 226 – 500 g (8 – 18 oz). As for red mullet, grey mullet should be fresh, and old or emaciated fish rejected.

Description: A round white fish, silvery-grey in colour, with firm flesh and a good flavour. At its best in the summer months.

Uses: Grill (suprêmes), bake whole (stuffed).

Herring (bloater, kipper)

Specification: Order whole by number and weight, between 226 – 340 g (8 – 12 oz). They should be as fresh as possible.

Description: A medium-sized oily fish, with silver-blue skin. Best in the summer months, herring is a cheap and versatile fish. Smoked herring is called, rather unfortunately, a 'bloater' and salt-cured and smoked is known as a kipper. The best bloaters come from Great Yarmouth and the best kippers from Scotland. Herring is a very oily fish and is therefore not easy to digest. It should always be cooked/served with sharp-tasting fruit or accompaniments e.g. lemon, vinegar, or a mustard-based sauce. Herrings can be bought ready prepared as rollmops or Bismark herrings, the main difference being that the former is rolled and the latter is served flat.

Uses: Breakfast (kippers), grill, bake, shallow-fry in oatmeal, soused, or serve cold as rollmops and Bismark herring.

Skate

Specification: The skate wings are ordered by number and weight. The wings should have an average weight of approximately 736 g (1 lb 10 oz), they will be supplied skinned.

Description: A white flat fish which is a member of the ray family. Skate is at its best from September to April. The body is never eaten, only the triangular shaped sides of the body are used; these have an extremely high bone content and in smaller wings the ratio of flesh to bone can make it unacceptable for consumption. The flesh has a soft texture and a good, sweet flavour.

Uses: The wings are cut into thick slices and usually poached in a *court bouillon* and served with black butter and lemon juice; the dark, slightly bitter butter offsets the sweetness of the flesh. Skate can also be shallow- or deep-fried.

Dogfish (flake, huss, nurse)

Specification: Order by weight and it should be as fresh as possible. Dogfish should measure approximately 60 cm (2 ft) in length and weigh approximately $1^1/_2$ kg ($2^1/_2$ lb).

Description: A shark-like round white fish, best from October to March. The white or pinkish flesh has a good flavour.

Uses: Shallow- and deep-fry.

Monkfish

Specification: Order by number and weight of tails. The weight should suit the required application – normally $2^1/_2$ – 5 kg (5 – 12 lb). It will have had the head and skin removed. Beware of suppliers who provide small tails, usually with the skin still on: the relatively high price of this fish merits a fair size and a good level of preparation.

Description: A round white fish with close-textured flesh, similar to that of shellfish. It has an excellent flavour and can be prepared in slices, as medallions, fillets and steaks.

Uses: Poach, grill, shallow- or deep-fry, braise.

The different cuts of fish

Fillet

A cut from a flat or round fish which is free from bone.

Preparation

Flat fish: Place the flat fish on a board with the head facing away from you. Draw the filleting knife down the middle of the fish, to one side of the backbone. Then, starting at the head end, with the tip of the knife gradually ease the flesh away from the bone by pressing firmly onto the bone and moving down the length of the fish at the same time moving outwards. The fillet should always be held in place with the knife-free hand, until separated from the bone. Repeat the same procedure on the other side of the backbone. Turn the fish over and do the same to the other side. A flat fish will yield four fillets.

Round Fish: Once gutted, lay the fish flat on a board and starting at the head end, draw the tip of the filleting knife down the length of the backbone making a cut approximately $1/2 - 1$ cm ($1/4 - 1/2$ in) deep. Hold the edge of the top fillet with one hand and with the tip of the knife gradually separate the flesh from the bone as with a flat fish. Turn the fish over and repeat the process. A round fish will yield two fillets.

Skinning fish fillets

Lay the fillet of fish on or along the edge of a board with the wider portion facing away from you. Hold the filleting knife in one hand and take the tail end of the fish between your thumb and first finger with your free hand, the thumb should be uppermost and facing away from you. Cut through the flesh of the fillet taking great care not to cut through the skin. Turn the blade of the knife away from you at an angle of 45°, draw the skin towards you and ease the knife forward and gently from side to side parting the flesh from the skin until the end of the fillet is reached. If by accident you cut through the skin, turn the fillet round and repeat the process from the other end. Trim off any rough edges and lightly scrape away any black congealed blood with the edge of your thumb and salt.

When preparing fish for grilling the skin is normally left on.

Suprême

A portion of fish cut at an angle across a large fillet of fish.

Preparation

Lay a fillet of a large fish on a board and cut at an angle across the fillet to produce 'steak'; the width of the suprême will depend on the thickness of the fillet and the size of the portion required.

Medallion

Prepare a suprême as above but trim off the corners to produce an oval or round medallion. The trimmings can be saved for forcemeat, pies, fish cakes, etc.

Delice

A fillet of fish folded over two or three times.

Preparation

A fillet has two sides, the skinned side and the presentation side; a delice is prepared by laying the fillet of fish with the presentation side down onto a board, then folding the fillet over two or three times so that the skinned side is on the inside. As an aid to remembering this, the rhyme 'skinned side inside', should help. For folding in two, the fillet is folded directly in half; for three, one end is folded to the middle of the fillet and the other is folded over the top. The fillet is then turned so that the presentation side is on top.

Paupiette

A fillet which is rolled, or stuffed with forcemeat and then rolled.

Preparation

Trim the fillet and place it presentation-side down on a board; lightly flatten with the side of a large knife. Roll the fillet from the tail to the head. Alternatively, after flattening spread with a thin layer of fish forcemeat then roll. Both styles of paupiette may be wrapped in greased, greaseproof paper and stood on end, packed, quite tightly together in a sauté pan or high-sided tray prior to poaching, or else tied (see Trussing/tying, p.61).

Goujons

Fillets which are cut into thin strips. The term '*en goujon*' comes from gudgeon, a small fish which may be deep-fried whole. Goujons should only be prepared from smaller fillets of prime white fish, usually sole or plaice, as larger fillets tend to break up easily.

Preparation

Starting at the tail end of the fillet, cut across at an angle to make strips 6 cm ($2^{1}/_{2}$ in) long and a $^{1}/_{2}$ cm wide. The goujons are then dipped in seasoned flour, egg and breadcrumbs – roll between the palms of the hands in the breadcrumbs to give them an even, rounded shape.

Goujonettes

Are prepared in exactly the same manner as goujons but are cut smaller.

Plait/*en tresse*

Plaited fillets of fish.

Preparation

Place the fillet of fish (Dover sole, lemon sole, plaice) presentation-side down on a board with the tail-end facing away from you. Make two cuts lengthways at a slight angle towards the tail to divide the fillet into three equal strips leaving them joined together by approximately 2 – 3 cm (1 in) at the tail, then plait one with the other. Poach or pané and deep-fry. Another method is to use different coloured fillets; cut each into four strips and plait. Poach or steam.

Darne

A cut across and through the bone of a large round fish.

Preparation

Lay the gutted fish on a board and remove the fins with fish scissors and any bones/rough edges at the flaps of the belly. Cut across and through the tail-end of the fish, approximately

8–10 cm (3–4 in) from the tip of the tail. Remove the tail. The exact point at which the tail is removed will depend on the size of the fish and the required portion size of the darne as the first darne is cut at a point were the fish is just thick enough to give a suitable sized and shaped portion. Once the tail is removed slice across and through the fish parallel to the first cut, both sides of the cut should be parallel to give an even thickness.

Troncon

A cut across and through the bone of a large flat fish.

Preparation

Remove the head, guts and fins of a large flat fish and, depending on the size of the fish, either cut in half lengthways down the backbone, or if a small fish, leave intact. Remove the tail and slice across in thickish slices through the bone as for a darne.

Note: It is essential for good portion control that each portion or slice of fish cut is weighed before the next is cut; in this way the width and size of the cut can be adjusted to ensure evenly sized portions.

Trussing / tying

This method is mainly used for paupiettes, in which case they are tied with string or thin strips of blanched leek leaf. Stuffed fish can also be tied with string to help keep the stuffing enclosed.

Roe

There are two types of roe: Hard roe (*oeufs de poisson*), the eggs of the female and soft roe (*laitance*) the sperm of the male fish. The type that is most commonly used is soft herring roe, while the most famous is caviar and comes from the sturgeon.

Hard cod's roe is often smoked and used on hors-d'œuvre. Salmon roe is eaten the same way as caviar and may be used on hors-d'œuvre, canapés, and so on. Lumpfish roe is available in two colours, orange and black. The black roe is the most commonly used as it resembles caviar but is a fraction of the price; it is often served as an alternative to caviar on hors-d'œuvre and canapés.

The preparation of whole fish

Sole colbert

This dish may be prepared with other kinds of fish, but it is at its most appealing when made with Dover sole. The presentation is meant to represent a man's tuxedo or dinner jacket with wide lapels.

Preparation

A medium-sized sole should be used weighing between 340–453 g (10–16 oz). The sole should first be prepared by removing the skin, gut, fins and eyes. Then cut down the backbone on the 'white side' as for filleting; cut each fillet to approximately 3 cm (1¼ in) of the side leaving the fillets attached. Turn the fillets back at the edges and cut through the backbone twice with a pair of fish scissors. The sole is then seasoned and panéed through flour, egg and crumbs ready for deep-frying.

Curled whiting (*merlan en colère*)

Preparation

Remove the skin, eyes, guts, gills and fins, then place the tail into the mouth of the fish and secure with half a wooden cocktail stick, pané and deep-fry – removing the cocktail stick once cooked.

The thicker part of the body of the whiting may be incised (ciseler) prior to pané. This will allow even cooking and help shorten the overall cooking time. It will also assist in preventing the whiting being undercooked in the middle, frequently a problem with this dish.

Turbot for the cold buffet

In the past, turbot was often used on cold buffets, almost as much as salmon is today. Salmon seems to have become something of an obsession with chefs. There's no doubt that salmon is a magnificent fish when presented cold, and due to salmon farming it is very economically priced, however, in my opinion it is part of the chef's job to try and widen the range of options that are available to the diner. In former times, passing from one end of a cold buffet to the other end was a voyage of discovery for the diner, who would often be presented with something outside the range of his or her regular dining experience. Today, when customers are coming in contact with a wider range of produce than ever before, the cold buffet seems to be presenting them with less variety. This is one reason why I would recommend turbot.

Preparation

The whole fish is cleaned, trimmed and washed, then poached in a *court bouillon*, with enough white wine added to enhance but not overpower the delicate flavour of the fish. Allow 20 minutes per ½ kg, and allow to cool completely in the cooking liquor. Turbot can then be presented in the same manner as salmon.

Salmon for the cold buffet

Over the years I have cooked hundreds of whole salmon for serving cold, and I have tried many different methods. None has been as successful as the first method shown to me by a local fish and game merchant; it may not be entirely classical, but in my opinion it gives the best result.

Preparation

Remove the scales by holding the salmon by its tail and scraping with the back of a knife, from the tail towards the head, then rinse with cold water. Remove the gills with a pair of fish scissors and remove the entrails by cutting along the middle of the belly starting at the waste hole. Wash out the cavity with plenty of cold running water, making sure that any blood is removed from along the backbone. This may be removed by rubbing with salt, then rinsing.

Prepare the following *court bouillon*:

Vinegar *court bouillon*

To every 4 litres of cold water add the following:

2 large sliced onions	4 bay leaves
4 sliced carrots	25 g (1 oz) parsley stalks
20 white peppercorns	300 ml (1/2 pt) vinegar
300 ml (1/2 pt) white wine	light vegetable oil

1. Place the fish in a fish kettle and cover with cold *court bouillon*. Cover the surface of the liquid with a thin layer of oil.
2. Cover with a tight fitting lid and place several weights on top of the lid to keep it firmly secured.
3. Place on the stove and bring slowly to the boil, allow to simmer gently for 8 – 15 minutes depending on the fish size.
4. Do not uncover. Leave overnight in a cool place.

Trout for the cold buffet

The trout should be very fresh, scaled, gutted and have the gills removed.

Preparation

1. Prepare a *court bouillon* similar to the one for salmon but replacing the vinegar with white wine (see above, vinegar *court bouillon*).
2. Bring the *court bouillon* to the boil and add the trout, do not cover.
3. Simmer for 2 – 5 minutes depending on the size of the fish, then allow to cool in the cooking liquor.
4. When cold, the skin and the dark flesh running along the top of the backbone should be removed with the tip of a sharp knife.
5. Lift the top fillet away from the bone, remove the bone and replace the top fillet.
6. Coat in a layer of aspic jelly or chaud-froid and decorate, then glaze once more with aspic.

Sardines

Sardines must be used while still very fresh.

Preparation

Trim, clean and wash, then grill or shallow-fry.

Herring

Preparation

To grill:

Scale, clean, remove the fins, gills (some people prefer to remove the head) and trim the tail with a pair of fish scissors. Make three incisions (approximately ¹/2 cm / ¹/4 in deep) at an angle on both sides of the thicker part of the fish.

  The roe may be left in the fish during cleaning, but I prefer to remove it and reserve it for later use. The soft roe from the male are used to garnish other fish and for savouries. It also means that the customer does not come across it unexpectedly.

Scaling a whole fish

Remove the scales by holding the fish by the tail, preferably in a sink (to contain any flying scales); scrape with the back of a knife from the tail towards the head to remove the scales, turning from side to side and then over when one side is completed. Rinse with cold water.

Stuffing whole fish (see also Stuffings below and Trussing/tying, p. 61)

Round fish

Remove the insides of the fish and rinse clean, scale the outside. Sprinkle with course grain sea salt and pepper. Stuff the inside of the fish and skewer the opening to close it. Wrap the fish in greaseproof paper and tie and poach in *court bouillon* for approximately 20 – 25 minutes (for a 1 kg fish).

Flat fish

Make a cut down the centre of the entire length of the fish as for filleting. Loosen the flesh with the tips of the finger but do not detach it entirely. Prepare the stuffing and fill the prepared pockets of fish either side of the backbone; place the fish in a buttered earthenware dish and brush with butter, cover with a buttered cartouche of greaseproof or foil and bake at 190°C for 20 – 30 minutes (for a 300 g fish).

Stuffings

All recipes are for ten portions.

Mushroom and herb

120 g (4 oz) butter	15 g chopped parsley
220 g (7 oz) white breadcrumbs	500 g finely diced mushrooms
2 chopped medium onions	250 ml (¹/2 pt) red wine (approx.)
6 eggs	10 g chopped chives

1. Sweat the onion in the butter without colour until soft, add the herbs and mix in the breadcrumbs.
2. Beat the eggs and gradually add to the above. Add the mushrooms, moisten with the wine until a firm paste is achieved, season and mix thoroughly.

The recipe may be altered with the addition of other herbs, for example *fines herbes*, chervil, tarragon, etc., and crushed garlic. The mushrooms can be replaced with wild mushrooms such as cepes, shitake, morrels, etc.

Basic fish stuffing

100 g (3¹/₂ oz) butter.
2 teaspoons fresh herbs (chopped)
200 g (6¹/₂ oz) white breadcrumbs
Grated zest of 1 lemon

10 g (¹/₂ oz) chopped parsley
2 eggs
pinch of grated nutmeg
sea salt and freshly ground pepper.

1. Melt the butter and mix in the breadcrumbs. Add the nutmeg, herbs, and lemon zest. Season and bind with the beaten egg.

The texture of the stuffing will depend on the dryness of the breadcrumbs. If too dry, add an extra egg or liquid such as milk, lemon juice or fish stock to make a soft paste.

Prawn/shrimp stuffing

Modify the basic fish stuffing by adding 200 g (6¹/₂ oz) of whole shrimps or roughly chopped prawns with the breadcrumbs then mix with the butter.

Forcemeats, mousses, mousselines and quenelles

Fish forcemeat (*farce de poisson*)

500 g (1 lb) white fish,
   e.g. sole, whiting, pike
300 ml (¹/₂ pt) double cream

1 × flour panada
2 egg whites
seasoning

1. Mince the fish finely and pass through a sieve or place in a food processor.
2. Gradually add the panada and beat till smooth, slowly add the egg whites. Chill the mix thoroughly by placing in a very cold fridge or in a bowl on top of a bowl of ice, water, and a good pinch of salt.
3. Beat in the chilled cream till the mix is thoroughly combined. (The mixture must be ice cold before adding the cream or else the texture will be too soft.

Fish mousse (*mousse de poisson*)

500 g (1 lb) raw white fish,
   e.g. sole, whiting, pike
2 – 3 egg whites

500 ml (1 pt) double cream
salt, pepper and nutmeg to taste

1. Pass the fish through a mincer or food processor.
2. Gradually add the beaten egg whites and mix till thoroughly combined.
3. Thoroughly chill or place the mix over ice as for fish forcemeat (see above), and gradually add the ice cold cream.
4. Place in a well-buttered seasoned soufflé/ramekin dish and cook *en bain-marie* in a moderate oven or steam at low pressure.

It is better to prepare mousses in small moulds as larger containers require a firmer consistency to prevent collapse.

Mousselines

1. Prepare the mix for mousse or *farce de poisson*, then shape with two dessert spoons and poach in salt water or stock.

Quenelles

1. Prepare the mix for mousseline or *farce de poisson*, then shape with two teaspoons and poach in salt water or stock.

Mousses, mousselines and quenelles are all made from similar mixtures, it is the manner in which they are shaped, cooked and presented which differs.

Mousse

Cooked and presented in a container such as a dariole mould, ramekin or small soufflé mould, cooked in the oven *en bain-marie*.

Mousselines and quenelles

Moulding and shaping

Method one

The most common method is to place one of two spoons in a bowl of hot water and, taking a spoonful of the mixture with the cold spoon, pass the mix from one spoon to the other. The aim is to achieve a rounded shape.

Method two

The second method is to brush a tray with melted butter, and once cool pipe the mixture onto the tray using whatever size of nozzle is preferred.

Method three

Roll the forcemeat on a floured board, then cut across for the size required, these may be then rolled between the fingers until they are elongated in shape.

Cooking

To cook spoon-moulded and piped mousselines and quenelles: place on a buttered tray, pour over boiling stock or salt water until they are three-quarters covered. Place the tray on the edge of the stove and allow to poach gently, moving the tray occasionally until they are firm but still soft to the touch.

Hand-moulded mousselines and quenelles are poached by placing them in a pan of simmering salted water or stock.

Note that the texture and seasoning of forcemeats should be assessed by poaching a little of the mixture prior to moulding and adjusting the mixture by adding more cream if too stiff and more egg white if too loose.

Preservation

Fresh fish is usually delivered chilled in boxes of crushed ice; once delivered it should be kept chilled, in other words as cold as possible without actually freezing. Fish should never be allowed to lie in water and if frozen, should be kept at a minimum of $-18°C$ and defrosted slowly.

Listed below, with examples, are the different methods used for preserving fish.

1. **Chilling**   Most types of fish
2. **Freezing**   Most types and some cuts of fish
3. **Drying**   Bombay duck, Pedah
4. **Canning**   Oily fish e.g. sardines, salmon, anchovies
5. **Smoking**   E.g. trout, mackerel, salmon
6. **Pickling**   Rollmop / Bismark herrings
7. **Salting**   Caviar, lumpfish roe

Often fish is preserved by combining salting and smoking methods to produce 'cured' fish.

French terms

Below is a list of French names for some well-known types of fish.

Cod	Le Cabillaud	Salmon	Le Saumon
Plaice	La Plie	Salmon Trout	La Truite Saumonée
Whiting	Le Merlan	Sardine	Les Sardines
Brill	La Barbue	Whitebait	La Blanchaille
Halibut	Le Flétan	Mackerel	Le Maquereau
Bream	La Breme	Conger Eel	La Congre
Turbot	Le Turbot	Grey Mullet	—
Tuna	Le Thon	Red Mullet	Le Rouget
Coley	—	Herring	Le Hareng
Dover Sole	La Sole (de Douvres)	Skate	La Raie
Lemon Sole	La Limande	Monkfish	La Lotte
Haddock	Èglefin	Trout	La Truite
Finnan Haddock	Èglefin Fumé	Hake	Le Colin

Shellfish

If fish is the ocean's 'main crop' then shellfish is its 'fruit'. Shellfish has several advantages for the chef in that it is rich in flavour and simple to cook and present. It requires little preparation from its natural raw state and is highly versatile, suitable for the simplest of snacks or the most deluxe of meals. Shellfish is available all the year round, but it is most reasonably priced when in season. However, due to various factors such as over-fishing and pollution certain types of shellfish are much scarcer than once was the case and are therefore expensive.

Nutritional value

Shellfish is high in protein and trace elements as well as in calcium, iodine and sodium.

Classification

Shellfish is divided into two main groups: crustaceans and molluscs.

Crustaceans

Characterized by their external skeleton and articulated (movable) limbs, most crustaceans have five pairs of jointed legs, the front two being pincers or claws. The outer-shell is usually black with a tinge of green prior to cooking; this turns red when subjected to heat. The hard outer-shell is made from calcium secreted by the crustacean. Some examples include lobster, prawn and crab.

Molluscs

Molluscs are soft-bodied animals enclosed in a hard shell. Bivalves, such as mussels and oysters, are molluscs which have an upper and lower half to their shells which is joined at the rear allowing the shell to open and close. Molluscs with a single solid shell are called univalves. Squid, cuttlefish and snails are also classified as molluscs.

Quality

The wide variety of shellfish that is available means that most will have some specific points which are applicable only to that species, but the following can be used as a general guide to the purchasing of shellfish.

1. Fresh shellfish should be alive when purchased.
2. Crabs, lobsters, scampi, prawns, crawfish, etc. should be active, the most lively will be the freshest. The tails of lobsters and crawfish should curl up tightly when picked up.
3. Crustaceans should feel heavy in relation to their size and any with broken or cracked shells, or missing claws should be avoided.

4. Oysters, scallops, mussels, clams and other bivalve molluscs should have tightly closed shells, or they should close immediately when tapped. Bivalves that have open shells are dead and should be discarded.
5. Cooked crustaceans should feel heavy in relation to their size, have a clean fresh smell and have no trace of stickiness on their shell.
6. A clean fresh smell is the best guide to all shellfish, both fresh and cooked.

Storage

Shellfish – both raw and cooked – is a highly perishable commodity and should not be stored for any length of time. The reason for purchasing shellfish in its live state is to ensure freshness. All shellfish should be purchased from reputable suppliers to avoid the possibility of obtaining seafood from contaminated waters.

(a) Purchase alive if possible; crustaceans may be kept for a short while in a refrigerator covered with wet sacking or similar. Prawns and shrimps are normally purchased cooked.
(b) Cooked prawns, shrimps etc. may be kept for a short time in a refrigerator, but prolonged storage must be avoided as this can lead to contamination and severe food poisoning.
(c) Cook all shellfish as soon as possible after purchasing.

Purchasing/grades

- Crustaceans such as lobsters, crabs, crawfish, etc. are normally ordered by number and weight.
- Oysters are ordered by the dozen and are graded from 1 to 3 according to size (1 being the largest).
- Raw cockles and mussels are bought by capacity, i.e. pint, litre, gallon, or by weight.
- Scallops are purchased by number.
- Fresh shrimps and prawns are ordered by capacity or weight; cooked or frozen are ordered by weight.
- Squid is ordered by weight.

Cleaning and preparation for cooking

All molluscs should be put into clean salted water, which should be changed several times to remove any sand, grit or mud from inside the shells. Mussels can be kept overnight by placing in cold salt water (preferably sea water) and adding one handful of oatmeal to every 5 kg (gallon) of mussels, this will both feed and fatten up the mussels. Mussels should be scraped or scrubbed with a stiff brush to clean the shells. The fine hairs along the hinge of the shell of the mussel is used to anchor it to rocks and is known as the 'beard': remove this by holding between the thumb and a knife and pulling sharply.

Mussels and clams

After scraping, mussels and clams should be soaked in cold salted water for 2–3 hours to aid the removal of sand. Rinse well prior to cooking.

Prawns, shrimps and crayfish

Remove the head, shell (the carapace), legs and the black vein (the intestines) from the length of the back.

Scallops and oysters

Remove the membrane or beard/skirt from around the meat prior to cooking, or in the case of oysters which are to be served raw, prior to presentation.

Lobsters and crabs

To kill a crab, insert a trussing needle into the soft flesh behind the mouth and then through the hole located beneath the tail flap, stabbing several times. In the case of lobster, place the point of a sharp knife through the shell at the 'cross' of the lateral line at the rear of the head.

It is especially important that lobsters are not overcooked otherwise the flesh can become hard, tough and fibrous.

Cleaning cooked lobster
1. Remove the claws and legs by pulling away close to the lobster's body.
2. Cut in half lengthways, stretch out the tail, then insert the knife through the head at the cross of the lateral line; cut through the tail along the lateral line.
3. Remove the sac (stomach bag) from the head leaving the creamy parts, then remove the black trail from the tail. (The black trail can contaminate lobster so it is important that it is removed and if broken or damaged, the area is washed carefully.)
4. Pull back and out the small pincer of each claw and then crack the claws and remove the flesh in one piece if possible.

Cutting live lobster

For Américaine: Cut through the head of the lobster at the cross of the lateral line on the top of the head, discard the sac and reserve the coral. Remove and crack the claws, cut the tail at its natural sections into collops (slices).

For grilling: Cut into two halves, starting at the cross on the lateral line; remove the sac from the head and the black trail from the tail.

Squid, cuttlefish and octopus

Separate the head and tentacles from the body/tail of the squid/cuttlefish by pulling gently; discard the head, and inner organs and remove the thin cuttlebone. Wash under running water, rubbing vigorously to remove the reddish-coloured outer membrane. Small squid, etc. can then be cut into sections.

To prepare octopus, cut away the beak and anal parts and remove the ink sac. Turn the octopus inside out and remove the internal organs, suckers and tips of the tentacles. Older octopus will require pounding and should be stewed for 2–3 hours until tender.

Gutting

Scampi and crayfish require gutting just prior to cooking, this is done by holding the scampi or crayfish by the head and in the middle of the tail and twisting while gently pulling to separate one from the other; this will expose the trail/gut which should be discarded.

Extracting the flesh

After gutting, place the tail of the scampi or crayfish across a board and bat firmly with the side of a large knife or gently with a cutlet bat to open up the underneath and expose the flesh. The flesh should be gently pulled out in one piece.

Cooking liquors

Court bouillon

It is not necessary to prepare as elaborate a *court bouillon* for shellfish as it is for, say, poached salmon; a simple cooking liquor containing sliced onion, peppercorns, a little salt, sliced carrot and parsley stalks is quite sufficient. The texture of shellfish is improved by the addition of a little vinegar to the *court bouillon*, this will soften the fibres of the shellfish, especially in cases where the texture of the flesh tends to be quite course.

All shellfish is improved by the judicial use of seasoning. Often such items as prawns and shrimps are used in cocktails, seafood platters, omelettes, etc. without first being seasoned; shellfish lose a lot of their natural salt due to the cleaning process, and especially when using frozen shellfish, seasoning with sea salt will greatly enhance the flavour.

Purchasing (crustaceans)

Crab

Specification: Male (cock) crabs should be supplied in at least equal numbers to females (hens). If supplied cooked, the shell should be bright pink and show no signs of bleaching or stickiness; the crab should feel heavy in relation to its size and have a clean fresh smell.

Weights: For dressing: 1/2 – 1 kg; other uses: 1 – 2 1/2 kg.

Description: A reddish-brown coloured, oval-shelled crustacean with two pincers and four pairs of legs. It is important that the crab has two good-sized claws as the majority of the white meat comes from the claws. The male usually contains more white meat and can be distinguished from the female by a smaller tail flap. Crab has an excellent flavour: the smaller crabs are the sweetest whereas the meat from larger crabs can sometimes have a course texture.

Preparation/Cooking: Place in warm water for half an hour prior to cooking then kill by piercing with a skewer just above the mouth (both of these methods will assist in preventing the crab shedding its claws during cooking). Place in boiling liquid, cover and boil gently for 6–8 minutes per 1/2 kg (1 lb) depending on size, then allow to cool in the cooking liquor.

Uses: Dressed crab (see hors-d'œuvre), hors-d'œuvre, salads, sandwiches, soups, sauces.

Lobster

Specification: Order by number and weight, alive and as fresh as possible. Claws and shell will be intact. Numbers of male (cock) lobsters should be at least equal to numbers of females (hens) supplied. If cooked, the shell should be bright pink and show no signs of bleaching or stickiness; the lobster should feel heavy in relation to its size and have a clean fresh smell.

Weights: 1/2 – 1 kg (1 – 2 1/2 lb).

Description: A highly-prized crustacean, with an excellent flavour; blue/black when uncooked, bright red when cooked. The lobster has two large pincers/claws, and the flesh of the male (cock) is considered superior to that of the female (hen). The hen is distinguished from the cock by a broader tail.

Uses: Salads, hot dishes (lobster cardinal, thermidor, newburg), buffets, soups, sauces, hot and cold mousses, hors-d'œuvre, lobster mayonnaise, lobster salad, lobster butter (for lobster salad and mayonnaise, see Salads, p. 251). For certain dishes lobster coral from the hen is used for the colouring and flavouring of sauces.

Crayfish

Specification: Order by number and weight, alive and as fresh as possible. Claws and shell will be intact.

Weights: 50 – 100 g (1 1/2 – 2 1/2 oz).

Description: A small fresh-water lobster found in streams and rivers. Bluey-black coloured when raw, turning bright red when cooked. Crayfish has an excellent flavour, especially the Polish 'red legged' crayfish.

Uses: Soups, buffets, garnishing of dishes and as for lobster.

Crawfish (rock lobster, spiny lobster)

Specification: Order by number and weight, alive and as fresh as possible. The shell will be intact.

Weights: 1 – 2 1/2 kg (2 – 5 lb).

Description: A large lobster-like crustacean, but without claws; light reddish-brown in colour that reddens after boiling. A good mild lobster flavour. The flesh is quite course in texture. Due to its size and appearance it is mainly offered cold but may be served hot as for lobster.

Uses: Hot as for lobster, seafood cocktails, seafood platters, soups, sauces, buffets, hors-d'œuvre.

If presented cold, the tail should be stretched out and tied to a board prior to cooking.

Prawns

Specification: Order by weight or capacity (pint/litre). Shell-on prawns will have an average length of between 8 – 10 cm (3 – 4 in).

Description: A small crustacean, greyish in colour when raw, turning bright pink when cooked. Fresh prawns are far superior in flavour to frozen. King prawns are sourced from warmer seas and are larger than the more common cold water varieties. The texture and flavour of king prawns is slightly inferior but still very good and is ideal for stir-fries.

Uses: Hors-d'œuvre, cocktails, garnishing of fish dishes, soup, salads, sandwiches, hot salads, stir-fries, bouchées, omelettes, savouries.

Scampi (Dublin bay prawn)

Specification: Order by weight, alive or as fresh as possible; shell-on scampi should have an average size of 12 – 20 cm (4½ – 8 in).

Description: Resembles a small lobster, orange-pink in colour, apart from its white legs which do not change their colour when cooked. Scampi normally comes from the Mediterranean or from off the coast of Scotland. It has an excellent flavour and texture. Only the flesh from the tail is used.

Uses: All seafood applications, fried scampi, scampi Provençal, brochettes.

Shrimps

Specification: Order by weight or by capacity (litre/pint). Shell-on shrimps will measure between 5 – 7 cm (2 – 3 in).

Description: Similar to a prawn but smaller; brown/grey in colour turning pink when cooked. Firm dry flesh with an excellent flavour.

Uses: Hors-d'œuvre, potted shrimps, cocktails, garnishing of fish dishes, soup, salads, sandwiches, bouchées, omelettes, savouries.

Purchasing (molluscs)

Oysters

Specification: Order by shell size and number (see Grades, p.70). Native oysters such as Colchester (River Colne), West Mercia and Helford oysters should be supplied between

September and April; Belon or Brittany oysters and French varieties of 'Portuguese oysters', such as Huîtes de parc and Fines de Claires are acceptable alternatives. Pacific oysters (for cooking) are to be supplied only on request. All the above will be supplied live and as fresh as possible with tightly closed shells.

Description: Round flat bivalve mollusc, with a soft to chewy texture and excellent flavour. Native British oysters, which are undoubtedly the best, are expensive and available only when there is an 'R' in the month, the non-breeding period. Portuguese varieties of oysters mature quicker than native varieties and are cheaper but do not possess the same excellent flavour. Pacific oysters are raised commercially in the UK and are available all year round; these are the cheapest but also the poorest in flavour and suitable only for cooked dishes.

Uses: Mainly eaten raw, lightly cooked (poached) oysters may be served mornay, Florentine, deep-fried in breadcrumbs, or used in steak and oyster pies/puddings, hors-d'œuvre, soups, buffets and savouries.

Preparation: Oysters are opened by using a blunt short oyster knife which is specially designed for the purpose: hold the oyster in a thick cloth (to protect the hand) and insert the blade between the shells, move the knife from side to side to sever the muscle and open the oyster. Care should be taken when opening oysters – if done roughly, pieces of sharp shell may be left behind which can cut the inside of the mouth.

It is important that the natural juice contained in oysters is retained as it greatly adds to the flavour. Oysters presented cold in the half shell are served in their natural juices; if oyster are dry, lightly rinse and allow to stand, this will encourage them to produce more natural juices. When cooking oysters, reserve the juice and either add to the dish/sauce or use in other shellfish applications.

Mussels

Specification: Order by weight or capacity (litre/pint). The average shell size will be 5 – 8 cm (2 – 3 in). They will be supplied live with tightly closed shells and free from excessive amounts of encrusted debris. Mussels bought from a reputable supplier come from uncontaminated waters. Also available vacuum-packed.

Description: A thin oval bivalve, with blue/black coloured shell, a soft chewy texture and very good seafood flavour.

Uses: Hors-d'œuvre, soups, hot dishes (e.g. mussels marinière and Paulette). Often eaten pickled.

Scallops

Specification: Great or deep-sea scallops will be supplied by number, with an average shell size of 10 – 13 cm (4 – 5 in). Bay scallops will be acceptable should deep-sea scallops be in short supply, average shell size is 8 cm (3 in). Small queen scallops should be supplied only on request. All the above will be supplied live with tightly closed shells and free from excessive amounts of encrusted debris, mud, etc. Bay scallops bought from a reputable supplier come from uncontaminated waters.

Description: Large round bivalve with white flesh and an orange-red coloured roe, chewy texture with an excellent flavour. Scallops are named after the fluted shape of their shells, which are in two halves, one rounded in shape and the other flat.

Scallops are normally available from autumn to winter but are at their best during January and February. There are three varieties of scallops: the largest is the great or deep-sea scallop, the next is the bay scallop which is medium-sized, the smallest is the queen scallop. If scallops are purchased with the shell removed they should be plump and the roe should be brightly coloured and moist.

To remove from shell: place rounded shell downwards onto a hot solid top stove until the shell opens, then separate the flesh from the flat shell with a sharp knife. Alternatively, hold in a thick cloth and with the flat shell uppermost, insert a sharp firm-bladed knife between the shell at the front, cut through the muscle to allow the shell to open. Scallops are presented in the rounded half of the shell.

Uses: Hot dishes (mornay, *bonne femme*) deep-fry in breadcrumbs, buffets.

Cockles

Specification: Order by weight or capacity (litre/pint); average shell is between 3 – 5 cm (1 – 2 in). They will be supplied live with tightly closed shells free from excessive amounts of encrusted debris. Cockles supplied from a reputable source will come from uncontaminated waters. They should be allowed to soak in clean salted water prior to cooking.

Description: Small round bivalve with a chewy texture and good flavour, eaten mainly in the UK. Cockles are at their best during the summer months.

Uses: Soups (cockles may be used as a substitute for clams in chowder), salads, fish and pasta dishes. Often eaten pickled.

Squid (calamare) (technically not a mollusc but a cephalopod)

Specification: Purchase by weight, average size should be 15 – 20 cm (6 – 8 in). Will be supplied as fresh as possible.

Description: White flesh with a mottled skin, squid has two tentacles and eight arms. It is important that squid is prepared correctly and that only the smaller squid are used for the quicker methods of cookery, otherwise it can be rubbery and unpleasant to eat. Cuttlefish and octopus can be cooked in the same way as squid, but in their case tenderization and correct use is even more important.

Uses:
Squid/Cuttlefish: deep-fry, stir fry, hot seafood dishes, poach or stew.
Octopus: boil/stew then deep-fry or grill.

Sea urchin (technically not a mollusc but an echinoderm)

Specification: Order by number. Both white or black urchins are acceptable; they will be as fresh as possible.

Description: Until recently sea urchin, like squid, was not well known in the UK. However, it has gained in popularity among chefs. The white sea urchin is regarded as a great delicacy but the black species is also acceptable. A hard outer spiny shell encases the orange and yellow coloured roe which has a salty, raw egg-like texture and creamy seafood flavour; it may be eaten raw or used as a flavouring in sauces, soups, omelettes, scrambled eggs, seafood stews, etc.

Cooking times (boiling/poaching)

Shrimps   Simmer in salt water for 5 minutes.

Prawns   Simmer in salt water for 10 minutes.

Scampi   As for prawns.

Crayfish   As for prawns.

Lobster   500 – 750 g (1 – 1½ lb) simmer for 15 – 20 minutes.
(Allow to cool in cooking liquor).

Crawfish   As for lobster.

Crabs   750 g – 1 kg (1½ – 2½ lb) simmer for 15 – 25 minutes.
(Allow to cool in cooking liquor).
1 kg and above, 25 – 30 minutes.
(Allow to cool in cooking liquor).

Oysters   Cover and bring to the boil for a few seconds, remove from heat and allow to cool in the pan.

Scallops   Poach in water/wine for 3 – 4 minutes.

Mussels   Cover, bring to the boil and cook for 5 minutes until shells open.

Methods of preservation

Freezing   Most varieties of shellfish are available frozen including:

Prawns	Lobsters
Scampi	Mussels
Shrimps	Scallops
(cooked	Crawfish
and potted)	

Pickled   Cockles   Mussels

Canned	Oysters	Clams
	Mussels	Shrimps
	Prawns	Squid
	Crabmeat	

Smoked	Oysters	Squid
	Clams	

Dried	Squid	Abalone
	Cuttlefish	Octopus

Fresh shellfish can be frozen but only the freshest should be used. Molluscs should first be washed and removed from their shells. Frozen shellfish should preferably be used within four to six weeks after freezing.

French terms

Crab	Le Crabe	Mussels	Les Moules
Crawfish	La Langouste	Oysters	Les Huîtres
Crayfish	L'Écrevisse	Scallops	La Coquille Saint-Jacques
Lobster	Le Homard	Squid	Le Calmar
Prawns	Les Crevettes Roses	Cuttlefish	La Seiche
Scampi	La Langoustine	Octopus	Le Poulpe
Shrimps	Les Crevettes Grises	Sea Urchin	L'Oursin

FIVE

Meat

The specifications used in this chapter for meats are based on the diagram set out below.

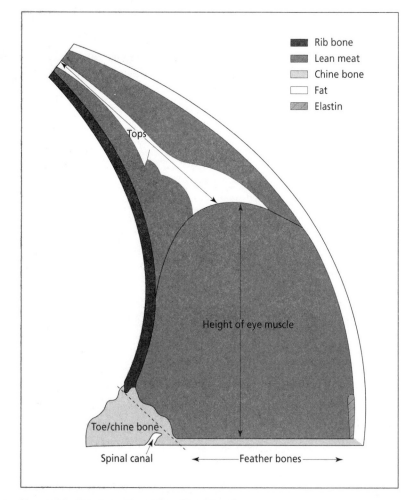

Figure 5.1 **Cross-section of a rib of beef**

The following list of technical terms will assist in the purchasing of cuts of meat.

Table 5.1 **Butchery terms and definitions**

Term	Meat type	Definition
Aitchbone	B, L, P, V	Bone that joins pelvis to the leg (femur).
Back fat	P	White fat covering loins and part of shoulder
Backstrap gristle	B, L, V	Elastin. Yellow fat running along the eye of the meat
Bark	L	The brown skin on lamb
Blade bone	B, L, P, V	Shoulder blade, flat scapula bone
Chain	B	Knobbly strip of meat running along sirloin/fillet.
Chine bone	B, L, P, V	Backbone, running along loins, ribs, etc. (toe bone)
Chump bone	P, L, V	Thick end of loin, part of pelvis fused into one bone
Eye of meat	B, L, P, V	Round long muscle running along backbone, e.g. loin
Feather bones	B, L, P, V	Small bones running under the eye of meat
Flaps	L	Breast meat
'Flare'	P	White fat from kidney, fillet and belly
Frenched	L	French-trimmed ends of rib bones exposed and clean
Kidney knob	B, L, V	Kidney and its covering of suet
Rib fingers	B, L, P, V	Strips of meat between ribs
Scoring	L, P	Parallel knife cuts, through rind (P) or fat (L)
Scrag/scrag end	L	The neck and its bones
Silver sheen gristle	B	Bluish gristle on thick end of fillet
T-shaped bone	B, L, P, V	Back bones (lumbar vertebra)
Toe bone	B, L, P, V	Pointed part of 'chine bone'
'Tops'	B, L, P, V	The length between the edge of the eye of meat and where the breast, flank, belly etc. has been removed

Key: B = Beef   L = Lamb   P = Pork   V = Veal

Beef

Introduction

Beef is one of the most widely consumed meats in the UK, yet it is difficult to obtain top quality or even consistent quality regularly in this country. The purchaser must be able to recognize signs of quality, age, breed, the method of rearing and the length of time the carcass has been matured by hanging: remember, Age, Breed, Care and Feed.

Age

The older the animal is when slaughtered the more extractives will have built-up in its tissue (depending on the type of feed it has been given,) therefore the more tasty the beef will be. The average age in the UK for the slaughter of cattle used to be 18–21 months; in Europe the preference is for older beef – three years is normal, but 4–5 years is not unusual. Under present UK government regulations, no cattle over 30 months old can be slaughtered for human consumption. A large amount of the beef produced for home consumption is slaughtered as young as twelve months, with it perhaps reaching the ripe old age of sixteen months.

Different breeds mature at different rates and the recent cross-breeding of continental breeds with British animals has complicated matters even further; this was done to provide a leaner product, but as fat distributed through the animal's tissue assists in tenderizing and flavouring the meat during cooking, the addition of extra fat is needed with some cuts.

Breed

The main breeds of British beef are: Shorthorns, Herefords and Aberdeen Angus.

Care

In the past, cattle were reared mainly on grass in mixed herds. Modern intensive farming methods mean that the majority of cattle are now separated shortly after birth and transported, sometimes for long periods, to be reared intensively. Some of these cattle may never come in contact with their natural diet – grass (see Feed, below).

The treatment of cattle before slaughter and the processing of the carcasses afterwards all have a bearing on the quality of beef that is produced, i.e. if the animal has to travel a long way to the abattoir the stress caused by this will affect the required hanging time. This is because if the animal is tired or nervous at the time of slaughter, its muscles tense up and thus it requires an extended hanging time.

Hanging is the maturation of the carcass after slaughter and this and diet are the main influences on the quality of the meat. An older animal that has been hung for three to four weeks will be deliciously tender and full of flavour. Hanging allows the enzymes that naturally occur in the meat to break-down the connective tissue making the meat more tender and increasing the flavour. However, long maturation has various drawbacks for the producer: storage costs money, evaporation of water means that the carcass loses weight, and the well-matured meat is a deep red, sometimes almost approaching black colour. This is unacceptable to major retail outlets such as supermarkets who have grown used to bright red meat and even install coloured lights in their stores to enhance the beef's bright red colour. Fresh beef may be pleasing to the eye but to the professional caterer it is taste and texture that counts.

Most meat in the UK is hung for a maximum of seven to ten days, in other countries it may be hung for anything up to eight weeks. In my experience two or preferably three weeks is ideal; to achieve this special arrangements may have to be made with your suppliers.

Feed

In the UK three-quarters of all beef is produced by intensive farming. This involves calves bred for milk production being separated from their mothers soon after birth then fed on milk powder and given various antibiotics.

Cheap additives have been used to enhance proprietary feeds including animal protein sources. These have been linked to the outbreak of BSE (bovine spongiform encephalopathy or 'mad cow disease') that has so devastated British farming, and this is the reason why the addition of animal protein to cattle feed was banned in the UK in 1989. This intensive system continues until the calf reaches the age of approximately 5 – 6 months, when it is put on a mainly cereal-based diet consisting of crushed barley or other cereal (and before the ban, combined with protein-rich ingredients including bonemeal, fishmeal and dried blood). Finally, the calf may be put out to grass for a short time before being slaughtered.

The intensive system is suited to major retailers and supermarkets; the advantages are consistent-sized animals and therefore cuts, little fat which is white in colour, low production costs, minimal hanging/storage time and a short production time. However, producing beef in this way has several disadvantages to the professional caterer, these are:

(a) The product is practically tasteless.
(b) Cattle bred for milk production do not produce the best beef.
(c) Cows are vegetarian and are not equipped to process non-vegetable food sources; this can lead to contaminated meat as proved by the BSE affair.
(d) The texture of barley-cereal-fed beef is much softer than traditionally-reared beef.

Thus intensively-produced beef may have advantages for producers, suppliers, retailers and amateur cooks, but not for the professional caterer or connoisseur.

A good larder chef must be able to distinguish between 'real beef' and 'barley beef': barley beef is very pale coloured, has little fat, and what fat there is is white, and the texture when raw is soft; real beef is produced in a more humane way, which is better for the animal and for the consumer (and certainly safer).

In non-intensive farming traditional breeds are reared using an age-old system. Calves are left with their mother and fed on her milk, they are then gradually weaned onto grass, their natural diet. Once weaned, the calves may, depending on the season, be brought inside or turned out to pasture. After two or three years on a varied diet, including hay and silage, they are ready for slaughter. Once correctly slaughtered and hung the traditional method will produce the highest standard of beef.

The priority now is to eradicate BSE from the food chain; this can be done only by removing the tissue found in cattle most likely to contain the infective agent, i.e. the brain, spinal cord and intestine, and by selective slaughter/culling of cattle with a high possibility of developing the disease, such as cattle from infected herds and cows that are over 30 months old. Caterers can still obtain beef from herds that have been unaffected by the BSE epidemic; pure bred herds such as Aberdeen Angus and beef supplied through the 'Q' guild of butchers are a safe source of beef, and bear testimony to the necessity for traditional rearing methods. However, the regulations to do with beef on the bone outlined below, apply to all sources of beef, regardless of origin.

Beef Bones Regulations 1997

These came into force on 16 December 1997. They require the de-boning of British beef over six months old, prior to it being supplied to the ultimate consumer (see Definition of terms, below). The regulations allow British beef with the bone in to be supplied to food businesses such as caterers, but it is the obligation of the caterer to ensure that no beef on the bone is supplied to the ultimate consumer. The regulations also prohibit the cooking of beef on the bone or the use of bones to prepare food products, for example stocks. De-boning must be carried out in a hygienic manner so as to avoid the contamination of any other foods or ingredients. All tools used for de-boning must be sterilized so as to avoid cross-contamination.

Storage of bones

Bones must be stored in a hygienic manner separate from other products, preferably in a lidded, labelled container in a chilled area. They must be disposed of without undue delay; but it is permitted to store bones in order to accumulate an appropriate amount for disposal. Storing bones for too long a period prior to disposal is an offence.

Bone disposal

Beef bones must be disposed of through approved methods by the local government authority. Commercial arrangements can be made for the disposal of bones, but this is usually at a high cost. See below, Record-keeping.

Definitions of terms used in the regulations

Bovine animal All bovine animals over six months old at the time of slaughter.

Bone-in-beef Any carcass or fresh meat, including, chilled-frozen, or vacuum-packed meat, which contains any bones or has bones attached to it.

Bone Any part of the animal that contains bone, including marrow, tail and feet, but excluding cartilage and gristle.

Ultimate consumer Anyone who buys beef for other than a food business. In the case of caterers this means the diner. It is an offence to provide beef on the bone or beef cooked on the bone, regardless of whether or not the meat has been cooked on the premises or supplied to the premises already cooked.

Record-keeping

It is the duty of the occupier of the food premises to keep records that show the source of any bones, i.e. the premises where the bones came from and their destination. These records must be available for inspection by environmental health officers and should be kept for a minimum of two years.

Penalties

The penalties are the same as for those in the Food Safety Act 1990.

> In a magistrates' court: up to £5,000 fine and/or up to six months imprisonment.
> In a crown court: up to two years imprisonment, and/or an unlimited fine.
> In Scotland: equivalent penalties after trial and conviction.

The above regulations should be temporary, I have therefore chosen to include in this chapter the joints, offal and applications which include bones.

Quality

There are various things to look out for when buying beef. These include:

1. Lean meat should be a deep red colour with small flecks of white fat (marbling).
2. The fat should be firm, a brittle texture, creamy white colour and odourless.
3. Beef from old dairy cattle (cowbeef) has yellow fat which is often soft.
4. Beef should be hung a minimum of fourteen days at 1°C, with a relative humidity of 90 per cent.

Convenience beef

Beef is available vacuum-packed fresh, chilled or frozen as boneless, wholesale cuts, this process is called 'cryovac'. The airtight packaging keeps the meat in very good condition and means a longer shelf-life than ordinary meat (as long as the seal is not broken). The packs must be stored the right way up, so that the blood does not stain the fat surface, at a temperature of 0°C to −1°C, and used in strict rotation. When required for use, the pack should be punctured and the blood drained away. On opening the seal a sour odour is noticeable, but this should disappear shortly after exposure to the air.

Storage

1. After hanging, beef should ideally be stored at 1°C, with a humidity of approximately 90 per cent; at this temperature beef may be safely kept for up to three weeks.
2. Beef that has been vacuum-packed has three advantages over non-sealed beef as it prevents:
   (a) drying out, which discolours the beef
   (b) growth of bacteria – this is inhibited by the vacuum-packed atmosphere
   (c) the fat becoming rancid due to contact with the air.
3. Vacuum-packed beef has a life of approximately six weeks from the date of production.
4. Beef that has been blast frozen and sealed will keep for six months if held at a minimum temperature of −18°C.
5. Frozen beef should be completely thawed in a refrigerator before use and should always be clearly labelled, dated and include the weight.

Portion control

Portion sizes are given in this chapter for each specification of cut. As a general rule, the amount allowed per portion for a joint of meat is 230–340 g (8–12 oz).

Buying specifications

An excellent catalogue of meat specifications is contained in *The Meat Buyers' Guide for Caterers* by John Stone, Roger Moore and Henry Tattersall, International Business Pubishing in association with the Meat and Livestock Commission, but it is possible to compile your own using a checklist such as the one given here:

Breed of animal:
Country of origin:
Type of carcass, including specification:
Length of hanging time:
Exact location of cut:
Trim level:
Fat level:
Method of preparation (e.g. boned, rolled or trimmed):
Thickness (if applicable):
Method of packaging:
Labelling:

Butchery

Few caterers have the capacity to process a whole carcass therefore in this section I will instead concentrate on the quartered carcass and the different grades. As well, a description is given of the various cuts and their uses.

Carcass

This is the whole body of the animal excluding all inedible offal but including all edible offal.

Side

A carcass split laterally in equal halves.

Quarter (fore and hind)

A side split between the eleventh and twelfth ribs, each side will yield two quarters, one forequarter (the front of the beast) and hindquarter (the rear half).

Hindquarter

The hindquarter is the part of the carcass that is of particular interest to the larder chef as the majority of first class joints (joints which may be roasted or broken down into smaller cuts for grilling or frying) come from it.

Shin/leg (hindleg)

Specification: Cut at the joint between the tibia and fibula bones and the patella; 90 per cent visual lean (this means that to look at the meat should be 90 per cent fat-free).

Weight: including bones, approximately 7 – 8 kg (14 – 16 lb).

Description: Lean, dark-coloured meat with a high proportion of intra-muscular connective tissue (collagen) which breaks down (hydrolyzes) during slow, moist cooking into gelatine. A hard-worked muscle containing a high level of extractives and is therefore well-flavoured.

Uses: Mainly used minced for the clarification of consommés but may also be used in brown stews, pre-cooked pie fillings, for enriching stocks and in speciality soups.

Topside

Specification: Inside muscle of the top piece after separation of silverside and thick flank (toprump) through natural seams, leg and all bones removed.

Weight: excluding bones, 8 – 10 kg (16 – 20 lb).

Description: A very lean piece of meat, the muscles have not been as highly worked so it has medium amounts of connective tissue and extractives.

Uses: Diced and used in stews, sliced, batted out and braised as beef olives, sliced and braised, cut, tied and braised in one piece, minced for bitocks/hamburgers, second-class roasting joint (see Topside – Rolled), beef *sautés*.

Topside (rolled)

Specification: Inside muscle of the top piece after separation of silverside and thick flank (toprump) through natural seams, leg and all bones removed. A whole topside is cross-cut into two or three joints, depending on the weight required and is trimmed of all elastin (gristle), then tied or netted.

For roasting, fat is normally tied around the joint (this should not be necessary if there is natural fat present or if the joint has been prepared in-house; topside that has been bought in prepared for roasting usually has excessive added fat and is charged at the price of beef).

Description: A very lean piece of meat, the muscles have not been as worked, so it contains medium amounts of connective tissue and extractives.

Weight: As specified in recipe. Normally 5 – 8 kg (10 – 16 lb).

Uses: As for topside.

Silverside

Specification: Outside muscle of the top piece, separated from thick flank and topside, should be well trimmed.

Weight: 10 – 14 kg (20 – 28 lb).

Description: Reasonably hard-working muscle, therefore it contains a moderately high level of connective tissue and extractives and is therefore quite well flavoured. Long slow cooking is required.

Uses: The traditional use for this joint is salting and boiling for which it is ideal, it may also be used in stews, braised in slices, or in one piece, the whole joint may be divided into two and roll/tied to make the cooking/processing easier.

Thick flank (top rump)

Specification: Middle muscle of top piece between topside and silverside with all bones removed.

Weight: 12 – 14 kg (24 – 28 lb).

Description: Hard-worked muscle, high in connective tissue and extractives, making it full-flavoured. Requires long moist cooking.

Uses: This has become one of the most popular joints for stewing and braising.

Rump (whole)

Specification: Separated from sirloin at the point of the hip bone and the sixth lumbar vertebra, including hip bones and rump fillet. Suet content should not exceed 2 per cent of the initial weight, no portion of thick flank or silverside will remain on the posterior section of the rump.

Weight: 10 – 12 kg (20 – 24 lb).

Description: Lean and fairly tender cut, which has slightly more flavour than sirloin but must be correctly hung and matured to reach an acceptable eating quality (texture) level.

Uses: Grilling and frying (steaks), may also be sliced thinly and used in beef stir-fries or minced for hamburgers/bitocks.

Figure 5.2 **Rump**

Rump (boneless)

Specification: Taken from the whole rump after removal of fillet, skirt and all the bones.

Weight: Boneless 8 – 10 kg (16 – 20 lb).

Description: As for rump.

Uses: As for rump.

Sirloin (long/whole/rump and loin)

Specification: The remaining part of the hindquarter after removing the top piece including the long fillet, wing rib and part of the rump (the sirloin is removed from the rump by cutting between the last T-shaped bone and the hip bone). Channel fat, suet and kidney knob will be removed. The thin flank is removed by a cut running parallel close to the chine bone, so that the length of the 'tops' do not exceed the height of the eye muscle. The surface fat should not exceed a thickness of 25 mm (1 in).

Weight: 10 – 14 kg (20 – 28 lb).

Description: Tender and well-flavoured if allowed to mature correctly.

Uses: First-class roasting joint both on and off the bone, mostly used for cutting into steaks for grilling and frying. (See also Beefsteaks)

Sirloin (short)

As for sirloin but with whole rump and wing rib removed. Excess thin flank is removed by cutting parallel to the chine bone 25 mm (1 in) above the eye of muscle. Tops at wing-rib end of sirloin do not exceed the height (diameter) of the eye muscle. Including fillet.

Sirloin (chump end)

As for sirloin but remove the wing rib by cutting between the first and second lumbar vertebrae.

Figure 5.3 **Sirloin rump**

Figure 5.4 **Sirloin loin**

Figure 5.5 **Sirloin entrecôte trim**

Sirloin (boneless)

As for sirloin but with all bones removed, the inclusion of the long fillet is optional.

Striploin (standard)

As for sirloin but without the long fillet.

Striploin (short cut)

As for sirloin but with flank removed by cutting 13 mm (½ in) from eye muscle at rump end and 25 mm (1 in) at rib end. Chain should be removed.

Striploin (entrecôte trim)

As for sirloin but with all gristle removed, including the strip of elastin/backstrap gristle and its covering of fat.

Weight: (Whole) 10 – 12 kg (20 – 24 lb); (Short) 8 – 10 kg (16 – 20 lb); (Striploin) 5 – 7 kg (10 – 14 lb).

Description: Tender and well-flavoured if allowed to mature correctly.

Uses: Ideal first-class roasting joint both on and off the bone, used mostly for cutting into steaks for grilling and frying. (See also Beefsteaks, p.94)

Fillet

Whole
Specification: Situated on the underside of the whole sirloin, extending to the rump at its thickest part (head), continuing along the sirloin and tapering to its thinnest part (tail) at the last T-shaped bone; all deposits of fat and suet should be removed.

Loin
Specification: This is the portion of the fillet that extends along the sirloin and excludes the head (rump fillet).

Figure 5.6 **Whole fillet of beef**

Weight: (Whole) 3 – 4 kg (6 – 8 lb). (Loin) 2 – 3 kg (4 – 6 lb).

Description: Probably the least used muscle on the carcass, this means that it is the tenderest cut and therefore highly prized and priced.

Uses: Roasting, grilling, frying. First-class roast, usually encased in pastry, brioche, etc. to protect its delicate texture and to conserve moisture and flavour. Fillet for roasting is normally prepared by inserting strips of fat into the meat (see Larding, p. 90) then poêled (pot roast).

Head/châteaubriand

The head of the fillet is grilled for two or more persons, and should weigh 500 – 600 g (16 – 20 oz). Usually carved at the table.

Middle

The middle of the fillet is used for fillet steaks/tournedos (see Beefsteaks, p. 98).

Tail

This is normally cut into strips and used for beef stroganoff, alternative uses include beef/steak tartare and spaghetti bolognaise (used minced or finely chopped).

Wing rib/wing end of sirloin

Specification: Cut from the anterior end of a whole sirloin at the chump end between the first and second vertebrae. The thin flank will be removed parallel to the chine bones so that the tops do not exceed the height of the eye muscle; the wing rib should contain 3 – 4 rib bones, approximately two T-shaped bones, and the chine bone (toe-bone) should be removed.

Weight: 4 – 5 kg (8 – 10 lb).

Description: See sirloin (whole). The wing rib is part of a long/whole sirloin and is processed in exactly the same way except when prepared as above and roasted as a joint.

Uses: Roasting, grilling, frying.

Thin flank

Specification: This is the thin piece of meat cut along from the wing end to edge of the topside/silverside.

Weight: 8 – 9 kg (16 – 18 lb).

Description: A fairly lean and tender piece of meat, but not the most convenient shape.

Uses: Mincing, stewing, boiled or braised (rolled in one piece), sausages.

Larding

Larding is when strips of fat are inserted in roasting joints such as fillet or sirloin. It is often used with beef that has little natural fat content. Inserting strips of pork fat will increase moisture and flavour. Strips of pork fat measuring 6 – 12 mm ($^1/_4$ – $^1/_2$ in) are chilled, a hole is made along the grain of the meat, and the fat is placed into the needle and inserted in the meat.

Forequarter

The forequarter contains fewer prime joints than the hindquarter but it has the advantage of providing some of the more highly flavoured joints for braising and stewing.

Forerib

Specification: This is cut from the last three – four ribs of a forequarter, by cutting between the sixth and seventh ribs, the flank/flat ribs are removed by a cut parallel to the chine bone (toe-bone) leaving the height of tops less than 106 mm (4 in) at the ninth and tenth ribs. The amount of flank should not exceed the diameter of the eye muscle. There will be an even covering of fat not exceeding three-quarters of an inch.

There are various alternatives to the above cut, all of which relate to the roasting process; these include cutting between the fifth and sixth ribs to give a five-bone forerib and removal of the chine bone (toe-bone), feather bones, blade bone and elastin (known to butchers as backstrap gristle or paddiewax gristle). The joint is then tied with string around the girth between the ribs.

Weight: 7 – 8 kg (14 – 16 lb); five-bone prepared for roasting will weigh approximately the same amount but will have a better meat to bone/gristle ratio.

Description: A well-flavoured, reasonably tender joint, ideal for roasting if matured correctly.

Uses: Roasting, grilling, frying. This joint has replaced sirloin as the most popular roasting joint, mainly due to its price and convenient size. However, forerib also provides rib-eye steaks: these are the eye muscles of the forerib trimmed and cut across the grain and are used as an alternative to the traditional steak cuts.

Middle rib

Specification: The cut between the chuck rib and the forerib cut between the second and third ribs, sawing through the shoulder blade to include four rib bones. The brisket and flank are removed.

Weight: 8 – 9 kg (16 – 18 lb).

Description: An 'in-between' joint – too good for stewing but not quite good enough for a first-class roast.

Uses: Roasting (second class), braising (in joints).

Chuck rib

Specification: The remaining cut which contains the rib bones between the sticking piece (neck) and middle rib; the brisket should be removed.

Weight: 12 – 14 kg (24 – 28 lb).

Description: A lean and well-flavoured joint, ideal for stewing. Butchers refer to it as 'chuck steak' or 'steak meat', although it is not used whole.

Uses: Stewing, braising, fillings for pies. Ideal for dicing and stewing, slicing and braising and for pie fillings; can be minced, but the high price makes this an expensive option.

Sticking piece

Specification: The remaining section of the forequarter after the brisket has been removed, cut through the shoulder ball joint and containing six neck bones.

Weight: 7 – 9 kg (14 – 18 lb).

Description: A hard-worked muscle and therefore well-flavoured, but fiddly to prepare due to the presence of neck bones.

Uses: Stewing, mincing, sausages and pie fillings.

Plate

Specification: Portion of flank situated beneath the forerib between the leg of mutton cut and the end of the forequarter. Bones should be removed.

Weight: 8 – 9 kg (16 – 18 lb).

Description: A well-flavoured tough joint, economical but restricted in its applications.

Uses: Stewing, mincing, sausages. Boiling: plate can be rolled, tied and boiled but only when the quality is first class.

Brisket

Specification: Located beneath the leg of mutton, cut across the rib bones from the point of the sternum to the sixth and seventh ribs.

Weight: 16 – 18 kg (32 – 36 lb).

Description: Similar to plate, brisket is supplied on or off the bone (rolled), and tends to have a high amount of fat (how much fat is acceptable must be made clear to your supplier).

Uses: Boiling (pickled in brine or plain), pressed beef, boiled beef French style.

Leg of mutton cut

Specification: Located above the brisket and separated from the blade bone and chuck at the natural seam, to produce a joint roughly similar in shape to a leg of mutton.

Weight: 10 – 12 kg (20 – 24 lb).

Description: A well-flavoured often ignored joint as it tends to be quite tough, and therefore requires a long period of slow moist cooking.

Uses: Stewing, braising (both whole and in one piece).

Shank

Specification: The shank is removed from the forequarter by cutting through the joint at the elbow.

Weight: 6 – 7 kg (12 – 14 lb).

Description: Lean, dark-coloured meat with a high proportion of intra-muscular connective tissue (collagen) which breaks down (hydrolyzes) during slow, moist cooking into gelatine. A hard-worked muscle containing a high level of extractives and is therefore well-flavoured.

Uses: As for shin: the clarification of consommés, pre-cooked pie fillings, enriching stocks and in speciality soups.

Beef offal

The term offal comes from the expression 'off falls' – meaning pieces that fell off or out of the carcass; it has come to mean all the ancillary parts of an animal other than the main joints. The range of offal available has recently been reduced because of worries about transmission of BSE (see Beef Bones Regulations, p. 82). In this section I have also included bones, fat and marrow as these too have valuable uses.

Quality

All offal should be as fresh as possible, with an even colour, there should be no unpleasant smell, discolouration or stickiness.

Bones (see also Beef Bones Regulations, p. 82)

If ordered separately these should be the large marrow bones from the legs sawn into manageable pieces. They should be fresh and have a pleasant smell.

Uses: White and brown beef stocks and meat glaze, trivets for roasting joints.

Fat

Fat from around the kidneys (suet) should be reserved for other uses for example pastry, puddings and stuffings. All other fat should be melted (rendered) and used as below and for first-class dripping.

Uses: Roasting fat, sealing meat for stewing/braising, Yorkshire pudding, roasting potatoes.

Marrow (see also Beef Bones Regulations, p. 82)

Beef bone marrow is a valuable asset to the chef, it is removed by sawing the bones into sections then laterally on both sides until the semi-circles of bone can be separated leaving the marrow intact; this process is made easier by chilling the marrow bones well beforehand. If ordered pre-prepared it should be whole, firm and have a fresh smell.

Uses: Savouries, speciality soups, enriching sauces, grill garnishes.

Kidney

Ox kidney is prepared by removing the skin/membrane tubes, gristle and fat (the fat assists in keeping the kidney moist and for this reason should be kept on for as long a time as possible prior to cooking), then cut as required. It should have a firm texture and a fresh smell with no odour of ammonia or traces of stickiness.

Uses: Diced, steak and kidney pie, sliced and braised, kidney soup.

Heart

Less popular today, ox heart tends to be dry and tough; calves heart is preferable. It should not have too much fat or too many tubes and should be moist when cut.

Uses: Braise – remove arterial tubes by cutting round inside of the heart, remove excess fat. Marinate inside with oil and lemon juice and stuff with parsley and thyme stuffing or forcemeat and sew the top up with a trussing needle and string.

Liver

Good quality, fresh liver should have an even colour and be moist with a pleasant smell.

Uses: Braise – remove skin/membrane, tubes and gristle, cut on an angle into thin slices and slightly bat out with a steak hammer.

Tongue

It should have a firm texture with a pleasant smell and no sign of stickiness. The majority of ox tongue to be served cold is bought ready-prepared – home-pickling/brining of meats is not recommended because of the risk of contamination.

Uses: Braised ox tongue (fresh), boiled ox tongue (salted).

Fresh ox tongue should have all bone and gristle from the throat end removed and be soaked in salt water overnight. Pickled ox tongue should be soaked in water overnight then boiled.

Tail (see Beef Bones Regulations, p. 82)

Oxtail free from bone or marrow is still permitted. It should have no signs of stickiness and have a pleasant smell. The proportion of fat should not be too high or too yellow. Oxtail is one of the most richly-flavoured meats you will find, it has a high level of extractives and a gelatinous texture when cooked.

Uses: Braised oxtail, oxtail soup. Purchased skinned, it is cut between the natural joints and trimmed of excess fat.

Tripe

Honeycomb tripe is considered the best, it should be creamy white with no discolouration, traces of stickiness or a bad smell.

Tripe is less popular than it used to be but prepared correctly it can be a nutritious addition to a menu. Because as it is easily digestible it is popular with some elderly people.

Uses: Hot – tripe and onions, tripe *à la mode de Caen*. Cold – cooked and dressed with vinaigrette as an hors d'œuvre.

Tripe is prepared by the tripe dresser, (cleaned, washed, blanched) then soaked in cold water and cut into even-sized pieces; unless it is to be used for tripe *à la mode de Caen* in which case it is left in its natural state.

Steaks

All beef steaks (apart from rib-eye steaks) come from the hindquarter. The specifications given here are intended both for the butcher and for the larder chef.

I have included standard sirloin steak which is now seen as distinct from entrecôte steak, which it once mirrored. Weights given for cuts are average portion sizes, depending on the course.

Weight tolerances

To maintain a consistent level of quality and profit it is important that weights for steak remain within pre-set tolerances.

These are set maximum variables to a plus and minus limit.

Specified weight	Tolerance
Under 170 g (6 oz)	+/– 5 g (¹/₄ oz)
Over 170 g (6 oz), under 340 g (12 oz)	+/– 10 g (¹/₂ oz)
Over 340 g (12 oz), under 510 g (18 oz)	+/– 15 g (³/₄ oz)
Over 510 g (18 oz)	+/– 25 g (1 oz)

For example, if 226g (8 oz) portions are ordered, then individual items weighing between 216 – 236 g (7¹/₂ oz – 8¹/₂ oz) would be acceptable.

Sirloin steak (standard)

Cut from striploin.

Fat: Should not exceed 13mm ($^1/_2$ in).

Weights: 170 g (6 oz); 198 g (7 oz); 226 g (8 oz); 283 g (10 oz).

Preparation: Cut across the grain of the eye muscle, at an even thickness. Remove elastin/backstrap gristle but leave side chain intact. Length of tops should not exceed 25 mm (1 in).

Figure 5.7 **Standard sirloin steak**

Entrecôte steak (sirloin steak, specially trimmed)

Cut from striploin entrecôte.

Fat: Should not exceed 13 mm ($^1/_2$ in).

Weights: 170 g (6 oz); 198 g (7 oz); 226 g (8 oz); 283 g (10 oz).

Preparation: Cut across the grain of the eye muscle, at an even thickness; all gristle/elastin should be removed, including that which runs through the eye muscle at the cut end of the loin. Remove chain. The tops should not exceed 13 mm ($^1/_2$ in).

Entrecôte minute (minute steak)

Cut from striploin entrecôte.

Fat: Should not exceed 6mm ($^1/_4$ in).

Weights: 113 g (4 oz); 141 g (5 oz); 170 g (6 oz).

Preparation: Cut across the eye of the muscle, at an even thickness, all gristle/elastin should be removed. Flattened with a cutlet bat or steak hammer to a thickness of no more than 6 mm ($^1/_4$ in).

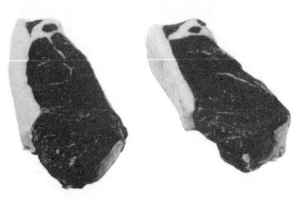

Figure 5.8 **Entrecôte steak**

Entrecôte double

Cut from striploin entrecôte.

Fat: Should not exceed 13 mm (¹/₂ in).

Weights: 340 g (12 oz); 394 g (14 oz); 454 g (16oz).

Preparation: Cut across the eye of the muscle, at an even thickness; all gristle/elastin should be removed, including that which runs through the eye muscle at the cut end of the loin. Remove chain. Length of tops should not exceed 13 mm (¹/₂ in).

T-bone steak

Cut from sirloin-chump end.

Fat: Should not exceed 13 mm (¹/₂ in).

Weights: 283 g (10 oz); 340 g (12 oz); 394 g (14 oz); 454 g (16 oz).

Preparation: Cut across the grain of the eye of both the fillet and sirloin, making sure both are of an even thickness. Remove all gristle/elastin plus any bone/meat fragments. The length of tops should not exceed 25mm (1 in). The eye of the fillet should be a minimum of 38 mm (1¹/₂ in) when measured from the chine bone.

Figure 5.9 **T-bone steak**

Porterhouse

Cut from sirloin-chump end.

Fat: Should not exceed 13mm (¹/₂in).

Weights: 453 g (16 oz) (minimum); 509 g (18 oz); 566 g (20 oz).

Preparation: Cut across the grain of the eye of both the fillet and sirloin, making sure both are of an even thickness. Remove all gristle/elastin plus any bone/meat fragments. The length of the tops should not exceed 25 mm (1 in). The eye of the fillet should be a minimum of 38 mm (1¹/₂ in) when measured from the chine bone. The porterhouse is practically identical to the T-bone steak; this is a recent development, formerly the porterhouse was cut at the joints of the lumbar vertebrae giving a steak with a thickness of approximately 2 inches or more. To maintain the spirit of the original, a porterhouse should be heavier and thicker than an ordinary T-bone steak.

Rump steak

Cut from boneless rump.

Fat: Should not exceed 13 mm (¹/₂ in).

Weights: 170 g (6 oz); 198 g (7 oz); 226 g (8 oz); 283 g (10 oz).

Preparation: Cut across the grain of the meat, at an even thickness; all excess gristle flank and skirt is removed so that the length of the tops does not exceed 13 mm (¹/₂ in). Any suet should not exceed a thickness of 6mm (¹/₄ in).

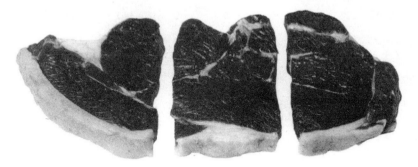

Figure 5.10 **Rump steak**

Point steak (rump)

Cut from triangular part of the rump.

Fat: Should not exceed 13 mm (¹/₂ in).

Weights: 170 g (6 oz); 198 g (7 oz); 226 g (8 oz).

Preparation: Cut from the triangular part of the rump, at an even thickness (minimum thickness is 25 mm (1 in). Remove all gristle.

Châteaubriand (head)

Cut from the head of a whole fillet.

Fat: Remove.

Weights: A minimum of 226 g (8 oz) per portion; traditionally prepared for 2–4 portions: 453 g (16 oz) = 2 portions, 679 g (24 oz) = 3 portions, 906 g (32 oz) = 4 portions.

Preparation: Cut across the grain of a prepared whole fillet at the thick/head end then lightly flatten with a cutlet bat. Finish by carving at the table.

Fillet steak

Cut from the middle of a prepared whole fillet/thick end of a sirloin fillet.

Fat/suet: Remove along with silver sheen tissue.

Weights: 170 g (6 oz); 198 g (7 oz); 226 g (8 oz).

Preparation: Cut across the grain of the muscle, at an even thickness (minimum thickness 25 mm (1 in)); the diameter of the cut steak should be not less than 50 mm (2 in) excluding chain – the chain may be left on or removed according to requirements.

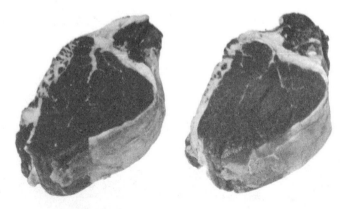

Figure 5.11 **Fillet steak**

Tournedos

Cut from the middle of a prepared whole fillet/thick end of a sirloin fillet.

Fat: Remove along with silver sheen tissue.

Weights: 141 g (5 oz); 170 g (6 oz).

Preparation: Cut across the grain of the muscle, at an even thickness (minimum thickness 25 mm (1 in)); the diameter of the cut steak should be not less than 50 mm (2 in). Remove the chain and tie the middle with string.

Figure 5.12 **Tournedos**

Medallions of beef

Cut from middle/end of trimmed fillet.

Fat: None.

Weight: 50 – 60 g (2 oz).

Preparation: Cut from the middle/tail of fillet, at an even thickness. Gently bat out with a cutlet bat to 5 – 6 cm (2 – 2¹/2 in) in diameter and ¹/2 cm (¹/4 in) thick. Serve three per portion.

Special joints, steaks and cuts

Steak tartare

Finely-chopped tail of fillet, shaped like a tournedos. Place on a flat surface and make a small depression in the centre of the steak, fill with a very fresh egg yolk (pasteurized); surround with onion rings and fill these with finely-chopped onion, parsley and capers. A halved clove of garlic may be included for rubbing around the sides of the mixing bowl.

This dish is finished at the table in the restaurant; the above ingredients are mixed to the customer's taste in a wooden bowl, with the addition of various seasonings, for example mustard, Worcester sauce, Tabasco sauce, salt and mignonette pepper. Serve accompanied with side salad and warmed sliced French bread or toast.

Carpet bag steak

Traditionally prepared for two or more persons. Double entrecôte is sliced laterally to form a pocket, stuffed with six oysters and then sewn-up with a strip of beef fat.

Wing-rib steaks

Cut like a large cutlet from a prepared wing-rib, including bone; prepare for two or more people.

Beef olives

Ingredients for ten portions:

1¹/₂ kg (3 lb 6 oz) topside of beef	50 g (2 oz) butter
400 g (1 lb) sausage meat	25 g (1 oz) chopped parsley
2 large onions (finely-chopped)	Seasoning

Cut from the topside of beef, across the grain in 6mm (¹/₄ in) slices, batted out with a cutlet bat or steak hammer to a thickness of 3 mm (¹/₈ in). Stuff with a combination of sausage meat, sweated onion and parsley. Fold in the edges, roll up and tie with string.

Hamburger or hamburger steaks

Ingredients for ten portions (75g (3 oz) per portion).

1 kg (2 lb 4 oz) finely minced rump or topside of beef	50 g (2 oz) butter
2 large onions (finely-diced)	2 large eggs
10 g (¹/₂ oz) chopped parsley	salt and mignonette pepper

Minced rump or topside is mixed with sweated onion, chopped parsley and seasoning; bind with a beaten egg.

Bitocks

Follow instructions as for hamburger, but replace 100 g (4 oz) of meat with 100 g (4 oz) of fresh white breadcrumbs soaked in 125 ml (¹/₄ pt) of milk. Shape into round balls and slightly flatten, pass through seasoned flour just prior to shallow-frying.

Beef for stroganoff

Ingredients for ten portions:

1 kg (2 lb 4 oz) tail of fillet (cut into 5 cm/2 in-long by 1 cm/¹/₂ in-wide strips)	150 g (6 oz) butter
100 g (4 oz) finely-chopped shallots	426 ml (³/₄ pt) double cream
¹/₂ clove of garlic (optional, to suit customer's taste)	Juice of one lemon
	Chopped parsley

This is normally finished at the table but preparation may take place from the larder. The ingredients are neatly arranged on a silver flat.

Baron of beef

Long: Two rump and loins and foreribs joined together.

Short: Two rump and loins joined together.

French terms

Hindquarter of beef	
Shin	La jambe
Topside	La tranche tendre
Silverside	La gite à la noix
Thick flank	La tranche grasse
Rump	La culotte de boeuf
Sirloin	L'aloyau
Boned sirloin (striploin)	Le contre-filet
Fillet	Le filet
Wing-rib	La côte de boeuf
Thin flank	La bavette

Forequarter of beef	
Fore-rib	Le côte première
Middle-rib	Le côte découverte
Chuck rib	Le côte du collier

Forequarter of beef (continued)	
Sticking piece	La collier
Plate	Le plate de côte
Brisket	La poitrine
Leg of mutton cut	La tallon du collier
Shank	La jambe

Beef offal	
Marrow	La moelle
Kidney	Le rognon
Heart	Le coeur
Liver	Le foie
Tongue	La langue
Tail (Ox)	La queue
Tripe	La tripe
Bones	Les os

Technical terms

Aitchbone:	Hipbone, part of the pelvic girdle directly connected to the femur.
Backstrap gristle:	Strip of yellow elastin/fibrous tissue directly adjacent to the eye muscle.
Blade bone:	Shoulder blade – scapula.
Chine bone:	A collective term for back bones/toe bone – lumbar vertebrae.
Eye muscle:	The largest muscle in the carcass/joint which lies on each side of the backbone and runs the full length of the back.
Entrecôte:	Trimmed sirloin steak.
Feather bone:	The extended part of the chine bone, situated beneath the eye muscle.
Flat ribs:	Thin tops, thin ribs and cut top of rib bones.
Kidney knob:	The kidney and its surrounding covering of suet.
Point end of rump:	The part of the rump adjacent to the sacral vertebrae.
Side chain:	(sirloin) The strip of muscle running parallel and closely attached to the eye muscle.
	(fillet) As above, but attached to the fillet muscle.
Silver sheen gristle:	The thin sheet of bluish-coloured tissue situated on the uppermost part of the fillet muscle.
Striploin:	Boneless sirloin, strip sirloin, contre-fillet.
T-shaped bones:	Backbones – lumbar vertebrae.
Tail end of fillet:	The tapering end of the fillet.
Thick flank:	Top rump, bed, end, first cutting,
Toe bone:	Chine bone, the protruding portion.
Tops:	The distance between the outer tip of the eye muscle and the point where the flank has been removed.

Preservation

Beef is available vacuum-packed (cryovac), chilled, frozen, dried, cured and tinned.

Corned beef

This is also known as salt beef; it is cured and spiced brisket of beef, available in tins and in a range of sizes/weights.

Dried beef

Beef which is usually cured with salt and spices then dried; examples include *bunderfleish* (Swiss-dried beef), *bresaolo* (Italy) and air-dried beef (UK).

Smoked beef

This is cured beef that has been smoked, and is known as pastrami. The original version comes from Romania, but the better known is the American pastrami.

Kosher salami

This is an all-beef Italian salami.

Veal

Introduction

Veal that can be shown through the correct documentation to have come from calves under six months old at the time of slaughter are exempt from the present UK regulations (see p. 82).

Veal is the meat from dairy calves that have been slaughtered at approximately three months old. The French prefer veal which has been fed solely on a diet of milk, making the meat white and tender. UK-produced veal is usually more pink than continental veal, as the animals are fed on grass or solid food. In addition, unlike in Europe, veal crates are not used in the UK.

Veal that has died very young or been slaughtered at too early an age is loose textured and very gelatinous. This is often called 'bobby veal' and is not suitable for first-rate cookery; it should be purchased at a reduced price and used only for stews, pies and processed items such as forcemeats and kromeskies. Older veal tends to be more pink with creamy white fat. Veal with a dry texture or brown colour should be refused as it has most likely come from an older animal and the flesh will be tough and lack flavour.

Quality points

1. The flesh should be white to pale pink in colour.
2. The flesh should be very lean with little or no fat, except around the kidneys.
3. The flesh should be firm textured, not loose and gelatinous.
4. Surfaces when cut should be moist not dry.
5. The bones should be white tinged with pink and contain blood.

Storage

Store at a temperature of $-1/2°C$ for 1 – 3 weeks.

Order of dissection

Veal may be purchased as a whole carcass and jointed in a similar manner to that of lamb, but more often it is split into two sides. The order of dissection given below is for a side of veal.

1. Remove the shoulder as for lamb.
2. Remove the breast as for lamb.
3. Remove the leg by cutting directly above the aitchbone.
4. Separate the loin and best end from the neck and scrag by cutting between the fifth and sixth ribs.
5. Separate the loin from the best end.

Dissection of a leg of veal

1. Remove the knuckle by separating it at the knee joint, taking a line across to skirt the edge of the cushion.
2. Remove the aitchbone as for a leg of lamb.
3. Remove the surface skin and fat to expose the muscles and the muscle seams, the three muscles should be visible with two-thirds (cushion and under-cushion) on one side of the thigh bone and one-third (thick flank) on the other side.
4. With the thick flank at the bottom divide the cushion and under-cushion at the natural seam working towards the thigh bone.
5. Carefully remove the thigh bone. The three muscles should be clearly visible; remove the smaller, finer-grained of the two muscles (the cushion) from above the hole left by the thigh bone, then remove the under-cushion and finally the thick flank.
6. Trim the cushion and the under-cushion of any membrane, gristle, etc. The under-cushion may also be divided into three at the natural seams. Trim the thick flank and make an incision into the flatter side to find the natural seam and trim.

Joints

Veal may also be ordered as the following:

Short forequarter

Contains two shoulders, middle neck and scrag.

Hind and end

The remaining part of the carcass after the short forequarter, breast and thin flank have been removed.

Haunch

The leg and chump-end of the loin in one piece. The loin and end removed by cutting between the fifth and sixth T-shaped bones.

Loin and end

The loin and best end in one piece, removed from the haunch between the fifth and sixth T-shaped bones.

Leg

Weight: 7 – 9 kg (14 – 18 lb).

Specification: The haunch with the chump end of loin removed.

Description: A tender and versatile joint which may be used whole (roasted) but most often is split into four, i.e. cushion, under-cushion, thick flank and hind knuckle.

Uses: Roasting, pot-roasting (poêle), braising, escalopes, diced for sautés.

Preparation for roasting – Remove the aitchbone and clean approximately 8cm (3in) of the knuckle lard or bard with fat and tie three times with string.

Preparation for escalopes – see Dissection of a Leg of Veal, p. 103.

Cushion/topside

Weight: 3 kg (6 lb).

Specification: Cut from the leg at the natural seam (see dissection of a Leg of Veal, p. 103).

Description: The prime joint of the leg, tender and very lean, provides escalopes, paupiettes, and grenadines.

Uses: Roasting, braising, escalopes, diced for sautés.

Under-cushion/silverside

Weight: 3¹/₂ kg (7 lb).

Specification: Cut from the leg at the natural seam (see Dissection of a Leg of Veal, p. 103).

Description: Larger but less tender than the cushion.

Uses: As for the cushion.

Thick flank

Weight: 3 kg (6 lb).

Specification: Cut from the leg at the natural seam (see Dissection of a Leg of Veal, p. 103).

Description: The smallest and least tender of the three muscles that come from the leg.

Uses: Roasting, braising, escalopes, steaks, grenadines, diced for sautés.

Knuckle (hind)

Weight: 2¹/₂ kg (5 lb).

Specification: Cut from a leg of veal separated at the knee joint, and cut across and away from the cushion edge (see Dissection of a Leg of Veal, p. 103).

Description: A bony but sweet-flavoured joint usually cut across into thick slices for osso buco (see Cuts, p. 107).

Uses: Stewing, braising, osso buco.

Loin

Weight: 3¹/₂ kg (7 lb).

Specification: Cut from a loin and end containing approximately six T-shaped bones, or cut from the saddle. The thin flank should be removed as closely as possible parallel to the chine bone so that the length of the tops do not exceed the height of the eye muscle.

Description: A prime cut of veal which has similar applications to a loin of pork as it may be used whole, boned or cut into chops.

Uses: Pot-roasting, roasting (whole or boned, stuffed and rolled), frying and grilling (chops).

Preparation for roasting – on the bone: as for pork loin. For stuffing and rolling: remove all the bones, trim away the back sinew, roll or stuff with lemon and thyme stuffing, then roll and tie with string. The bones are chopped and used as a trivet.

Best end

Weight: 3 kg (6 lb).

Specification: Cut from a whole carcass to give a double best end or cut from a loin and end, separated from the middle neck or short forequarter between the fifth and sixth ribs, separated from the loin at the end of the rib bones.

Description: A prime joint with similar characteristics to best end of lamb.

Uses: Pot-roast or roast whole, fry or grill (cutlets).

Shoulder

Weight: 5 kg (10 lb).

Specification: Remove at the natural seam (as for lamb).

Description: A medium tender joint boned and used in a similar fashion to lamb shoulder.

Uses: Pot-roasting, roasting (stuffed or not), diced for stews, fricassees, sautés.

Neck end/middle neck

Weight: 2 kg (4 lb).

Specification: Cut from a short forequarter as for lamb.

Description: A very bony joint, often cut into neck chops and braised, or diced for blanquette, fricassees and other stews. May be minced and used for forcemeats.

Uses: Stewing, braising (chops), forcemeats, pojarskis.

Scrag

Weight: 1¹/₂ kg (3 lb).

Specification: Cut from a short forequarter as for lamb.

Description: The poorest cut on a carcass of veal, it is very bony and is ideal for making stocks.

Uses: Boned and diced for stewing, chopped with the bones for preparation of first-class stocks.

Breast

Weight: 2 – 3 kg (4 – 6 lb).

Specification: Remove as for lamb.

Description: A bony but sweet piece of meat which can be boned and stuffed, boned, stuffed and rolled or boned, trimmed and diced. When roasted it is best barded to prevent drying out.

Uses: Pot-roast (stuffed), roasting, stewing.

Escalopes

Weights: (average-sized portions) 85 g (3 oz); 113 g (4 oz); 141 g (5 oz); 170 g (7 oz).

Specification: Cut from the cushion and across the grain; any internal fat should be completely removed, as should all sinew, tendon, etc. Each escalope is batted out between sheets of cellophane.

Uses: Sauté.

Cheaper escalopes can be had by cutting them from the under-cushion or thick flank.

Figure 5.13 **Veal escalopes**

Chops

Weights: As for lamb chops (see p. 116).

Specification: Cut from the loin and prepare as for lamb chops (see p. 116).

Uses: Grilling, sauté.

Cutlets

Weights: As for lamb cutlets (see p. 115).

Specification: Cut from the best end and prepare as for lamb cutlets (see p. 115).

Uses: Grilling, frying, braising.

Steaks

Weights: As for beef sirloin/entrecôte steaks (see p. 95).

Specification: Cut from a boned and trimmed loin, cut and prepare as for sirloin steaks (see p. 95).

Uses: Grilling, frying, sauté.

Osso buco

Specification: Cut from the fore and hind knuckles, saw across into slices of an even thickness, 3 – 6 cm (1 – 2 in) thick. Make sure it is free from bone fragments and sinews.

Uses: Osso buco.

Offal

Due to the regulations to do with the BSE outbreak in the UK, certain veal offal is not available, for example calf's brains and spinal marrow. Therefore, the items listed below are only those that are available.

Kidneys – Prepare as for lamb's kidneys (see p. 119). *Uses:* Sauté, pies and puddings.
Liver – Prepare as for lamb's liver (see p. 120). *Uses:* Frying/ sauté.
Sweetbreads – Soak and prepare as for lamb's sweetbreads (see p. 120). *Uses:* Braising frying.
Bones – *Uses:* Stocks.

French terms

Joints		Cuts	
Knuckle	Le jarret	Escalopes	L'escalope de veau
Leg	Le cussot	Cutlet	La côtelette de veau
Loin	La longe	Chop	La côte de veau
best end	Le carré	Grenadin	La grenadin de veau
Shoulder	L'épaule		
Neck end	Le cou	**Offal**	
Scrag	Le cou	Liver	Le foie de veau
Breast	La poitrine	Kidneys	Les rognons de veau
		Sweetbreads	Le ris de veau
Leg Cuts		Bones	Les os
Cushion	La noix		
Under-cushion	La sous-noix		
Thick flank	Le quasi		

Lamb and mutton

Introduction

Lamb is widely enjoyed in the UK, which makes sense as the best lamb is produced here. However, the majority (approximately 60 per cent) of the lamb eaten in this country is not British but comes instead from New Zealand and Australia. The main reason for this is that the UK is one of the few countries where people eat lamb the whole year round, not just as a seasonal luxury. Although British lamb is available throughout the year, price rather than quality dictates people's choice for cheaper, imported, frozen lamb, even when home-produced lamb is at its best and priced competitively.

Grading

Lamb

Lamb is graded according to the following criteria:

Age: All 'lamb' is under one year old; imported lamb is slaughtered in general earlier than UK-produced lamb – usually under six months old.
Weight: The weight of the dressed (prepared) carcass.
Conformation (shape): The amount and distribution of muscle and fat.

New Zealand lamb is graded under two basic classifications.

'**P**' – A well-muscled carcass in the legs, loins and forequarters, with an adequate but not excessive fat cover over the whole carcass.

'**Y**' – A moderately-fleshed carcass with a light fat cover.

The above grades are further subdivided by weight: a range from 9 – 12$\frac{1}{2}$ kg in the 'P' grade is classified as 'PL'. The most popular grade for all-round cooking is 'PX', which is 16$\frac{1}{2}$ – 20 kg.

These are the main guides to quality, but other factors such as excess or yellow fat and dark-coloured meat is assessed prior to grading, and may exclude the meat from the grading process.

Mutton

The same criteria as for lamb applies to mutton, the major differences being that mutton is over twelve months old, and boneless mutton has the fat content expressed on a visual lean basis.

It is of vital importance to the professional caterer that meat is ordered by specific grade otherwise time and money will be wasted. The various types of catering require different grades, for example lamb to be diced for a hotpot or Irish stew does not need to be of the same grade as lamb intended for serving as cutlets in a first-class restaurant. The British Sheep Carcass Classification Service provides a common system for carcass specification. This is as follows:

Weight category: L (lamb); YS (clean sheep under one year); NS (clean sheep over one year)

Fatness: 1, 2, 3L, 3H, 4, 5 (1 = very lean; 5 = very fat)

Conformation: E (extra); A (average); C (poor); Z (very poor)

Further information about grading may be obtained from the Meat and Livestock Commission and the New Zealand Lamb Catering Advisory Service.

Dissection of a carcass

1. Remove the legs by cutting with a large knife 25 mm (1 in) from the round of the aitchbone (the exact position depends on whether a long or short leg is required), then saw through the bones and remove any bone dust.
2. Remove the breasts by cutting from the cod fat (just in front of the elbow at the shoulder) to the thirteenth rib to free the breast from the loin; cut and saw through the ribs, repeat on the opposite side.
3. Remove the forequarters by cutting between the fifth and sixth ribs then sawing through the backbone.
4. Remove the shoulders by cutting the forequarter either side of the backbone, then turn the forequarter over and cut down from the ribs at the natural seam to separate the shoulders from the middle neck and scrag-end.
5. Remove the saddle by cutting down to the backbone, between the twelfth and

thirteenth ribs, then sawing through the bone to separate the pair of best ends from the saddle (a best end must contain at least six rib bones). Both joints should be rectangular.
6. Split the legs by cutting through the meat and cartilage connected to the aitchbone, then saw through the aitchbone.
7. Remove the scrag-end by cutting through where the neck (scrag) joins the middle neck bones, then saw through.
8. Split the middle neck by sawing through the backbone where it joins the two sets of ribs.

Quality

1. Lamb is under one year old, mutton is twelve months or over.
2. The carcass should be a compact shape and evenly fleshed.
3. The flesh should be lean, deep red with a fine grain and have traces of intra-muscular fat (marbling).
4. There should be an even covering of surface fat which should be pure white, and have a hard, brittle, flaky texture. Soft off-white (pasty) fat is an indication that the animal has been bred primarily for wool production.
5. The bones in a young animal will be pink, porous and contain a degree of blood when cut; as the animal ages the bones become more solid, white and splinter when chopped.

Storage

Fresh lamb should be stored in a chill refrigerator at a maximum temperature of 2°C. It may be stored for ten to fifteen days, but is best used within three to four days. Frozen lamb should not exceed −18°C and will keep for up to twelve months.

Thawing

For large joints: 2°C for 24–36 hours. For small cuts (cutlets, etc.): 7–8 hours at 2°C.

Hanging

The lamb carcass should be hung for between five to seven days; this should be specified to the supplier. After this time, it should not require further hanging and should be used as soon as possible.

Purchasing

Leg

Specification: Remove by a perpendicular cut approximately 25 mm (1 in) from the round of the aitchbone.

Weight: $2^1/_2 - 3$ kg ($4^1/_2 - 6$ lb).

Description: The leg is one of the prime cuts for roasting; alternatives such as sawing through the leg to obtain slices (lamb steaks) have not proved as practical, and roasting remains the best option.

Uses: Roasting (lamb/mutton), braising (whole); Mutton – boiling or roasting.

Preparation for roasting lamb or mutton on the bone

1. The shank bone should be exposed (Frenched*) for approximately 51 mm (2 in) from the posterior end; this enables the leg to be held firmly while carving and will enhance presentation.
2. The aitch is removed and this portion of the leg is strung securely around the girth to enable maximum carving yield.
3. The tailbones should be removed.

* 'Frenched' refers to French trimming whereby the bone or bones are shortened; a cut is made round the bone and the flesh removed, the bone is then scraped with a knife to leave a portion of clean bone.

Stuffing a leg of lamb

Prepare as for roasting, then using a sharpening steel and with help from a boning knife, loosen the bone by sliding the steel along the bone, removing any sinew, etc. attached to the bone with the knife; fill with stuffing then tie.

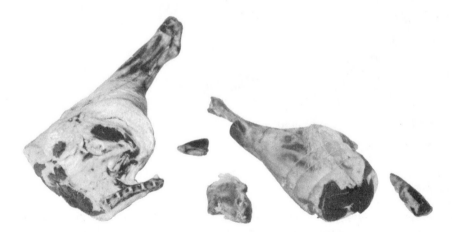

Figure 5.14 **Leg of lamb prepared for roasting**

Shoulder

Specification: Remove by cutting between fifth and six ribs, and at the natural seam between the middle neck muscle and the shoulder; only the internal bones (scapula, humorous, radius and ulna) should remain, the scrag, cervical vertebrae and rib fingers will be removed. Note that some butchers may attempt to substitute a half forequarter for a round cut shoulder, this is unacceptable as it includes half the cervical vertebra (bones), middle neck and scrag-end.

Weight: 1¹/₂ – 2 kg (3 lb 6 oz – 4 lb).

Description: The shoulder is primarily a roasting joint, but can be boned and diced for other applications such as stews, kebabs and curries.

Uses: Roasting, stewing, kebabs, mutton curries.

Preparation for roasting

Remove all bones apart from the tip of the knuckle (radius and ulna) so that no fragments or rib fingers remain. The internal fat adjacent to the breastbone should be removed along with backstrap gristle (elastin). Roll the joint securely (with the eye muscle lengthwise), then tie or net with the tip of the knucklebone tied vertically to enable the shoulder to be held in place while carving.

To stuff a shoulder

Prepare as for roasting, season the inside of the shoulder and fill with stuffing, roll and tie.

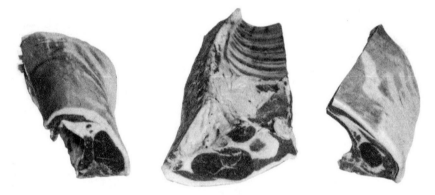

Figure 5.15 **Whole loin of lamb**

Whole loin

Specification: Cut approximately 25mm (1in) from the round of the aitchbone to remove the leg and between the sixth and seventh ribs to remove the shoulder. The breast is removed by cutting parallel close to the chine bone so that the tops do not exceed one and a half times the height of the eye muscle. The kidney knob should be removed.

Weight: 1¹/₂ – 2 kg (3 lb 6 oz – 4 lb).

Description: A whole loin including the best end is probably the most versatile prime joint on a carcass of lamb as it can be used whole for roasting and poêling or it can be butchered into several smaller cuts for grilling, frying and sautéing.

Uses: Roasting, poêling, grilling/sautéing (see cuts, cutlets, chops, noisettes, rosettes, p. 117).

To prepare for roasting

Skin and bone completely, remove backstrap and silversheen gristle. The fillet will be left in place, roll and tie or net around the girth, stuffed or unstuffed.

Best end

Specification: A whole loin separated into the loin end and the best end by cutting between the thirteenth rib and the first T-shaped bone, the best end should have seven ribs and corresponding chine bones.

Weight: 1¹/₄ kg (3 lb 3 oz).

Description: The prime joint for roasting and poêling, often referred to as a 'rack' especially when roasted, also used for several smaller cuts (see Whole loin, p. 112).

Uses: Roasting, poêling; use smaller cuts for grilling and sauté.

Preparation for roasting

Skin and completely remove the chine bone in one piece; the tip of the blade bone should also be removed. Backstrap and silversheen gristle should be removed from under the fat covering the eye muscle. The length of the tops should not exceed one and a half times the height of the eye muscle. Expose the extreme ends of the rib bones (Frenched) to a depth of 2 cm; score the fat in a trellis style.

Middle neck

Specification: Remaining part of the forequarter after the shoulder and scrag have been removed.

Weight: 1 – 1¹/₂ kg (3 lb 6 oz).

Description: A well-flavoured but relatively tough joint, suitable for slow moist cooking methods.

Uses: Stewing-in cutlets for Lancashire hotpot, boneless for Irish stew, brown lamb stews (navarin).

Preparation for stewing

(Bone in) split middle neck down the centre of the backbone, then between the bones to produce small cutlets, trim if necessary.

(Boneless) split as above then bone out completely, trim excess fat and sinew.

Saddle

Specification: The saddle is removed by a cut commencing at the tail and continuing at an angle approximately 30° towards the chump. All excess flaps should be removed and the remainder to meet in the middle, removing the best ends between the twelfth and thirteenth ribs. The kidney knob will be removed or left intact as specified, the length of tops should not exceed 10 cm (4in). Skin will be removed.

Weight: 3¹/₂ – 4 kg (6 – 8 lb).

Description: A double loin (chump end) roasted whole or used for cutting into double loin chops/crown chops/barnsley chops.

Uses: Roasting, poêling, double loin chops.

Preparation for roasting

Skin and remove kidney, excess fat and sinew. The aitchbone should be removed, and score the fat trellis-style. Reform the saddle and tie securely around the girth; for special presentation the tail may be left on and the fat may be cut and plaited along the chine bone. The saddle may also be boned, stuffed, rolled and tied.

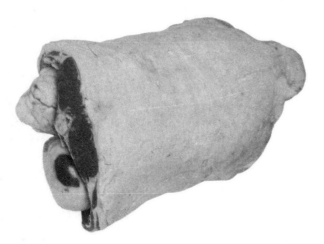

Figure 5.16 **Saddle of lamb**

Short saddle

The chump should be removed just clear of the hip bone, between the sixth and seventh vertebrae.

Scrag-end

Specification: The cervical vertebra (neck) and all attached meat.

Weight: ¹/₂ – 1 kg (8 oz – 1 lb).

Description: Well-flavoured but tough and bony joint only suitable for long moist cooking, stocks, etc.

Uses: Braising, stewing, stocks.

Preparation for stewing

Cut across the neck to produce round disks, or cut down the middle to produce semi-circles; scrag may also be completely boned out for stewing.

Breast

Specification: The thin flank running from the shoulder to the thirteenth rib. Surplus fat should be removed.

Weight: 1 – 1¹/₄ kg (2 – 2¹/₂ lb).

Description: A strip of meat with a coating of fat on both sides, and a few small bones.

Uses: Roasting, stewing, epigrammes.

Preparation for roasting

Chill well to aid removal of skin, completely bone out and trim any excess fat, roll length-wise and tie, or stuff, roll and tie.

Small cuts

Lamb cutlets ('Frenched')

Specification: Cut from French trimmed best end (rack). Cut in between individual rib bones; length of tops should not exceed one and a half times the height of the eye muscle. A best end should yield a minimum of six cutlets and each cutlet should contain a complete rib bone.

Weight: 85 – 113 g (3 – 4 oz). 'Frenched' cutlets should be priced by weight and not by unit.

Description: Lamb cutlets are one of the most popular cuts of lamb, however, all gristle and excess fat must be trimmed so that all that remains after eating is the rib bone. Only quick, dry cookery methods should be applied to cutlets.

Uses: Grilling, frying, sauté.

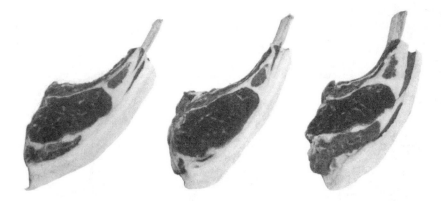

Figure 5.17 **Lamb cutlets**

Loin chops

Specification: Cut from a trimmed loin (excluding chump), all gristle should be removed before cutting, including backstrap gristle (elastin) and silver sheen gristle. Cut in between the vertebrae/T-shaped bones; both cut surfaces should be parallel to ensure that each portion is of an even thickness. Length of tops should not exceed the height of the eye muscle. Surface fat should not exceed 6mm (¹/₄ in). Excess suet should be removed to a maximum thickness of 6mm (¹/₄ in).

Weight: 85 – 113 g (3 – 4 oz).

Description: The ratio of meat to bone on a chop is less than on a cutlet, so slightly larger portions are usually provided.

Uses: Grilling, braising.

Figure 5.18 **Loin of lamb chops**

Chump chops

Specification: Cut from the chump of a trimmed loin, across the grain and through the chump bone 2 – 3 cm (¹/₂ – 1 in) thick. Both cut surfaces should be parallel so as to ensure a consistent thickness. All gristle should be removed and excess fat from the flank should be trimmed to a maximum thickness of 13mm (¹/₂ in). Excess suet should be removed to a maximum thickness of 6 mm (¹/₄ in). Each loin will yield approximately two chops.

Weight: 113 – 141 g (4 – 5 oz); 170 – 226 g (6 – 8 oz).

Description: A well-flavoured cut that will require longer cooking than chops or cutlets.

Uses: Grilling, braising.

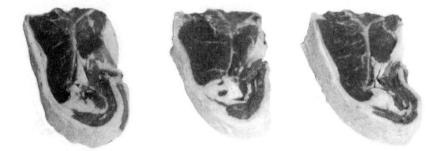

Figure 5.19 **Chump chops**

Barnsley/crown chops

Specification: Cut from a saddle on the bone which has been skinned and the flaps removed, along with the kidneys and any internal fat or suet. Cut approximately 3 cm (1 in) thick and of an even thickness. External fat will be trimmed to a maximum of 7 mm (¹/₄ in).

Weight: 300 – 400 g (10 – 12 oz).

Description: A double loin chop but cut from a trimmed whole saddle. After trimming two halves of kidney may be skewered in position on the underside.

Uses: Grilling, braising.

Lamb rosettes

Specification: Remove the chump end and fillet from a boned whole loin; remove all gristle and excess fat/flank. Roll girthwise, tie and cut into round slices approximately 4 cm (1¹/₂ in) thick between the strings.

Weight: 75 g (2¹/₂ oz) per portion.

Description: A prime cut of lamb, used for only the most delicate of cooking methods. Always served 'pink', often on a lightly fried crouton of bread.

Uses: Grilling, frying, sautè.

Lamb noisettes

Specification: Remove the chump end and fillet from a boned whole loin; remove all gristle and excess fat. The flank should be removed by cutting from the eye of the meat at an angle then cutting across the loin on a slant so as to produce a teardrop shape.

Weight: 75 g (2¹/₂ oz) per portion.

Description: As for rosettes

Uses: As for rosettes

Both rosettes and noisettes can be lightly cooked, decorated and served cold on a first-class buffet, they may be glazed with aspic or meat glaze.

Lamb fillet

Specification: Remove the fillet(s) from the inside of the loin/saddle and trim any gristle or fat.

Weight: 120 – 150 g (4 – 5 oz).

Description: The most tender cut on a carcass of lamb, with a delicate flavour so suitable for only quick, dry methods of cookery. Served with rich flavourings and sauces and suitable for cold buffet presentation.

Uses: As for rosettes and noisettes, kebabs; can be baked in pastry (*en croûte*) or in a bag/envelope (*en papillote*). It is important to stress loin fillets when ordering as latterly butchers have invented a 'shoulder fillet'.

Lamb *epigrammes*

Specification: Cut from a cooked breast of lamb and prepared in-house. The whole breasts are poached flat in white stock with various flavourings until tender (approximately one hour). All bones, gristle and excess fat is removed, then the cuts are placed between trays and weighted, cooled and put in a refrigerator until completely chilled and set. Cut into diamond or triangular shapes, pass through flour, egg and breadcrumbs and shallow-fry.

Weight: 50 – 75 g (1^1/2 – 3^1/2 oz).

Description: An excellent use of a lesser quality cut, suitable for any recipes that calls for breaded lamb cutlets, e.g. napolitaine.

Uses: Frying/sauté.

Diced lamb (kebabs, brochettes, etc.)

Specification: Cut from the loin fillet into 2 – 3 cm (1 – 1^1/4 in) cubes, trim all fat and gristle. If any other cut is used, for example loin or shoulder, it must be marinated overnight to achieve the required tenderness.

Weight: Several pieces to make a total weight of 150 g (5^1/2 oz).

Description: Use only the most tender of cuts, however, lesser cuts may be used if tenderized in an acidic marinade.

Uses: Grilling.

Diced lamb/mutton (curries, stews, etc.)

Specification: Cut from leg, loin or shoulder; all fat and gristle should be removed. Cut meat into 2 – 3 cm (1 – 1^1/4 in) cubes. Only prime mutton may be used.

Weight: 100 – 150 g (3^1/2 – 4^1/2 oz) per portion or 1^1/2 – 2 kg (2^1/4 – 4 lb) for ten portions.

Description: Lamb is used for both brown and white stews and curries; prime mutton (just over one year old) is becoming more popular for use in curries.

Uses: Navarin, blanquettes, curries.

Medallions

Specification: Cut from the eye of the loin or loin fillet. Cut across the grain into round slices. All gristle and fat should be removed. Ensure that both cut surfaces are parallel thus guaranteeing an even thickness. Once cut, medallions may be batted out between plastic or with a steak hammer to form a rounded shape approximately 50 mm (2 in) across and 6 mm (1/4 in) thick.

Weight: 56 – 85 g (2 – 3 oz), three per portion.

Description: A prime cut of lamb used for only the most delicate cookery, ideal for *à la carte* cookery.

Uses: Sauté, frying (as for medallions of veal and noisettes but excluding grilling).

Lamb and mutton mince

Specification: Cut from leg, shoulder, breast. All gristle and excess fat removed.

Weight: As required.

Description: Lamb/mutton mince is well flavoured but it can be fatty if not properly trimmed. Only the above cuts should be used otherwise the mince can be 'chewy'.

Uses: Moussaka, shepherd's pie, samosas, kebabs.

Offal

I have not included individual quality points in this section as most offal is purchased as fresh as possible, and apart from the few general points listed below, is usually of a consistent quality.

1. Offal should be purchased as fresh as possible.
2. A fresh smell is a good guide to quality.
3. A good depth of colour denotes freshness and quality.
4. Any excess fat or gristle should be removed (kidney suet is the one exception).
5. Offal should have a firm texture and show no signs of stickiness.

Kidney

Lamb's kidneys are the most popular type of kidney. They have a mild flavour and a pleasant texture. All suet should be removed before preparation.

To prepare for grilling: Make a horizontal cut towards the core as if to cut the kidney in half, but do not cut completely through. Remove the skin (transparent membrane) on the outside of the kidney, then carefully cut out the central core of gristle and fat. Still leaving the two halves of the kidney joined, use cocktail sticks or skewers to keep the kidney open and flat while grilling.

To prepare for sauté (turbigo, etc.): Prepare as for grilling by cutting and removing the skin and central core. Cut the kidney in half and slice each half into three pieces on a slant.

Uses: Grilled (by themselves or mixed), devilled kidneys, sautéed, soup, brochettes of kidneys (skewered sautéed kidneys).

Heart

When prepared and presented well lamb's heart is one of the most delicate types of offal.

To prepare for braising: All excess fat should be removed as should the tubes and valves inside the heart: remove carefully with a small sharp knife, taking care not to pierce the heart. Stuffed hearts are filled with parsley and thyme stuffing with the addition of chopped suet, and cohered with a beaten egg. The heart should then be sewn up with split butcher's string and a trussing needle, making every effort to retain its shape.

Uses: Braised lamb's heart (unstuffed or stuffed).

Liver

Along with calf's liver, lamb's liver is the most tender, delicately flavoured and popular offal. However, the correct preparation is necessary: liver should be purchased whole, not in slices as this makes the preparation much more difficult, and lamb's liver is not at its best when cut into thick slices.

To prepare for grilling/sauté: First 'skin' by inserting two fingers through and underneath the transparent membrane (skin) covering the liver; gently separate the skin from the liver and remove. Trim off any gristle, then slice thinly by cutting at an angle along the liver. The slices may then be flattened by placing between dampened polythene and patting gently with a cutlet bat; alternatively, a few gentle taps with a steak mallet will be sufficient. The resulting slices will be very tender and require the minimum of cooking. Lamb's liver can also be marinated prior to cooking in various preparations such as orange juice and zest, oil, garlic and chopped parsley. If prepared as outlined above, the slices will require the minimum of marinating since they will already be very tender, and the marinade is simply used to add flavour.

Uses: Grilling, sauté.

Sweetbreads

These are glands taken from the neck and near the heart of the animal: the one nearest to the heart is considered superior as it has a nice plump round shape as opposed to the one from the neck which is more elongated and uneven in shape. Most sweetbreads are delivered pre-packed containing a mixture of both neck- and heart-breads. Sweetbreads are easily digested and are nutritionally rich. This makes them a valuable addition to the diet, especially for the elderly and the sick.

To prepare for braising/sauté: Soak in salted cold water to clean and whiten, then blanch in boiling water for two minutes. Refresh under cold running water, drain and trim off any fat or membrane.

Uses: White/brown braising, sauté.

Tongue (lamb's/sheep's)

Once quite popular but now seldom used, particularly salted lamb's tongue which is rarely seen on menus. Sheep's tongue is used fresh.

Uses: Boiling and braising.

French terms

Joints

Leg	Le gigot d'agneau
Shoulder	L'épaule d'agneau
Loin	La longe d'agneau
Best end	Le carré d'agneau
Saddle	La selle d'agneau
Middle neck	Le basse côte d'agneau
Scrag-end	Le cou d'agneau
Breast	La poitrine d'agneau

Cuts

Cutlet	La cotelette d'agneau
Loin chop	La côte d'agneau

Cuts (continued)

Rosettes	Les rosettes d'agneau
Noisettes	Les noisettes d'agneau
Fillet	Le filet d'agneau
Epigrammes	L'epigrammes d'agneau
Medallions	Les medaillons d'agneau

Offal

Kidneys	Les rognons d'agneau
Heart	Le coeur d'agneau
Liver	Le foie d'agneau
Sweetbreads	Le ris d'agneau
Tongue	La langue d'agneau

Note: *D'agneau* means lamb; in the case of joints, if mutton is used in place of lamb, the term 'mouton' should be used.

Parsley and thyme stuffing for lamb (1 kg)

500 g (1 lb) white breadcrumbs
300 g (10 oz) suet
10 g (^{1}/$_3$ oz) chopped parsley
10 g (^{1}/$_3$ oz) rubbed thyme
Grated rind of half a lemon

250 g (10 oz) diced onion
50 g (2 oz) butter
4 eggs
Nutmeg, salt and pepper

1. Sweat the onion and thyme in the butter until the onion is soft.
2. Apart from the eggs, place the rest of the ingredients in a mixing bowl.
3. Add the onion and butter it was cooked in, and mix.
4. Lightly beat the eggs and add, season with salt and pepper and a pinch of nutmeg.

Pork and ham

Introduction

The Chinese are believed to be the first people to have introduced pork into their diet, and most of the pigs we eat today are strains that have come originally from China. Pork was regarded for a long time as a staple diet of the poor, especially in the Middle Ages, and was frowned on by the rich. Today the eating of pork is considered taboo by certain religions – including Judaism and Islam. This is because pigs were seen as unclean animals and in hot climates it was practically impossible to store the meat, this meant that people became ill from eating pork and thus it made sense to avoid it. Pork used to be infected with a parasitic worm known as *trichinella spiralis*, and still can be, although the last recorded case in the UK was in 1952. Most of the pork available in the UK is home-produced (see note on p. 122) and any imported meat is rigorously inspected for signs of infection. However, it is still important for caterers to beware of *trichinae* and to minimize the risk of infection by making sure all pork is cooked well done or for a minimum of 25 minutes per $1/2$ kg (1 lb) plus 25 minutes extra. That said, as long as an internal temperature of 77–80°C is achieved, all the parasites will have been killed and the pork can be safely served while still moist and tender.

Pigs are omnivorous, in other words they will eat almost anything from vegetables to meat, which is the reason why they are known as 'nature's vacuum cleaners'. Pigs cannot live on grass alone, and need cereals and protein to supplement their diet. The flavour and texture of pork is very much dependent on their diet: if pigs are fed on bland cereals then the flesh will have little flavour; if fed mainly a liquid diet then the flesh will be 'wet' or 'sloppy' in texture (this was the case in the past when swill – liquid kitchen waste – was the mainstay of many small pig farmers). It is important, then, that pigs are fed a varied diet; in the past when most pork was free range, it is likely that it would have been tougher and have had more fat but would have tasted much richer than today's commercially-farmed pork. Perhaps this is one of the reasons for the widening availability of wild boar which has a much stronger flavour than pork.

The richness and fattiness of pork meant that for many years it was not considered suitable for the highest levels of cookery (haute cuisine), and to counteract the fattiness most countries have traditionally served sharp-tasting accompaniments or sauces with pork: apple sauce (UK), sweet and sour sauce (China), sauce Robert/charcutière (France) and sauerkraut (Germany). Other flavourings which go well with pork include, prunes, white wine or cider reductions, mustard, lemon juice and calvados. Boiled bacon may be served with mustard sauce and grilled gammon with pineapple or peaches. Fortified wine reductions can be used with ham, for example made with madeira or marsala. These perform two functions: first, they counteract the sweet richness of the pork, and second, fruit- or vinegar-based sauces help break down the fat globules and greatly assist in digestion. Sage and onion stuffing is normally served with roast pork as the oil contained in the sage leaves also aids in breaking down the fat.

Note: Due to the recent improvement in the welfare standards of pigs kept in the UK, more and more cheaper pork is being imported from the continent. It is in everybody's interest to support home-produced pork, as the standards of husbandry are much higher.

Types and breeds

There are many breeds of pig, but these are usually split into two groups, depending on what they will be used for after slaughter:

Porker pigs: Used primarily for the production of pork and ham.

Baconer pigs: Used mainly for the production of bacon and gammon.

This is due to the physical characteristics of the animal which make it more suitable for one or the other application, and is normally decided after slaughter.

Some of the most popular breeds bred for the table are:

Heavy hog	Wiltshire
Welsh	Gloucester Old Spot

Suckling pig (sucking pig)

This is a young piglet aged 4 – 6 weeks and weighing 5 – 6 kg (10 – 14 lb). It is important that a suckling pig is exactly that, a piglet that is slaughtered prior to being weaned. It is normally roasted whole on a spit and this is the most suitable method for hot presentation. The ears and tail must be protected from burning by covering with tin foil, the skin is lightly scored to allow the heat to penetrate, then brushed with oil and seasoned. For oven roasting the belly may be stuffed, sewn up with string then prepared as for spit-roasting. An item such as a potato is placed in its mouth to keep it open and the pig is cooked for 2 – 3 hours in a moderate oven. It can be brushed with liquid honey towards the completion of cooking, this gives the skin a golden glaze. For hot service serve the pig with an apple in its mouth on a bed of spiced (cinnamon, mace) sweetened, grilled apples (quartered or sliced) with roast gravy.

Due to the fact that pig's/boar's heads are not as available or popular as once was the case, suckling pig is now a more favoured item for cold buffet presentation. Prepare and cook the suckling pig as for roast suckling pig. It may be glazed with a coat of aspic jelly but if already glazed with honey this should not be necessary; the service flat should, however, be set with a layer of aspic, the pig is then presented on a wedge-shaped trivet of deep-fried bread, with the head at the high point and a red apple (lightly glazed with oil) placed in its mouth. Garnish with apple quarters that have been lightly spiced with cinnamon and glazed by brushing with honey or sprinkling with brown sugar and colouring under the salamander/grill.

Grading

The grading of pork is not as clear as it is for other meats. The most expensive pork comes from carcasses weighing between 36 to 50 kg (approximately 80 – 100 lb). Heavier pigs can grow up to 68 kg (150 lb), these are known as 'cutters' as they are normally cut up at the abattoir before being dispatched to wholesale and retail butchers. Cutters tend to be higher in fat than their leaner smaller cousins. The objective of the caterer is to achieve a balance between fat, which enhances the flavour (especially intramuscular fat), and lean.

Grading is carried out on 80 per cent of pigs. This is done by various methods, including optical probes and ultrasonic meters which measure the depth of fat over two or three points; above the eye muscle the three points are known as P1, P2 and P3. The P2 is a single optical probe at a point level with the head of the last rib and $6^{1}/_{2}$ cm from the backbone, back fat and rind thicknesses are also measured. Using lean meat percentage a carcass can be allocated an EC grade.

Lean meat percentage and EC grades

EC grade	Lean meat percentage
S	60 % or more
E	55 – 59 %
U	50 – 54 %
R	45 – 49 %
O	40 – 44 %
P	39% or less

Marking of carcasses

The P2 or sum of P1 and P2 (in millimetres) is marked on the carcass.

Hanging

A side of pork is normally hung from the hole in the aitchbone for an initial twelve hours and then a minimum of four days. Bone-in loins require a minimum of seven days hanging, boneless loins need a minimum of twelve days.

Quality

1. The flesh should be pink, firm in texture and dry, not wet and sloppy.
2. The fat should be white, firm textured and smooth, without the remains of any stiff hairs or bristles.
3. The bones should be small and pink.
4. The skin should be smooth, without any stiff hairs or bristles.
5. Pork should be hung for $4-7$ days at $-1°C$.

Dissection of a carcass

Starting at the tail, split the first few vertebrae by steadily drawing the boning knife forward until the main spinal vertebrae are located by pressing firmly with the fingers; draw the knife along the middle of the spine, cutting through the skin to the nape of the neck or first spinal vertebrae. Cut round the head just behind the ear and follow the line of the jawbone around in a complete circle, thus removing the head – if the head is to be used for brawn or for presentation as a boar's head on a cold buffet it should be cut to include part of the neck. Separate the carcass into two sides by lightly chopping down the centre of the spine while pulling the two halves apart.

Note that it is rare nowadays to have to dissect a whole carcass complete with head; due to the rigors of meat inspection most pig's heads are sawn in half and often the brains are removed prior to sale. The process from this point details the dissection of the more commonly used cuts.

Side of pork

1. Remove the trotter by cutting through the sinew at the rear of the joint in the trotter and push forward firmly.
2. Remove the leg by cutting across the joint 25 mm (1 in) below the round of the aitchbone to a point $2^1/2 - 5$ cm ($2 - 3$ in) above the tail; cut through to the bone with a boning knife then saw through the bone, finish cutting through with a knife.
3. Remove the shoulder (cross-cut) by a straight cut between the fourth and fifth ribs.
4. Remove the belly by cutting parallel close to the chine bone of the loin so that the tops do not exceed the height of the eye muscle, normally about half the height of the rib bones. Do this by marking with the back of the knife a line parallel to the chine bone, then saw through the rib bones, finishing with a knife.

5. Remove the neck end/spare rib from the cross-cut shoulder by a cut running at right angles to the rib bones passing directly through the socket joining the blade bone to the shoulder bone to produce a rectangular-shaped joint.
6. The above will leave an intact short loin of pork which may be divided into two joints between the ninth and tenth ribs to give a chump end and a rib end (best end). The chump end is normally boned, tied and roasted. The rib end can also be roasted but is more suited to the cutting of chops and escalopes.

Storage

Pork should be stored in a chill refrigerator at a temperature of 0°C to −1°C; it will keep for one to two weeks.

Preservation

Pork can be preserved in several ways:

Salting/curing

In the past salt pork was used extensively, but it is rarely seen nowadays. Salting is still used in the production of ham and bacon.

Freezing

Pork is often frozen but this tends to increase moisture and can lead to a dry finished product, especially if allowed to become freezer burnt. All frozen pork must be allowed to thaw in a refrigerator.

Smoking

Many items containing pork are smoked, these include sausages, salamis, frankfurters, as well as hams and bacon.

Canning

Pork is often canned, and is usually combined with other flavourings, for example chopped ham and pork and luncheon meat. Ham is also available tinned, but the majority is not of a high enough quality to be used for anything but for dicing and combined with other ingredients, for example omelettes, bouchée fillings, chicken and ham pies.

Pickling

As with salting a great deal of pork used to be pickled in brine; this is not so much the case anymore, but belly pork is still the joint most commonly used for pickling. Leg of pork is cured with brine to produce ham.

Butchery (joints)

Leg (bone-in)

Specification: Remove by cutting across the joint 25 mm (1 in) below the round of the aitchbone to a point $2^{1}/_{2}-5$ cm (2–3 in) above the tail. The tail and foot should be removed and the rind should not be scored unless requested. The following bones will be included:

Shank bone	Thigh bone
Cramp bone (kneecap – patella)	Aitchbone

Weight: 5–6 kg (10–12 lb).

Description: The leg is a large prime joint, either cured and made into ham and boiled or served as roast pork with apple sauce and sage and onion stuffing. It is a joint where some caution is required as once roasted it should not be reheated and does not store well for any length of time. As a cold cut as it can quickly become dry. It is ideal for a roast joint where the number of portions required can be confidently predicted, for instance at set luncheons or parties.

Uses: Roasting, boiling as ham.

Preparation for roasting on the bone

The aitchbone should be removed and the end of the shank bone (cramp bone–patella) sawn off straight revealing it bared (Frenched) for 3 cm (1 in). The part of the leg which contained the aitchbone should be strung girthwise, thus maximizing the carving yield.

Leg (boneless, tied or netted)

Specification: Cut as for leg, all bones should have been removed cleanly so that there are no bone fragments or loose particles of meat. The shank muscle should have its direct covering of rind removed and then folded into the thigh bone cavity. All visible deposits of gristle should be removed. Skin/rind should be scored at 1 cm ($^{1}/_{2}$ in) intervals. The joint is then rolled and tied or netted securely.

Weight: 3–4 kg (6–8 lb).

Description: As for leg.

Preparation for roasting

The above specification should require no further preparation for roasting.

Figure 5.20 **Leg of pork**

Shoulder (cross-cut)

Specification: Separate from the head by a cut between the atlas bone (first cervical vertebrae attached to the skull) and the base of the skull. Separate from the loin by cutting between the fourth and fifth ribs. The foot should be removed. The rind is not scored unless required. All excess deposits of blood should be removed. The following bones will be included: hock bone, shoulder bone, blade bone, rib cage and neck bones.

Weight: 3 – 4 kg (6 – 8 lb).

Description: Shoulder of pork is an all-purpose joint; although not the first choice for roasting, it will suffice as a second-class roast. Because it contains quite a high amount of connective tissue it is more suited to applications that require trimming, slicing, dicing or mincing.

Uses: Second-class roast, pork cassoulet, pâtés, terrines, pies, sausages.

Figure 5.21 **Shoulder of pork**

Loin (short)

Specification: Cut from a side of pork, separate from the shoulder by cutting between the fourth and fifth ribs. The leg is removed by a perpendicular cut approximately 25 mm (1 in) from the round of the aitchbone. The belly/breast is removed closely parallel to the chine bone so that the lengths of the tops do not exceed the height of the eye muscle. The rind should not be removed unless requested. The back fat should not exceed 18 mm (3/4 in). The kidney and flare fat should be left intact. A short loin of pork should contain a minimum of ten ribs and corresponding chine bones, approximately six to seven T-shaped bones, the chump and blade bones.

Weight: 5 – 6 kg (10 – 12 lb).

Description: The loin is the most versatile prime cut on a side of pork and is suitable for most first-class applications. These include roasting (chump end), grilling and frying (rib end). The fillet, kidney, back fat and flair fat all have good culinary applications.

Uses: Roasting, grilling, frying (escalopes, cutlets, medallions), stir-frying, deep-frying (sweet and sour pork).

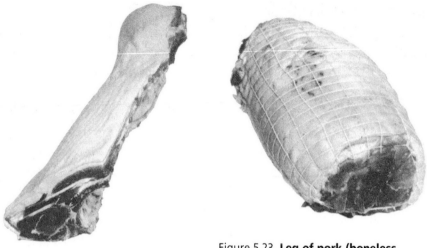

Figure 5.22 **Short loin of pork**

Figure 5.23 **Leg of pork (boneless and netted)**

Neck end / spare-rib

Specification: The spare-rib/neck end is cut from a cross-cut shoulder of pork. The 'hand' is removed by a cut (running at right angles to the rib bones) passing directly through the socket joining the blade bone to the shoulder bone, to produce a rectangular-shaped joint. The rind will not be scored unless requested. All deposits of congealed blood should be removed. The neck end may contain the following bones: blade bone, rib bones and corresponding chine bones, neck bones.

Weight: 2 – 3 kg (4 – 6 lb).

Description: The spare-rib or neck end is similar to the shoulder. It is quite a fat joint before trimming, and although it may be used as a second-class roast, it is preferable to use it in applications similar to those of shoulder, i.e. those which require the removal of fat and connective tissue, such as pies, etc.

Uses: Second-class roast, pies, spare-rib chops, rillettes.

Note that the term 'spare rib' can cause confusion: what is sometimes called 'spare-ribs' are in fact ribs cut from the pork belly/breast, and include individual rib bones (see belly pork, below). However, spare-rib chops, have a much higher meat to bone ratio, and some may contain little or no bone.

Belly / breast

Specification: The breast or belly is cut from a side of pork starting at the fore end. Cut between the fourth and fifth ribs towards the cartilaginous tip of the blade bone. At right angles to the rib bones, cut parallel to the chine bone of the loin so that the length of tops does not exceed the height of the eye muscle, to a point just opposite the tail. The rib bones are sawn through and the flesh cut with a knife. The belly/breast should contain the tips of approximately ten rib bones.

Weight: 2 – 3 kg (4 – 6 lb).

Note that belly pork is the term normally used to describe both the pork breast and belly: in fact the breast of pork is obtained from the rib area of the animal opposite the best end of loin, whereas the belly should be obtained from opposite the chump end of the loin and contains no rib bones.

Description: A well-flavoured but very fatty joint, useful in pâtés and terrines, sausages, forcemeats, etc. to moisten and enrich (due to its fat content). Often pickled in brine then boiled and served hot or cold.

Uses: Pâtés, terrines, rillettes, pies, sausages, barbecued spare-ribs, pickled and boiled.

Fillet

Specification: The pork fillet or tenderloin is cut from a loin. All fat and connective tissue should be removed.

Weight: 113 – 170 g (4 – 6 oz).

Description: The tenderest piece of meat on the pig, ideal for *à la carte* cookery; often removed from loins prior to further processing. The fillets may be saved until enough are gathered to be of use on the menu. Alternatively, boxes of pork fillets can be purchased in bulk, usually supplied frozen.

Uses: Medallions, escalopes, sweet and sour pork; may be used whole or diced to enhance presentation of pies and terrines.

Chop

Specification: Cut from a de-rinded short loin of pork (excluding chump), cut on or between each segment of the T-shaped bones. Both cut surfaces should be parallel to ensure each portion is of a consistent thickness. The minimum thickness should be 13 mm (1/2 in). The length of tops should not exceed the height of the eye muscle and the surface fat not exceed 13 mm (1/2 in). The toe bone is left intact. The blade bone should be removed with its direct covering of meat. The kidney and all deposits of flair fat are also removed.

Figure 5.24 **Pork chops**

Weights: 141 g (5 oz); 170 g (6 oz); 198 g (7 oz); 226 g (8 oz).

Description: A standard pork chop usually containing a portion of the fillet, with a T-shaped bone; suitable mainly for service at lunchtime.

Butchery (cuts)

Cutlet

Specification: Cut between and closely parallel to the rib bones; both cut surfaces should be parallel to ensure that each portion is of an even thickness. The minimum thickness will be 13 mm ($\frac{1}{2}$ in). The length of tops should not exceed the height of the eye muscle and the surface fat should not exceed 6 mm ($\frac{1}{4}$ in). The toe/chine bone should be removed. Each cutlet should contain an individual rib bone which will have the top 12 mm ($\frac{1}{2}$ in) bared (Frenched). The blade bone should be removed. All kidney and deposits of flare fat need to be removed.

Weights: 141 g (5 oz); 170 g (6 oz); 198 g (7 oz); 226 g (8 oz).

Description: This is an enhanced version of the pork chop, suitable for service at lunch or dinner.

Noisettes

Specification: Cut from a short loin (rib end) across the eye muscle; both cut surfaces should be parallel to ensure each portion is of an even thickness (minimum thickness 13 mm ($\frac{1}{2}$ in). All bones removed so that there are no bone fragments, loose particles of meat or rib fingers/bones. The blade bone should be removed. The length of tops will not exceed 13 mm ($\frac{1}{2}$ in). Surface fat will not exceed 6 mm ($\frac{1}{4}$ in).

Weights: 85 g (3 oz); 113 g (4 oz); 141 g (5 oz); 170 g (6 oz).

Description: A pork noisette can be described as a pork cutlet without a bone. It is more delicate than a chop or cutlet and suited to service at dinner and ideal for sauté of pork dishes and *à la carte* cookery.

Uses: Sauté of pork dishes, dishes applicable to fillet of pork, *à la carte* cookery.

Medallions

Specification: Cut from a fillet/eye of loin (as specified) trimmed of all fat and connective tissue. Both cut surfaces will be parallel to ensure even thickness (minimum thickness 6 mm ($\frac{1}{4}$ in). Lightly bat with a cutlet bat to a size of 6 – 8 cm (2 – $2\frac{1}{2}$ in).

Weights: 56 – 85 g (2 – 3 oz).

Description: Medallions of pork was once another name for noisettes, but it has come to mean small round slices taken from the fillet of eye of the loin of pork and lightly flattened with a cutlet bat into $\frac{1}{2}$ cm ($\frac{1}{4}$ in) thick rounds. These require little cooking and are ideal for *à la carte* cookery.

Uses: The uses of medallions are still being explored and it is up to the ingenuity of the chef to apply and invent suitable classic and individual garnishes, bearing in mind that the richness of pork needs to be balanced with fruit or sharp-tasting sauces. Popular examples include:

- Pork Normande with calvados, apple sauce, lemon juice and cream.
- Pork Dijonaise with white wine, Dijon mustard, lemon juice and cream.
- Pork Provençal with garlic, white wine, shallots, tomato concasse and chopped parsley.

Escalopes

Specification: Cut from the loin or loin fillet. Loin escalopes are cut from a short loin (rib end), across the grain of the eye muscle, at an angle. Both cut surfaces will be parallel to ensure each portion is of an even thickness. Cut on the slant into $1 - 1^{1}/_{2}$ cm ($^{1}/_{2}$ in)-thick slices, depending on size of loin. Each escalope should be flattened/batted out evenly between sheets of cellophane or with a moistened cutlet bat, to a thickness of $4 - 6$ mm ($^{1}/_{4}$ in), then trimmed.

Weights: 113 g (4 oz); 141 g (5 oz); 170 g (6 oz).

Description: A thin tender slice of meat, the name is usually applied only to white meats such as pork and veal. Escalopes are best cooked to order as they quickly become dry and tough. Ideal for *à la carte* cookery.

Uses: Recipes requiring veal escalopes may be substituted by pork, in which case it would be called escalope of pork, for example holstein, viennoise, *à la crème*, milanaise, cordon bleu. Fillet escalopes are cut from a fillet of pork and trimmed of all connective tissue. The fillet is split down the middle three-quarters of the way through, cut to size/weight, then opened out and flattened/batted out as above; or the fillet will be cut to size/weight on a slant across/against the grain and flattened as above.

Diced pork (stewing)

Specification: Cut from the shoulder or breast of pork, trimmed of all fat and sinew. Diced into $2^{1}/_{2}$ cm (1 in) cubes.

Description: Suitable for any stewing or braising applications requiring pork, including pâtés and terrines. If a shorter cooking method is to be used, e.g. shallow-/deep-frying, then fillet or loin of pork should be used.

Uses: Cassoulet of pork (braised pork and beans), pâtés, terrines.

Diced pork (frying)

Specification: Cut from the fillet of pork and trimmed of all fat and connective tissue. The fillet is split down the middle, lengthways, then cut across the grain into $^{1}/_{2}$ cm ($^{1}/_{4}$ in) slices.

Description: Fillet of pork is the tenderest cut of pork, so care must be taken not to overcook it as this will result in dry tough meat. It is ideal for shallow-/deep-frying and for use in Chinese dishes.

Uses: Sweet and sour pork, pork chow mein, fried rice combinations, stir-fries and pancake rolls.

Note: If fillet of pork is used for fried rice or pancake rolls then it should be further diced into 3 – 5 mm (1/4 in) pieces.

Offal

A much wider range of pig offal was once eaten than is the case today. Some examples include:

Chitterlings – Intestines, used as sausage skins.
Chaps – Cheeks, smoked then boiled and eaten like ham.
Melt – Spleen, once used in sausages, now mainly used as pet food.
Lights – Lungs, once added to pâtés, now used as pet food.
Ears – In the past were stuffed and grilled.
Heart – Braised in the same way as lamb's heart; not much larger than a lamb's heart
      but now little seen on menus.

Offal that is still eaten today includes:

Liver

Prepare by cutting out any tubes or gristle, remove the skin (where practical). Cut on a slant into thin slices and lightly bat out (should be no more than 1/2 cm (1/4 in) thick).

Uses: Grilled or sauté as for lamb's liver; has a much stronger flavour. Used as an ingredient in pâtés.

Kidneys

Prepare by making a small cut in the skin then peeling it off. Cut in half lengthways, cutting off the core (gristle and fat in centre). Usually skewered lengthways and grilled.

Uses: Grilled as for lamb's kidneys, ingredient in pâtés.

Head and brains

Apart from use as a buffet centrepiece, the head and brains used to be used for the making of pork brawn (head cheese), but concerns about soft tissue infection has led to problems with availability of these items. The production of brawn is also very labour intensive and not nearly as popular as it once was. Commercially-prepared brawn is readily available, and few people now prepare brawn in-house.

Trotters (feet)

Prepare by washing in boiling water for several minutes; cool then scrape to remove any hairs. Cook by simmering in a 'blanc' (water, lemon juice, flour and salt) to whiten.

Uses: Once cooked, the trotters are boned out, seasoned, rolled in butter and breadcrumbs (which may be flavoured with English mustard) and grilled; serve with *sauce diable* (devilled sauce). Stuff by filling a cooked, boned out trotter with pork sausagemeat/forcemeat, then bake or grill.

To braise – bone, stuff, tie and braise until tender.

In stocks: Trotters will give a gelatinous quality to stocks and consommés.

Caul

A pig's caul is a lace-like membrane found around the paunch of a pig. It is quite tough when raw but once cooked makes a delicate wrapping.

Preparation: Caul needs little preparation apart from washing, and soaking in cold water to whiten.

Uses: Wrapping faggots, creponettes, kromeskies.

Blood

Pig's blood is used in the making of black pudding.

Back fat

Not strictly offal, but back fat is an important product of pork with many applications.

Uses: Pâtés, pies, rillettes, lining terrines, larding of roast meats, barding of roast game birds.

French terms

Leg	Le cuissot	Cutlet	La côtelette
Shoulder	L'épaule	Medallion	Le médaillon
Loin	La longe	Escalope	L'escalope
Spare rib	La basse côte	Heart	Le coeur
Belly	La poitrine	Liver	Le foie
Breast	Le carré	Kidneys	Les rognons
Fillet	Le filet	Head	La tête
Chop	La côte	Trotters	Le pied

Rilletes (ten portions)

1 kg (2 lb) belly pork, with all	bouquet garni
the rind and bones removed	$^1/8$ litre ($^1/4$ pt) water
$^1/2$ kg (1 lb) pork back fat	salt, nutmeg, white
1 head of garlic	mignonette pepper

1. Rub the pork well with the seasoning, and leave overnight in the fridge.
2. Cut the pork along the grain into batons and dice the pork fat. Place into a large earthenware casserole dish with the water, bouquet garni and peeled whole cloves of garlic.
3. Cover with a lid and place in a slow oven, gas mark 2/150°C/300°F for $3^1/2 - 4$ hours. The meat should be very soft and swimming in its own fat.
4. Drain off the fat through a sieve and reserve the fat for later. Remove the bouquet garni. Partly pound, then shred the pork with two forks (rillettes should be in shreds not a paste).
5. Check the seasoning and adjust if necessary. Pile the pork lightly into small earthenware or ramekin pots and pour over the fat, leaving behind any sediment or juices.
6. Place in the refrigerator. Rillettes should be soft in texture, so while they should be served cold, they should be removed from the refrigerator approximately 30 minutes before service to soften.
7. Serve in their pots as an hors-d'œuvre garnished with parsley and accompanied by hot buttered toast or warm bread and butter.

Ham

Ham is the cured hind leg of a porker pig. A ham is cut from behind the aitchbone, and has a rounded end, whereas gammon (the cured hind leg of a baconer pig) is normally cut square. Ham is salted/cured and can also be smoked. Some hams such as Parma, Bayonne and Westphalian are sliced very thinly and served raw as hors-d'œuvre, often accompanied by a tranche of melon.

Preparation of ham for cooking

Wipe or scrape off any mould and soak in cold water for twelve hours. Cover with clean cold water, bring to the boil and skim. Cook simmering very gently for 20 minutes per $^1/2$ kg (1 lb) and 20 minutes over. To check if the ham is cooked, gently ease out and twist the small bone at the knuckle end (often called the mustard spoon bone), if this bone can be removed then the gammon is cooked. A 5 kg (10 lb) ham should take approximately $3^1/2$ hours to cook. Allow to cool in the cooking liquor and retain the liquor as it is ideal for use as a stock in the preparation of soups such as pea, pea and ham, and minestrone.

To prepare for cold service see Gammon (p. 137).

Bacon

Bacon is the salted/cured flesh of a baconer pig that is specially bred, or selected after slaughter, for its suitability to produce bacon. The ideal baconer pig has a long back and a small layer of fat, as this will produce more back bacon in relation to other joints from a carcass/side.

Bacon used to be dry-cured/salted with salt being rubbed into the meat and especially around any bones (ham is predominately dry-cured and served raw whereas bacon is cooked before serving). The salt draws moisture from the meat which combines with the salt to produce brine. This gradually penetrates the meat and 'cures' it. The term 'curing' means to cure the meat of its tendency to go bad. Due to the use of course salt, bacon could be hard and dry, and later other ingredients were used to improve the texture and consistency of the product. Sugar was used to soften and sweeten the meat and saltpetre to enhance the colour. The traditional pink colour of bacon is due to bacteria in the meat converting the salt into nitrite which stabilize the myoglobin (red pigment) contained in the blood. Saltpetre/potassium nitrate enhances the pinkness of the meat. Bacon is more often wet-cured nowadays as it is a lot less labour intensive, adds weight to the meat and gives a consistent product. Wet-curing involves immersing the flesh in brine and allowing the meat to soak up enough brine to penetrate the flesh, saltpetre is generally added for colour. Wet-cured bacon will often leak 'milk': as the protein coagulates during cooking, milky-coloured brine is squeezed out, this is most often witnessed during grilling.

Caterers should be aware that cheap 'wet-cured' bacon may not turn out to be as cheap as it appears due to the leakage and evaporation during cooking. In fact, it may be more profitable to purchase better quality or dry-cured bacon that does not leak.

There are two main categories of bacon:

Green bacon: Bacon that has been cured but not smoked.
Smoked bacon: Bacon that has been cured and smoked.

Smoking was first developed to enhance the keeping quality of meat. Wood smoke contains various antiseptic tar products which impart a particular flavour to the meat and help prevent the development of mould. Indeed, this may be where the term 'green bacon' originated as unsmoked bacon has a tendency to develop a green mould on the outside. This is especially true when bacon was stored in a cold larder and not under refrigeration.

Quality

1. Bacon should be lean and dry with a low salt content.
2. There should be no sign of stickiness or smell.
3. It should have a smooth thin rind with no wrinkles.
4. The flesh should be pink, firm and lean with no excess fat.
5. The fat should be smooth and white.

Storage

1. Whole bacon is best kept by storing sides hung on hooks in a cold room.
2. Sliced bacon is best kept in a refrigerator.
3. Vacuum-packed joints and rashers of bacon may be frozen or stored in a refrigerator, but once opened should be used quickly.

Classification

- Ham is the cured hind leg of a porker pig.
- Gammon is the cured hind leg of a baconer pig.

Dissection of a side of bacon

1. Mark a line with the back of a boning knife down the centre of the side lengthways from the middle of the aitchbone, across the ribs to the collar/hock end of the side.
2. Remove the gammon by cutting across the side 25 mm (1 in) below the round of the aitchbone, to a point $2^{1}/_{2} - 5$ cm ($2 - 3$ in) above the tail; cut through to the bone with a knife then saw through the bone and finish with a knife.
3. Split the side lengthways (following the mark made earlier) into back and streaky, starting at the end from which the gammon was removed, and cut through and down to the ribs. Saw through the ribs and finish cutting with a sharp knife.
4. Remove the collar by a cut across the 'back' half of the side, level with the tip of the first/second rib bone.
5. Remove the hock by a cut across the 'streaky' half of the side, level with the first or second rib bone.

Joints

Gammon (whole)

Specification: Removed from 25 mm (1 in) below the round of the aitchbone.

Weight: $5 - 6$ kg ($10 - 12$ lb).

Description: The gammon is the cured hind leg of a baconer pig. A versatile joint that can be boiled, braised, baked and served hot or cold. Gammon can also be cut into steaks and grilled. Gammon to be cooked whole is always soaked for at least 24 hours in cold water to remove excess salt.

Uses: Boiling, braising, baking and grilling (in steaks).

Preparation for boiling, braising and baking

The aitchbone should be removed and the end of the shank bone sawn off straight. Soak in cold water for 24 hours.

Boiling

Cover with clean cold water, bring to the boil and skim. Cook simmering very gently for 20 minutes per $1/2$ kg (1 lb) and 20 minutes over. Allow to cool in its cooking liquor. A 5 kg (10 lb) gammon should take approximately $3^1/2$ hours to cook. To check if the gammon is cooked, gently ease out and twist the small bone at the knuckle end (often called the mustard spoon bone), if this bone can be removed then the gammon is cooked. The knuckle part of the gammon, often referred to as a 'ham hock', may be ordered separately for the flavouring of soups.

Baking and braising

As for boiling but to allow for further cooking reduce the cooking time to fifteen minutes per $1/2$ kg (1 lb) plus fifteen minutes over, and allow to half cool in the cooking liquor. In this case, the removal of the mustard spoon bone will not apply until the cooking time is completed later.

To serve cold
English style: remove the small bone at the knuckle end and bare the bone, remove the skin and trim the fat to a smooth, even surface. Coat the surface of the fat with fresh breadcrumbs toasted to a golden brown in a slow oven. Place the gammon on a carving stand, cover the knuckle bone with a paper frill and surround with bouquets of picked parsley.

Continental style
As for English style but coat with honey and place in an oven at gas mark 6/200°C/400°F until golden brown, basting constantly. The gammon may also be studded with cloves prior to cooking. Place on a carving stand, cover the knuckle bone with a paper frill and garnish with peaches or pineapple and picked parsley.

Note that Brown/Demerara sugar is often used to coat gammon; this is suitable when gammon is to be served hot but not for cold service as the sugar becomes too hard and crunchy.

Gammon and ham may be coated with *chaud froid* sauce, decorated and glazed with aspic for service on cold buffets.

Braising

Prepare and cook as for boiling but reduce the cooking time to fifteen minutes per $1/2$ kg (1 lb). Allow to cool enough to handle easily. Remove the aitchbone, skin and excess fat to produce a smooth surface. Stud with cloves. Place on a bed of root vegetables, half cover with a mixture of Madeira and *jus lie/demi-glace*. Cover with a tight fitting lid and braise in a moderate oven for approximately one hour, or until the knuckle bone comes away easily. Baste occasionally with the sauce. When cooked, remove from the cooking liquor and glaze with honey or icing sugar in a hot oven or under a salamander.

Other fortified wines may be used instead of Madeira, for example Marsala, Port or Sherry, but Madeira is the most typical.

Baking (*jambon en croute*)

Prepare and cook as for boiling but reduce cooking time to fifteen minutes per $^1/_2$ kg (1 lb). Allow to half cool in the cooking liquor. Remove from liquor and remove the aitchbone, skin and trim the fat. The gammon can be enclosed in a sheet of short, rough puff or puff pastry, then decorated with trimmings and baked for approximately 15 – 20 minutes in a hot oven to colour the pastry, reducing to a low oven for 30 – 45 minutes to complete the cooking.

An enhanced method of presentation is to enclose the gammon in a sheet of pastry as above but cut into a trellis pattern. Modern trellis pastry cutters are ideal for this purpose. (If enclosing the gammon completely in a sheet of pastry, a hole must be made to allow the steam to escape, otherwise the pastry will become soggy. Enclosing in a trellis pattern of pastry makes this unnecessary.)

Collar

Specification: The collar is removed by a cut across the 'back' half of the side, level with the tip of the first/second rib bone.

Weight: 3 kg (6 lb).

Description: Apart from gammon, the collar is the most convenient joint for boiling as it contains little or no bone. It can be rolled and tied easily into a compact joint and boiled as for gammon.

Uses: Boiling, served with pease pudding and parsley sauce, grilling, boned and skinned, sliced into rashers across the grain.

Hock

Specification: The hock is removed by a cut across the 'streaky' half of the side, level with the first or second rib bone.

Weight: $3^1/_2$ kg (7 lb).

Description: The hock may be boiled as for collar but contains more bones.

Uses: Boiling, grilling (in rashers)

Gammon steaks

Specification: The gammon is removed by cutting across the side 25 mm (1 in) below the round of the aitchbone to a point $2^1/_2$ – 5 cm (2 – 3 in) above the tail; cut through to the bone with a knife then saw through the bone and finish with a knife. Gammon steaks are cut from the gammon joint that has been carefully boned out and the skin removed. Cut across the grain of the meat into 1 cm ($^1/_2$ in)-thick slices. Both cut surfaces should be reasonably parallel to ensure that each portion is a consistent thickness. All traces of bone and gristle should be removed and surface fat should not exceed 13 mm ($^1/_2$ in).

The fat should be nicked with the point of a sharp knife at $1/2$ cm ($1/4$ in) intervals to prevent curling during cooking.

Weights: 170 g (6 oz); 198 g (7 oz); 226 g (8 oz); 283 g (10 oz).

Description: Gammon steak is a simple yet popular cut, often prepared grilled with pineapple or peaches. If grilled in this way, marinate the steak in a little of the fruit juice prior to grilling as this will assist in keeping it moist. It may also be served with a devilled, piquant or Madeira sauce.

Uses: Grilled with peaches or pineapple; grilled and garnished with straw potatoes, watercress and a devilled or piquant sauce; grilled and garnished *à la maison*, e.g., with mushrooms and tomato.

Bacon rashers

Specification: Cut from 'back' or 'streaky' as specified. Should be cut across the grain to the required thickness, both sides being parallel to ensure even thickness. All traces of bone and gristle should be removed. Surface fat should not exceed 13 mm ($1/2$ in).

Weight: As specified.

Description: The price and quality of bacon rashers varies considerably (see Curing, p. 125). Bacon that is reasonably priced may be sold in uneven pieces making portion control difficult, or it may have a high water content which will mean weight loss during cooking. It is always advisable to check for weight loss during cooking by weighing before and after cooking. The thickness of rashers is dependent on their use.

Uses: Grilling/frying (in rashers), club sandwiches, grilled liver and bacon, bacon rolls with roast poultry.

Bacon pieces / bits

Description: The trimmings from any of the cuts of bacon. The only stipulation is that they should be either all green or all smoked –not a mixture – and that they should not contain too high a percentage of rind or fat. They have a very wide range of uses, some of the main ones are given here.

Uses: Flavouring of soups/sauces, lardons (sauté of chicken dishes), omelettes, Quiche Lorraine, potato dishes, pies.

SIX

Poultry and Game

Introduction

The term 'poultry' is used to describe domesticated birds that are bred and reared for eating. In other words, fowl kept in captivity for their flesh or eggs. Wild birds/fowl that are hunted come under the term 'game'. The domestication of poultry can be traced back some four thousand years. We eat more poultry today than any other animal or bird. All poultry is descended from wild species, such as chickens which come from the old jungle fowl and ducks which descend from the wild mallard, apart from the Muscovy. Poultry has come to include some birds that once would have been termed game, this is because more are raised or farmed than once was the case. Guinea fowl, for instance, is now mainly raised in captivity as opposed to being hunted in the wild or on private estates. Some varieties of poultry still have wild cousins, as in the case of ducks and pigeons. 'Poultry' now includes:

Chickens
Ducks and ducklings
Geese
Guinea fowl
Pigeon
Turkey

Farmed rabbit has also been adopted under the 'poultry' label, as it is closer to poultry than to any other classification; though not being a fowl, it is still a moot point. Rabbit caught in the wild, however, is still classed as game.

Quality

The age of the bird is the main guide to quality. A young bird will have a flexible end to the breastbone, and the spurs and scales on the legs become larger as the bird ages. Free-range birds may be a little older as they take longer to rear. There should be no excuse for purchasing old birds, as the 'table' chicken introduced from America in the 1950s and specially bred for its flesh rather than egg laying takes only six or seven weeks to reach the required weight of between $1^1/2 - 2$ kg (3 – 4 lb). The points laid out below are a guide for what to look for in a young tender bird.

1. The breast and legs of poultry should be plump and well fleshed.
2. The flesh and skin should have a natural colour and no discolouration. This should be white with a faint bluish tinge for chicken and turkey; ducks and guinea fowl are darker, and pigeons even darker.
3. The 'vent end' of the breastbone should be pliable.
4. The legs should have small scales and spurs.
5. Poultry should have a clean, fresh smell.

Food value

Poultry is more easily digested than red meat. It is high in protein which is used for building and repair of body tissues. Poultry such as chicken and turkey is also low in fat.

Classification

Poultry is classified into four main groups:

1. The type of poultry, e.g. chicken, duck, turkey.
2. The method of rearing, e.g. free-range, battery.
3. The condition of the meat, e.g. fresh, frozen, whole, portions.
4. Their catering use, e.g. roasting chicken, boiling fowl.

Grading

The grading of poultry is in my opinion one of the least developed areas of quality control. For instance, chickens are graded mainly by appearance into only three categories (see below), but the eating quality or availability of portions from a given weight depend on much more than what they look like. Other factors include: type of feed; method of rearing (free-range or intensively-reared); age; and if frozen, the frozen/thawed weight and thawed/cooked weight.

Poultry may absorb large amounts of water during the freezing process thus adding considerably to the weight of the product, and this may be lost during thawing and cooking. Although some weight loss is inevitable from frozen poultry, this in some cases can be excessive. Obviously it would be impracticable for all the above information to be stated on commercially-produced poultry, but if value for money is to be obtained, purchasers should take into consideration the various standards when comparing brands of frozen poultry.

Frozen poultry should be checked on arrival for broken packaging and any signs of freezer burn or thawing and re-freezing (look for misshapen birds or liquid frozen in the base of the packaging).

Grade A Is the top grade, good birds all within a small weight range.
Grade B These are chickens that have a few minor blemishes.
Grade C Chickens have some deformities and blemishes and will be unequal in size.

Hanging and storage

Fresh poultry

Should be hung by the legs in a fridge or cold room for at least 24 hours after slaughter to allow it to become tender. Then store in a fridge or cold room with a maximum temperature of 4°C. Most food poisoning organisms will not multiply below 4°C, and even those that do will grow only very slowly. Poultry should be kept *separate* from other meats to prevent cross-contamination, and should have a container placed beneath it to catch any drips.

Frozen poultry

Should be kept in a freezer at a minimum temperature of −18°C: the operating temperature of the freezer should be set at approximately −23°C so that it does not exceed the minimum of −18°C.

Thawing frozen poultry

This must be planned in advance as frozen poultry takes time to thaw (see Thawing times, below). Thawing may be carried out in a refrigerator, thawing cabinet or in a chilled cold room; poultry should *never be thawed in a warm place*. Thaw poultry in its wrapping, but puncture the seal and ensure that a container is used to catch any drips; any liquid must be thrown away as soon as possible.

The table below gives the approximate thawing times for poultry. This table is a rough guide only as fridge and cold room temperatures vary. Take extra care when thawing poultry from a commercial deep-freeze or blast freezer as the temperatures may be as low as −30°C to −40°C. If possible use a separate fridge for thawing, this may be set between 6°C and 8°C. At this temperature, allow approximately 3 – 4 hours per ¹/₂ kg (1 lb). Once thawed, cook immediately or transfer to a colder fridge.

Weight	Thawing in cold room (in hours)	Thawing in refrigerator (in hours)
900 g (2 lb)	8	24
1.35 kg (3 lb)	10	30
1.8 kg (4 lb)	12–14	36
3.2 kg (7 lb)	15–20	48

Use of frozen poultry

Always make sure that poultry is completely thawed before cooking. Check to see that there are no ice crystals left in the cavity, legs, or thighs. Cook as soon as possible after thawing and never refreeze frozen poultry once thawed, unless it has been thoroughly cooked. It is safe to freeze cooked poultry as long as it is cooled and frozen quickly, preferably in a blast freezer.

Types of poultry

Spring chicken (baby)

Specification: A fresh or frozen very young bird no more that 4 – 6 weeks old, with no broken bones, torn skin or deformities. If frozen, it should have a minimum of water content.

Weight: 400 – 500 g (14 – 18 oz).

Description: A very tender, one portion baby chicken that is ideal for quick, dry methods of cookery. It should never be overcooked as it will toughen and become dry.

Uses: Roasting, pot-roasting, grilling.

Double spring chicken

Specification: As for spring chicken.

Weight: 600 – 750 g (1 lb 5 oz – 1 lb 10 oz).

Description: A very tender, two portion baby chicken that is ideal for quick, dry methods of cookery. Should never be overcooked as it will toughen and become dry.

Uses: Roasting, pot-roasting, grilling.

Small young chicken

Specification: A fresh, free-range or frozen young bird no more that 12 – 16 weeks old, with no broken bones, torn skin or deformities. If frozen, it should have a minimum of water content.

Weight: 1 – 1^1/$_2$ kg (2^1/$_4$ – 3^1/$_2$ lb).

Description: Often called a small roasting chicken, ideal for all quick, dry methods of cookery. A 1^1/$_2$ kg (3^1/$_4$ – 3^1/$_2$ lb) bird will provide four portions.

Uses: Roasting, pot-roasting, grilling, sautés, suprêmes.

Medium-sized young chicken (broiler)

Specification: A fresh, free-range or frozen young bird no more that 16 – 20 weeks old, with no broken bones, torn skin or deformities. If frozen, it should have a minimum of water content.

Weight: 1^1/$_2$ – 2 kg (3^1/$_4$ – 4^1/$_4$ lb).

Description: Often called a medium roasting chicken, or a broiler (the American term for roasting), ideal for roasting and other methods of cookery apart from poaching (boiling).

Uses: Roasting, pot-roasting, grilling, sautés, suprêmes, fricassees, pies, forcemeats/mousselines.

Young fattened chicken

Specification: Fully-grown fat young bird no more than six months old. Fresh, free-range or frozen, with no broken bones, torn skin or deformities. If frozen, it should have a minimum of water content.

Weight: 2 – 2¹/₂ kg (4¹/₄ – 5 lb).

Description: Often called a large roasting chicken, it will provide 6 – 8 portions and has a good meat to bone ratio. It should not be confused with a boiling fowl which may be of a similar size but a lot older (twelve months plus) and tougher.

Uses: Poaching, pot-roasting, roasting.

Capon

Specification: A fully-grown fat young bird which has been specially treated (de-sexed/caponised). Six to eight months old, fresh, free-range or frozen, with no broken bones, torn skin or deformities. If frozen, it should have a minimum of water content.

Weight: 2¹/₂ – 3¹/₂ kg (5 – 7 lb).

Description: Capons used to be de-sexed (castrated), but modern practices mean that this can now be done using chemicals. This produces a fat, tender, large roasting bird.

Uses: Poaching, pot-roasting, roasting.

Boiling fowl

Specification: A fully-grown old bird, twelve months plus. Fresh, free-range or frozen, with no broken bones, torn skin or deformities. If frozen, it should have a minimum of water content.

Weight: 2 – 3 kg (4 – 6¹/₂ lb).

Description: Usually an old hen bird that has finished laying eggs. It is too tough for anything but boiling, but is full flavoured, reasonably priced and ideal for making stocks and soups.

Uses: Boiling, flavouring of stocks and soups, cooked, boned and diced for use in dishes that require boneless cooked chicken – hachis, vol-au-vents, risotto.

Turkey (young)

Specification: Fresh or frozen, with a plump breast, no broken bones or torn skin with a clean smell and no trace of stickiness. The legs should be dark coloured (almost black) and smooth with small scales and spurs. Pre-basted birds are not acceptable as they contain a large percentage of vegetable oil. If frozen, it should have a minimum of water content.

Weight: 4.5 – 6.3 kg (10 – 14 lb).

Description: The main use for young turkey is roasting, which is more suitable than older birds. The male bird (cock) is larger than the female but the female is often more tender. Turkey is low in fat, economically priced and has a vast range of uses. Raw and cooked turkey breasts are readily available and raw turkey may be prepared and used in recipes where once only chicken, veal or pork was considered suitable (see Uses). Cooked smoked turkey breasts also make a good addition to the range of cold meats available for hors-d'œuvre, salads and sandwiches.

Uses: Roasting, pot-roasting. Breast: sliced and lightly batted for escalopes (as for veal or pork), cut into strips for stir-fries, diced for grilled kebabs, sweet and sour (deep- or shallow-fried), risottos, quiches, club sandwiches, sandwiches. Smoked breast: hors-d'œuvre, assiettes and canapés.

Turkey (large, hen)

Specification: Fresh or frozen, with a plump breast, no broken bones or torn skin with a clean smell and no trace of stickiness. Older birds have lighter coloured legs with large scales. If frozen, it should have a minimum of water content. Pre-basted birds are not acceptable as they contain a large percentage of vegetable oil.

Weight: 7 – 10 kg (15 – 20 lb plus).

Description: Older turkeys are generally only roasted or pot-roasted, they tend to be drier and tougher than young ones. If roasting an old bird every effort must be made to conserve moisture in the flesh; this can be done by the use of 'micro-air' ovens, such as a mealsteam, which reduce the cooking time and hence moisture loss. If the turkey is not to be cooked in a micro-air oven then the legs should be removed and boned, all sinew removed, and then they are stuffed, rolled, tied and cooked separately – initially wrapped in buttered, seasoned tin foil. The breast can then be roasted for less time to conserve moisture. The cooking of turkey should always be monitored with a temperature probe so that it can be cooked for a minimum amount of time while still safeguarding against food poisoning bacteria.

Uses: Roasting, pot-roasting. Breast: diced for kebabs.

Note: There are a range of pre-prepared frozen turkeys on the market, for instance pre-basted and butter-basted turkeys. These may be of use to the inexperienced cook but in my opinion are to be avoided by the professional as they merely add weight to the bird which evaporates during cooking, thereby adding considerably to the cost per portion.

Turkey breast

Uncooked turkey breast is now available and the small and tender ones are reasonably priced and suitable for most styles of preparation, including escalopes, kebabs, pies and stir-fries. The thin white sinew must always be removed prior to cooking.

Duckling

Specification: Available fresh, frozen, farmed or wild (game); whole or in portions. It will be a young bird, approximately 6–8 weeks old, with a plump breast and no broken bones or skin. A fresh bird will have a brightly coloured bill and feet. The upper bill should break easily and the webbed feet should be easy to tear.

Weight: 1.6–1.8 kg (3¹/₄–4 lb).

Description: The quality of ducklings is dictated mainly by their age, and the quality of frozen ducklings is assessed by the weight as the main pointers will have been removed, i.e. the bill and feet. The age range should be between six weeks and three months. The weight range should be no more than 1.8 kg (4 lb).

Ducks and duckling are not easily digested due to their high fat content, and, like pork, need to be served with fruit-based or sharp sauces or sage and onion stuffing which helps to break down the fat.

Weight loss during cooking can be quite considerable due to the high fat content. Ducks/ducklings should never be overcooked as this leads to excessive weight loss and a tendency to become dry and tough.

Uses: Roasting, pot-roasting, pâtés, terrines.

Duck

Specification: Available fresh, frozen, farmed or wild (game); whole or in portions. It will be a young bird, approximately three months old, with a plump breast and no broken bones or skin. A fresh bird will have a brightly coloured bill and feet. The upper bill should break easily and the webbed feet should be easy to tear.

Weight: 1.8–2.7 kg (4–6 lb).

Description: As for ducklings, the quality is dictated mainly by age, and frozen ducks should be assessed by weight. The age range should be between eight weeks and three months. The weight range should be no more than 2.7 kg (6 lb), much larger than this and they tend to be tough.

Uses: Roasting, pot-roasting, braising, pâtés, terrines.

Goose

Specification: Available fresh or frozen; will have a plump breast, with no broken bones or skin. A fresh young bird will have brightly coloured, yellow bill and feet (these become more red in colour as the bird ages). The upper bill should break easily and the webbed feet should be easy to tear. The skin becomes tough after one year.

Weight: 5–7 kg (10–15 lb).

Description: Goose is once again becoming more popular due to the lack of flavour in modern-day chicken and turkey. It was once regarded as the finest of poultry and was traditionally served at Christmas. As with duck, goose has a high fat content. The flesh has a slight gamey flavour and a yellowish colour. The skin may be pierced prior to cooking to allow excess fat to run off.

Uses: Roasting, braising, *confit d'oie* (cut up pieces of goose, cooked and preserved in goose fat, see p. 159).

Guinea fowl

Specification: Available fresh or frozen, the breast and legs should be plump and well fleshed. The flesh and skin should have a natural yellow colour, not discoloured or torn in any way. The 'vent end' of the breastbone should be pliable. The legs should have small scales and spurs, and the bird should have a clean, fresh, 'gamey' smell.

Weight: 3/4 – 1 1/2 kg – (2 – 2 1/2 lb).

Description: Slightly smaller than a chicken, related to the pheasant, but not nearly as strong in flavour. Guinea fowl are halfway between poultry and game. Fresh guinea fowl should be hung for a few days before plucking, dressing and cooking. Care must be taken to keep the bird moist during cooking by covering the breast in fat (barding), otherwise it can be tough and dry.

Uses: All recipes that apply to pheasant may be prepared with guinea fowl, including roasting, braising, pot-roasting, shallow-frying (in suprêmes).

Pigeon / squab (young pigeon)

Specification: Available fresh or frozen, the breast should be plump, the flesh deep red, and the claws light pink. Squab will be 4 – 6 weeks old, pigeon 6 – 10 weeks old.

Weights: (squab) 350 – 500 g (12 – 16 oz); (pigeon) 350 – 675 g (12 – 24 oz).

Description: Pigeon is available as poultry (domesticated) and as game (wild wood pigeon): the wild version is larger. A squab is a young tender pigeon. Age is the main guide to quality as old birds may be tough and stringy. Young birds have a pleasant gamey flavour. Pigeons do not have a gall bladder so the liver may be left in place after drawing.

Uses: Roasting, pot-roasting, braising, grilling. Vacuum-packed pigeon breasts can be purchased separately and are good for sautéing.

Rabbit (tame / farmed)

Specification: Tame or hutch rabbits, fresh or frozen. Frozen will be skinned, eviscerated and de-headed. Fresh rabbits will be young, and medium sized and the ears should tear easily.

Weight: 1 1/2 – 2 1/2 kg (3 – 5 lb).

Description: Rabbit is at last becoming acceptable again as the memories of myxomatosis recede. The main guide to quality is age: if bought fresh then the main test to a rabbit's age is to tear the ears, the easier this is the younger and therefore more tender the rabbit. Frozen rabbits are available in boxes, imported mainly from China, usually skinned and eviscerated. The flesh is white, tender and 'chicken like'. Fresh rabbits should not be hung for any length of time as they quickly become tainted.

Uses: Stewing, blanquettes, fricassees, pies.

Offal / giblets

These are usually obtained from or supplied with the bird. If purchased separately they must be fresh; a clean, fresh smell is the best guide. Chicken livers are often bought separately (usually frozen), they should not be tainted with any 'green' from the gall bladder and they should not be surrounded by an excessive amount of blood.

Preparation: The majority of offal requires only washing and trimming.

Uses:

Giblets – stocks, soups and gravies.

Livers – garnishes, rice dishes, pâtés, terrines, kebabs, farces, savouries.

Hearts – as for giblets.

Gizzards – stocks; duck or turkey gizzards may be used in stews or pies.

Winglets – may be marinated and used in their own right, or as a garnish for consommés or incorporated into rice dishes. Turkey winglets may also be boned and stuffed.

Preparation of poultry

Plucking

It is not often that poultry will have to be plucked in-house as most birds are now plucked by machines at the suppliers. It is, however, a process that the chef should be acquainted with as game is becoming more popular and available and feathered game nearly always requires plucking. Plucking should be carried out away from other foods as the feathers may be carried by draughts and cause contamination. It should be done over a bucket or basin of water.

Spread the wings of the bird across your knee, hold the legs firmly, with the head hanging downwards. Dampen the outside feathers and with your free hand, pull the skin tight and grip the base of the feathers with the thumb and first finger, taking care not to damage the skin. Turn the feathers in a semi-circular motion from left to right giving a slight tug, and place the extracted feathers in the bowl or bucket of water. The bird should be plucked in the following order: breast, back, wings and legs. Small stub feathers should be removed by holding them between the thumb and a small knife, grip firmly, turn the knife to one side and tug gently.

Singeing

Singeing is used to remove any trace of feathers from the bird. First, 'pick' out any remains of pen feathers with your thumb and a small knife or with pliers. Then, hold the bird over a naked flame or apply a flame to the outside of the bird (in the past a candle was used, but today a gas jet or a hand-held butane blowtorch is the most usual appliance). Hold the plucked bird by the head and feet and pass over the flame, or lightly pass the torch over the surface of the bird turning it as you go. Care must be taken not to scorch or burn the skin. The feet may have more heat applied to them in order to help remove any scales which are wiped off with a cloth.

Blanching or scalding

Used to remove the scales from the legs of the bird. This is achieved either as above or by dipping the feet into boiling water and the scales removed by wiping with a cloth.

Removal of sinews

To facilitate carving, it is vital that in old or large birds the sinews are removed from the legs, this is especially important in the case of turkey. The skin is cut approximately halfway between the feet and the first leg joint, taking care not to cut through the sinews, the bone should then be broken with the back of a knife or small cleaver. The foot is twisted round to ensure complete separation. The sinews are then pulled from the bird by means of (a) a V-shaped sinew hook or (b) a butcher's hook, by placing the sinews over the hook and pulling the whole bird sharply downwards. Other birds such as game may have their sinews removed by breaking the bone as above and then inserting a skewer between the bone and the sinew and twisting it round to 'pull' the sinews.

Cleaning / evisceration

1. Lay the singed bird on the chopping board breast side down. Hold the neck firmly; pull the skin tight and with a small office knife cut open the skin at the back of the neck.
2. Remove the head with a 25 cm (10 in) chopping knife. Remove the crop. Separate the neck from the skin and cut through the neck close to the body. Remove the windpipe.
3. Insert the first three fingers through the opening in the neck and dislodge the organs from the carcass.
4. Cut a hole through the parson's nose at the rear of the bird with a small office knife. Loosen the insides with your fingers as before.
5. Carefully remove the intestines, taking great care not to burst the gall bladder (if it bursts it will taint the rest of the bird with bitter green bile).
6. Wipe the bird with a clean cloth.
7. Carefully separate the liver from the gall bladder (except with pigeon) and cut away any discoloured parts of liver. Discard the gall bladder and carefully cut open the stomach (gizzard) and clean under a running tap, except with duck or goose in which case the gizzard is not split but trimmed and wiped. Lastly, remove the heart and trim off any membrane and blood vessels. Discard all the inedible offal, clean and sterilize the area.

Drawing and cleaning of birds and rabbits is often carried out on clean sheets of paper, e.g. newspaper or grease-proof, so that the inedible entrails may be totally enclosed in the paper for disposal, leaving the preparation area uncontaminated.

Trussing

Birds are trussed to enhance the presentation of the finished product, giving it a pleasing, uniform shape; it is also important during the cooking process to keep the bird in shape and intact by securing with string.

Trussing for roasting

1. First, remove the wishbone by scraping away the flesh covering it and then gently pulling forwards, taking care if possible not to break it. (If the wishbone does break, care should be taken as the edges of the broken bone can be exceedingly sharp and may cause a nasty cut. If broken, a clean tea towel should be used to protect the fingers when pulling the bone away.)
2. Place the bird on its back and insert a stringed trussing needle through the flap of skin level with the joint (elbow) of the leg; pass through the bird to emerge through the other leg at the other side.
3. Turn the bird on to its side and pass the threaded needle between the bones of the winglet, along the bird securing the skin of the neck to the carcass and through the opposite side.
4. Tie the two ends of string together, pulling the string taut. Cut off the ends of the string close to the knot.
5. The legs may be secured for roasting by passing the threaded trussing needle through the hole in the carcass situated beneath the parson's nose over the top of the legs and tying securely.

Trussing for poaching, pot-roasting and braising

1. First, remove the wishbone by scraping away the flesh covering it then gently pulling forwards, taking care if possible not to break it. (See trussing for roasting).
2. Place the bird on its back and insert a stringed trussing needle through the flap of skin level with the joint (elbow) of the leg, pass through the bird to emerge through the other leg at the other side.
3. Turn the bird on to its side and pass the threaded needle between the bones of the winglet, along the bird, securing the skin of the neck to the carcass and through the winglet at the opposite side.
4. Tie the two ends of string together pulling the string taut. Cut off the ends of the string close to the knot.
5. Cut the tendon underneath the legs by the knuckle joint; make a small cut through the skin level with the knuckle joint, bend the joint parallel to the leg bone and insert through the incision.
6. The legs may then be secured as for roasting by passing the threaded trussing needle through the hole in the carcass situated beneath the parson's nose over the top of the legs and tying securely.

To stuff a bird for roasting

Follow the instructions for trussing for roasting up to the end of stage 2 (see p. 150). Then slide your finger under the skin of the breast at the neck end to make room for the stuffing. Place a sufficient amount of stuffing into the neck of the bird, pull the skin over it and tuck underneath the bird. Continue as for trussing for roasting from stage 3.

Except for ducks and geese, I do not see good reason for stuffing the cavity of a bird as opposed to the neck. If large amounts of stuffing are required then it should be cooked separately, either on trays or rolled in tin foil (eggs may be added for firmer stuffing). Stuffing the cavity increases the cooking time of the bird and can produce 'cold spots' which do not allow the inside of the bird to reach a sufficiently high temperature to kill any harmful bacteria.

To stuff the cavity (ducks and geese)

Fill the cavity with stuffing, fold over the parson's nose, and when securing the legs with a trussing needle (see Trussing for poaching, etc. stage 6) pass through the parson's nose instead of the hole in the carcass to secure it in place.

Cutting and cuts

Cutting a chicken for sauté, fricassee and so on is a fairly simple and logical process, but it takes time and concentration. The technique cannot be learnt with one chicken, but must be repeated over and over again to achieve a level of competence and speed essential to a professional chef.

Cutting for sauté / fricassee / pies

1. **Remove the winglets** by lifting the bird by the tip of the winglet so as to stretch the skin on the underside of the winglet. Cut through the flesh of the winglet to the bone parallel to the bird and as close as possible to where the winglet joins the bird. Hold the bone that is attached to the carcass and pull back the flesh of the winglet to the joint and break off by twisting against the joint, then repeat with the other winglet. (The advantage of removing the winglets in this manner is that the 'suprême' bone is left perfectly clean, which enhances the presentation of the wing and saves time scraping if suprêmes are to be cut from the bird; also the extra flesh attached to the winglet makes them suitable either for incorporating into the main dish or serving separately as Chinese-style/tikka winglets.)
2. **Remove the legs** by cutting the flap of skin between them and the carcass and bending them at right angles to the carcass to dislocate the bone that joins them to the carcass; with the bird on its side and the legs bent right back, the bulge of the 'oyster' should be plain to see. Cut through along the line of the carcass taking the flesh from the oyster cavity with the leg, and through the joint to detach the leg from the carcass. Repeat with the other leg. Then cut the legs into two through the joint, and cut through the bone above the joint at the foot end.
3. **Remove the wishbone** by scraping away the flesh covering the wishbone. To do

this, hold the carcass in one hand and scrape by placing a large knife in the middle of the wishbone and twisting the carcass against the knife. Once the wishbone is exposed, hold the carcass in one hand, slide the finger and thumb of the other hand up and behind the wishbone, pull the wishbone out and away taking care not to break it (see Trussing p. 150).

4. **Remove the wings** by cutting through the flesh halfway between the line of the breastbone and the outer edge of the flesh and cutting down and through the wing joint with the tip of the knife. Repeat with the other wing.

5. **Remove the breasts** by holding the carcass upright with one hand and chopping through the carcass along the line of the remaining flesh. Cut the breast into two diagonally across the middle of the breast. Cut the carcass across into three.

The above instructions will give you thirteen pieces: two winglets, two wings, two thighs, two drumsticks, two breasts and three pieces of carcass. These are normally cooked (sautéed) in the following order: drumsticks, thighs, carcass, wings, winglets and breasts. This is to ensure that each item has the required cooking time and that tender cuts, such as the wings and breast, do not become overcooked while waiting for the tougher cuts – drumsticks and thighs – to be cooked.

Often the cooking order for cuts of chicken is ignored as the chef will allow the chicken to boil for a period of time in the accompanying sauce. If the correct type of chicken is used, i.e. a young and tender bird, then boiling is unnecessary and will only toughen the chicken. Further cooking will cause the cuts to become tender again, but the flavour of the chicken will then be in the sauce and not the chicken. If using young and tender birds, all that is required is for the chicken to be 'held' in the sauce for a few minutes without boiling.

Presentation

For enhanced presentation and eating quality, chicken cut for sauté may be improved by removing the knuckles at the ends of the bones with a knife leaving only a straight short bone in the thighs, wings and drumsticks which the customer can easily push out with the tip of a fork. An alternative method of presentation is to turn the pieces of carcass upside down in an entrée dish and reform the chicken around the carcass so that it looks like the whole chicken prior to cutting/cooking. Of course, the carcass is never served. The following should be used as a guide to ensure that each customer has an equal portion of light and dark meat:

Drumstick + breast × 2   Thigh + wing × 2

The winglets may be used to enhance a portion which looks slightly smaller than another.

Suprêmes of chicken

A suprême of chicken is the wing and half the breast of a chicken with the clean wing bone attached. One chicken will yield two suprêmes. Suprêmes of chicken will keep their shape better if allowed to chill in a fridge after preparation and prior to cooking.

To prepare:

1. **Remove the winglets** by lifting the bird by the tip of the winglet so as to stretch the skin on the underside of the winglet. Cut through the flesh of the winglet to the bone parallel to the bird and as close as possible to where the winglet joins the bird. Hold the wing bone that is attached to the carcass and pull back the flesh of the winglet to the joint and break off by twisting against the joint; remove the tip of the winglet at the first joint, then repeat with the other winglet. (The advantage of removing the winglets in this way is that the wing/suprême bone is left perfectly clean, this enhances the presentation of the wing and saves time having to scrape the bone clean later.)

2. **Remove the legs** by cutting the flap of skin between them and the carcass and bending them at right angles to the carcass to dislocate the bone that joins them to the carcass; with the bird on its side and the legs bent right back, the bulge of the 'oyster' should be plain to see. Cut through along the line of the carcass taking the flesh from the oyster cavity with the leg, and through the joint to detach the leg from the carcass. Repeat with the other leg.

3. **Remove the wishbone** by first removing the skin from the breast, scraping the flesh covering the wishbone away, hold the carcass in one hand and scrape by placing a large knife in the middle of the wishbone and twisting the carcass against the knife. Once the wishbone is exposed hold the carcass in one hand, slide the finger and thumb of the other hand up and behind the wishbone, pull the wishbone out and away taking care not to break it (see Trussing, p. 150).

4. **Remove the suprême** by cutting lengthways along the breast parallel to the breastbone approximately halfway. Then, with the point of the knife follow the bone down to the wing joint and cut through the ball and socket joint. This should leave the cleaned wingbone attached. Turn the chicken on to its side; holding the fillet in the suprême firmly with the thumb, gradually pull the suprême away from the carcass, using the knife to hold the carcass and ready to cut away any flesh that may stick to the carcass. Repeat on the other side.

5. **Remove the fillet** from the suprême and remove the strip of white sinew that runs through it by holding the end of the sinew in one hand and gently scraping away the flesh with the tip of an office knife.

6. **Make a cut lengthways** along the underside of the suprême, approximately halfway through the thick part; open with the fingers and place the fillet inside. Fold the flesh over the fillet to enclose it, lightly flatten with a moistened bat, then neaten the shape, trim only if necessary.

Suprêmes of chicken (uses)

Suprêmes of chicken are ideal for most styles of service, including set menus, *à la carte* cookery, banquettes and cold buffets. They may be poached, shallow-fried or deep-fried. The poaching of suprêmes is mainly done in butter with a minimum amount of stock added. If suprêmes are to be served with a sauce or presented decorated on a buffet then the wingbone is normally removed. Suprêmes have a short cooking time and should be served 'just cooked', i.e. they should not be held for any length of time once cooked as they will become tough and dry. Suprêmes can be stuffed, as in chicken Kiev. Other popular styles of presentation include marechale (asparagus), princesse (white wine sauce and asparagus), florentine (spinach and mornay sauce) and chicken Maryland.

Preparation for Kiev

Follow the instructions for the preparation of suprêmes of chicken to the end of stage 6. Then make a cut lengthways along the underside of the suprême, approximately halfway though the thick part, turn the knife and cut horizontally out from the main cut towards the edges without cutting right through and open gently with the fingers to form a pocket. Lightly bat out the fillet with a dampened cutlet bat and place the tip of the fillet into the thin end of the pocket of the suprême. Fill the pocket with garlic butter and fold the fillet over the top of the butter, bring the edges of the suprême over the top of the fillet to completely enclose it in the pocket and neaten the shape. Chill in the fridge before passing through seasoned flour, egg and breadcrumbs.

Plain butter was once considered the only authentic filling for *suprême de volaille à la Kiev*, but garlic butter is now the accepted version. Other fillings can be used in suprêmes but the dish should not be called 'Kiev'.

Paupiettes of chicken (A large suprême may produce two paupiettes)

1. Remove the wing bone and fillet from the suprême. On the inside, cut down the centre no more than halfway through, and then towards the outside, both ways, so as to open out the suprême.
2. Lightly bat out, season, spread with stuffing or farce and roll up. Lightly bat the edges to seal and tie with string.

Escalopes of chicken

As stage 1 above, then bat out further using water/plastic. Use as for veal/ pork escalopes.

Goujons of chicken

As for stage 1 of paupiettes, then cut into strips diagonally across the suprême. Goujons are usually passed through seasoned flour, egg and breadcrumbs then rolled to shape. Deep-fry and serve with a sauce or dips, e.g. garlic mayonnaise.

Care should be taken not to fry chicken at too high a temperature as this can ruin the texture 165°C is ideal.

To prepare chicken for grilling

1. First, cut the tendon underneath the legs by the knuckle joint.
2. Make a small cut through the skin at the rear of the bird on both sides, level with the middle of the drumstick, and insert the legs through the cuts in the skin.
3. Remove the tips from the winglets, then turn the bird upside down and split down

the backbone with a large knife and open the bird out, flatten with a cutlet bat and cut away the backbone.

Note: The rib bones are removed once grilling is completed. To prepare for grilling *en crapaudine* (chicken spatchcock), prepare as for grilling to the end of stage 1, then cut horizontally from below the point of the breast at the vent end over the top of the legs and down to the wing joints, leaving the breasts attached. Fold back the breasts, then fold the backbone in the opposite direction and turn the bird over. With the point of the breast extended forward the shape should resemble a toad. Press lightly to flatten, the legs and wings may then be skewered in position prior to grilling. Portions of chicken may be used for grilling, but in my opinion it is preferable to use a smaller chicken and a whole or half a bird as opposed to quarters which limits the customer's choice to breast or leg as a portion.

Preparation of chicken ballotines

Ballotines are the boned and stuffed legs of birds, usually chicken. They may be served hot or cold. Below I have given two methods of preparation: the method for hot service is not suited to cold, but the method for buffet service may be applied to both hot and cold presentation.

Ballotines: hot presentation (braising and poaching)

1. Taking care not to break the skin remove the thigh bone from the leg.
2. Carefully loosen the bone in the drumstick from the flesh leaving the top 2 – 3 cm (1 in) of bone at the foot end still attached. Sever and remove all sinew.
3. Fill the spaces left by the removal of the bones with a savoury stuffing (preferably meat-based) or forcemeat.
4. Shape and bring the skin over to enclose the stuffing then sew up with a trussing needle and string.

Ballotines: cold or buffet presentation

1. Taking care not to damage or puncture it, pull the skin away from the flesh of the leg but leave it still attached at the foot end of the drumstick.
2. Cut through the flesh and bone approximately 2 – 3 cm (1 in) from the foot end of the drumstick, leaving approximately 2 – 3 cm (1 in) of bone still attached to the skin.
3. Bone out and remove all sinew from the flesh of the leg, then mince finely and make into fine chicken forcemeat.
4. Fill the skin with the forcemeat and shape the leg to resemble a small ham, sew up with fine string and poach gently in stock.

Once cold, ballotines for presentation on a buffet are coated with a layer of chaud-froid sauce, glazed with aspic jelly, decorated and finished with a coat of aspic. A typical mode of presentation is to surround a decorated whole chicken galantine with ballotines that have been decorated in a similar fashion. This means that the galantine centrepiece can remain intact while the ballotines provide individual portions.

Galantines

A boned and stuffed whole bird is called a galantine.

To prepare a chicken galantine

A fresh bird is preferable for this dish as the skin tends to be stronger than a frozen bird's. However, a perfectly acceptable product can be produced from a frozen bird. The bird should have unbroken skin with no remains of feathers or feather pins. If a fresh bird is used, it will have been drawn, singed and the feet removed.

To bone a whole bird

1. First, remove the wishbone without puncturing the skin, then remove the parson's nose and cut off the winglets at the joint where they join the wing bone.
2. Turn the bird upside down and cut through the skin along the middle of the backbone.
3. Using a small sharp knife cut sideways out from the backbone under the skin. Continue downwards until the joint which joins the leg to the carcass is reached; carefully cut through the joint with the tip of the knife to separate the leg from the carcass. Continue down one side until the joint which joins the wing to the carcass is reached; cut through as for the leg. Turn the bird round and repeat on the other side.
4. Carefully remove the carcass and flesh from the skin, taking care not to puncture the skin, especially the skin over the breast bone as this is where the flesh is at its thinnest.
5. Using the tip of a small knife, tunnel out the wing bones and holding the skin with one hand gently pull them inside the skin and away. Push the skin from the wings out again. Repeat with the legs.
6. Spread out the skin and very carefully cut/scrape away any remaining flesh or fat so that the skin is relatively clean.
7. Place the skin in cold water to whiten.
8. Separate the flesh from the bones taking care to remove all traces of gristle and sinew. Leave the breasts as whole as possible.

Just as there are two methods of preparing a ballotine, there are two ways of preparing and presenting a galantine. The one I have concentrated on here is the rolled galantine, the other method is to present the chicken 'whole', as near as possible to its original shape. In this case the bones are removed leaving the flesh attached to the skin, the space left by the removal of the carcass is filled with forcemeat, and the back of the bird is sewn up with string. It is then poached in stock, decorated and presented as for a rolled galantine.

Chicken galantine (*galantine de poulet*)

1¹/₂ kg (3¹/₂ lb) chicken

Chicken Forcemeat:

400 g (14 – 16 oz) chicken flesh	142 ml (¹/₄ pt) double cream (approx.)
400 g (14 – 16 oz) pork fat	3 – 4 eggs
200 g (7 – 8 oz) fillet of veal	seasoning (salt, pepper and nutmeg)
200 g (7 – 8 oz) fillet of pork	

Garnish:

the breast of chicken
(1 cm / ¹/2 in strips)

100 g (4 oz) cooked ham
(1 cm / ¹/2 in strips)

100 g (4 oz) cooked salted
ox tongue (1 cm / ¹/2 in strips)

100 g (4 oz) truffles/garnishing
paste (1 cm / ¹/2 in strips)

140 g (6 oz) pork fat
(1 cm / ¹/2 in strips)

100 g (4 oz) pistachio nuts

71 ml (2¹/2 fl oz) brandy

1. Cut the breasts lengthways into approximately 1 cm (¹/2 in) strips and marinate them in brandy, with the rest of the garnish apart from the garnishing paste (which will leak colour thus spoiling the appearance).
2. Prepare the forcemeat by passing the chicken flesh, fillet of pork and veal and pork fat through a mincer or food processor, *chill thoroughly*, then gradually add the eggs and cream, mixing thoroughly each time. Season with salt, pepper and nutmeg.
3. Lay out the drained skin on a clean tea towel (which may be lined with cling film). Spread a layer of forcemeat on to the inside of the skin and lay the strips of chicken breast, ham, tongue, pork fat, truffle/paste and nuts in a regular pattern on top. (The skin of the chicken may be lined with thin slices of pork back fat which, when the galantine is sliced, should give a nice white border around the forcemeat; however, this can be quite fiddly.)
4. Spread another layer of forcemeat on top and repeat the garnish; continue the process finishing with a layer of forcemeat.
5. Draw the skin over the filling and completely enclose. Roll up in the tea towel and tie the ends firmly with string; tie two strings around the cloth to help keep it in shape.
6. Poach in a good chicken or veal stock for approximately 1¹/4 – 1¹/2 hours.
7. Allow to cool slightly then unwrap the cloth a little, re-roll and tie firmly. Allow to cool under a weight of 2 kg (4 – 5 lb).
8. When thoroughly cool remove the cloth and coat with a layer of chaud-froid sauce followed by aspic. Decorate and finish with a coat of aspic jelly.

A flour panada may be added to the forcemeat to help it bind together. This is added before the eggs and cream (see Flour panada, p. 159).

Forcemeats, mousses, mousselines and quenelles

Chicken forcemeat

500 g (1 lb) chicken meat (boned,
skinned and free from sinew)

¹/4 litre (¹/2 pt) double cream

1 × flour panada

seasoning

2 egg whites

1. Finely mince the chicken flesh and pass through a sieve or place into a food processor.

2. Gradually add the panada and beat until smooth. Gradually add the egg whites. Chill the mix thoroughly by placing in a very cold fridge or in a bowl on top of a bowl of ice, water and a good pinch of salt.
3. Beat in the chilled cream until the mix is thoroughly combined.

Chicken farce

500 g (1 lb) chicken meat (boned, skinned and free from sinew)
2 – 3 egg whites
1/2 litre (1 pt) double cream
seasoning (salt, pepper and nutmeg)

1. Pass the flesh through a mincer or food processor.
2. Gradually add the beaten egg whites and mix until thoroughly combined.
3. Thoroughly chill or place the mix over ice as for chicken forcemeat, and gradually add the ice-cold cream.
4. Place in a well buttered seasoned soufflé or ramekin and place in a pan or tray with water two-thirds of the way up the sides. Cook *en bain-marie* in a moderate oven.

Mousselines

Prepare the mix for mousse or farce de volaille then shape with two dessertspoons and poach in either salt water or stock.

For further information on the shaping and cooking of quenelles and mousselines, see Chapter 4, p. 66.

Quenelles

Prepare the mix for mousse or farce de volaille then shape with two teaspoons and poach in either salt water or stock.

Mousse, Mousselines and Quenelles are all made from similar mixtures, what differs is in their manner of shaping, cooking and presentation.

Mousse – Cooked and presented in a container such as a dariole mould, ramekin or small soufflé mould. Cooked in the oven *en bain-marie*.

Mousseline – Moulded with large spoons such as tablespoons or dessertspoons. Poached in pans or on trays, with stock or salted water.

Quenelles – Moulded with small spoons such as teaspoons or coffee spoons. Poached in pans or on trays, with stock or salted water.

Soufflés are prepared in a completely different way from mousse, mousselines and quenelles. Soufflés use diced or puréed chicken, a velouté enriched with egg yolks, and aerated with beaten egg whites.

Flour panada (*panade à la farina*)

25 g (1 oz) butter	142 ml ($^1/_4$ pt) water
75 g ($2^1/_2$ oz) flour	seasoning

1. Place the water, butter and seasoning in a pan and bring to the boil.
2. Remove from the heat and gradually beat in the flour.
3. Return to the heat, beating well with a spatula for 3 to 4 minutes until smooth.
   Spread on a buttered tray, butter the surface and allow to cool before use.

It should have a smooth, creamy texture – this may be modified with extra flour or water
to give the required consistency which should be similar (when hot) to the texture of the
mixture to which it is to be added.

Confit d'oie

6 kg (12 lb) goose (makes 20 – 24 portions)

1. Remove any fat from the goose and put to one side.
2. Remove the two legs and suprêmes (as for chicken).
3. Prepare a mixture of 1 kg of salt, saltpetre (a pinch), mignonette pepper, nutmeg and
   thyme, and rub this over the pieces of goose. Leave for 24 hours. Remove from salt,
   wash and dry well.
4. Melt the reserved fat and add the pieces of goose, cook very gently for about
   $1^1/_2$ – 2 hours, until the bones come away from the flesh, but the flesh should not
   be overcooked.
5. Remove the pieces of goose from the fat and allow to cool slightly to allow the
   bones to be removed.
6. Place the meat into a earthenware dish and strain over the goose fat; the goose must
   be completely covered with the fat and if necessary top up with melted lard.
7. Place in the refrigerator and leave to mature for approximately 4 – 5 days. Present
   in slices as for pâté with hot buttered toast.

Chicken pie (10 portions, serve hot or cold)

3 × $1^1/_2$ kg ($3^1/_4$ – $3^1/_2$ lb) chickens	Worcester sauce
3 finely-chopped onions	25 g (1 oz) chopped parsley
250 g (8 oz) diced mushrooms	$^1/_2$ litre (1 pint) chicken consommé
(sweated in butter)	or fresh chicken stock
10 rashers streaky bacon	750 g ($1^1/_2$ lb) puff pastry
10 hardboiled egg yolks (halved)	egg wash (egg yolks and water)

1. Cut chicken for sauté and place in a pie dish with the sliced bacon, onions,
   mushrooms, egg yolks and parsley.
2. Season and add several drops of Worcester sauce.
3. Two thirds cover with the chicken consommé/stock.
4. Roll out the pastry. Eggwash the rim of the dish, then use a strip of paste to line the

edge of the dish, eggwash this strip, then cover with pastry.

5. Crimp the pastry edges. Cut a slit in the centre of the paste; use the point of a sharp knife to incise a trellis pattern on the surface of the paste, decorate with leaves using the pastry trimmings.

6. Eggwash two or three times with egg yolks and a little water while allowing the paste to rest (minimum 1 hour).

7. Cook in a moderate oven for approximately $1^{1}/_{2}$ hours, until cooked.

8. If the pie is to be served hot, pour a little thickened veal gravy into it after cooking. If for cold presentation, add a little liquid aspic jelly and allow to cool thoroughly.

Chicken tikka

Chicken tikka has become a very popular dish. It is an excellent addition to the larder chef's repertoire, and can be used for a range of applications including sandwiches, 'hot salads', salads, kebabs, hors-d'œuvres, and may be presented on various types of buffets. Tikka-flavoured chicken winglets can be offered on finger buffets or make an excellent bar snack served with salad and mint-flavoured yoghurt.

Chicken tikka marinade (10 – 20 portions)

3 teaspoons whole coriander seeds	100 g (4 oz) fresh ginger
$^{1}/_{2}$ × 200 g jar tikka paste	1 litre (2 pints) natural live yoghurt
2 teaspoons whole cumin seeds	juice of three lemons
50 g (2 oz) tomato puree	1 head of garlic
3 teaspoons chilli powder	

1. Peel and finely grate the root ginger, peel and crush the garlic to a paste.
2. Place the coriander and cumin seeds into a coffee grinder or pestle and mortar and grind/pound to a powder.
3. Mix together the yoghurt, tomato puree, tikka paste, garlic and ginger. Add the spices and lemon juice and mix well.

Chicken tikka

1. Remove the legs and suprêmes from the chicken and bone out completely. Cut into 2 – 3 cm (1 in) pieces and place in the marinade.
2. Leave to marinate overnight if possible, although a shorter time of 2 – 3 hours will produce an acceptable product.
3. Remove from the marinade and place on to lightly oiled skewers. Cook at a very high temperature, preferably in a tandoor (Indian clay oven) or in a very hot oven, or else grill over a char-grill.
4. Serve on a bed of lightly browned fried onions, accompanied with mint-flavoured plain yoghurt.

The above may be allowed to cool and served in sandwiches, accompanied with salad, or on a cold buffet.

Chicken winglets

Winglets, provided that they have a reasonable amount of meat on them, can be served tikka-flavoured as for chicken tikka or Chinese style as outlined below:

Chinese marinade

1 small bottle of dark soy sauce	6 bay leaves
1 demitasse cup of brown sugar	6 cloves garlic (crushed)
1 demitasse cup of vinegar	salt to taste
several drops of red colouring	a good pinch of Chinese five spice powder

1. Mix together the above and marinate the chicken as for tikka.

French terms

Spring chicken (baby)	Le Poussin	Turkey (young)	Le Dindonneau
Double spring chicken	Le Poussin double	Turkey (large, hen)	La Dinde
Small young chicken	Le Poulet de grain	Duckling	Le Caneton
Medium sized young chicken	La Poulet reine	Duck	Le Canard
		Goose	L'Oie
Young fattened chicken	La Poularde	Guinea fowl	La Pintade
Capon	Le Chapon	Pigeon/squab	Le Pigeonneau
Boiling fowl	La Poule	Rabbit(tame/farmed)	Le Lapin

Convenience and portion-controlled items

Poultry, especially chicken, is available frozen in a variety of cuts, including:

Suprêmes	Nuggets/Bites
Escalopes	Quarters
Drumsticks	Burgers
Pre-prepared Kievs	

Convenience duck items include:

Frozen breasts	Boil in the bag portions
Frozen quarters/halves	with sauce

Turkey:

Pre-rolled joints for roasting (frozen)

More and more convenience poultry goods are being produced all the time, as a look at any frozen food price list/brochure will testify. In my opinion very few frozen poultry items are suitable for hotel or restaurant service as they have a tendency to dry out during cooking and become tough. However, the advantages are that they require little or no preparation, so there is no waste; they are convenient; easy to store; do not need highly-trained staff to produce; and should give a consistent portion/product each time.

Many poultry items are now produced from 'formed meat', which is chopped scraps of meat pressed into various shapes. These are suitable for service in staff cafeterias, schools, cafés and so on, but not in hotels and restaurants, except perhaps on children's menus.

Cooked poultry items include:

Pre-roasted chickens, portions, quarters, legs.
Pre-cooked turkey breast, roll.

Chicken liver pâté (makes 2½ kg / 5 lb)

2½ kg (5 lb) chicken livers	1 kg (2 lb) onions
1 kg (2 lb) stewing veal	2 heads garlic
500 g (1 lb) fat bacon	50 g (2 oz) mixed spice
500 g (1 lb) pork (shoulder)	100 g (4 oz) dried mixed herbs
8 eggs	¼ bottle red wine
125 ml (¼ pt) brandy	250 ml (½ pt) cream
250 g (½ lb) butter	

1. Trim and remove all connective tissue, and cut the meat into approximately 2 cm (1 in) pieces. Chop the onions and crush the garlic.
2. Heat a large sauté pan and add the butter, pork, veal, onions and garlic and seal until half cooked in the butter.
3. Add the herbs, bacon and chicken livers. Fry until sealed, taking care not to overcook the chicken livers. Add the red wine and boil to reduce by one-third.
4. Remove from the heat and allow to cool slightly, then pass twice through the mincer.
5. Beat in the eggs, brandy and cream and check the seasoning.
6. Butter or line with bacon the earthenware dishes; add the pâté mix and cover with greased tin foil. Cook in a moderate oven in a *bain-marie*, gas mark 4/180°C/ 350°F, for 2 – 2½ hours.
7. When cold, seal with a layer of melted butter.

The pâté can be given a finer texture by rubbing through a sieve after mincing, or if a courser texture is desired, by mincing only once.

Mayonnaise of chicken

1. Garnish the bottom of a salad bowl/ravier with a layer of lightly seasoned chiffonade of lettuce.
2. Cover the lettuce with cold sliced chicken breast, free from all skin and bone.
3. Coat with a light mayonnaise, modified with cream.
4. Decorate with slices of peeled tomato, hardboiled egg, radish, strips of anchovies and stoned olives.

Mayonnaise of chicken Indienne

Prepare as above but flavour the mayonnaise with curry paste and chopped mango chutney and garnish with fruit (mango, peach, etc.) Finish with sliced almonds lightly browned under the salamander. An alternative is to substitute plain chicken with chicken tikka and natural/strained Greek yoghurt for the mayonnaise. This makes the dish suitable for 'healthy eating'.

Game

The term game applies to all animals and birds which are hunted in the wild to be eaten. Game is available as open-range or domestically-reared. It could be argued that pheasant, partridge, grouse and venison are not game as they are raised domestically on private estates, but as they live more or less 'in the wild', the term is still applicable. Gibier, the French for game, originates from the old French word for hunting, 'gibecer'; this probably derives from the Latin 'gibbosus' or hunchback – in reference to in the past when huntsmen would carry home their kill in a bag across their backs, giving them the appearance of being 'hunchbacked'. 'Venison' comes from the Latin word 'venari', which means to hunt and all game was once known as 'venison'.

Game differs from poultry in several respects:

Age – The age of a game animal cannot be controlled, therefore game birds or hares may be of different ages and so suitable for different methods of cookery.

Texture – Animals that have to range far and wide in search of food will inevitably have more developed muscles than poultry and are therefore tougher.

Fat content – Because wild animals have constantly to search for food, they use up any small reserves of fat during hard times; this means that they do not have a high fat content (the exception being ducks).

Storage – Game have much higher levels of enzymes in their meat which help break down the connective tissue; this makes the meat more tender, moist and enhances the 'gamey' flavour.

In addition, organisms found in the game carcass prevent the formation of harmful bacteria; this means that, so as long as the flesh is not subjected to any outside contamination, it will be safe to eat when poultry and other meats have long since gone bad. This process is not open-ended however, so the chef must learn to judge the length of time game is improved by 'hanging' and to cook it before it starts to deteriorate. Game requires much more judgement and preparation by the chef for cooking than almost any other commodity. Below is a guide to some of the considerations needed when preparing game.

Hanging

All game except quail must be hung to allow it to become tender and develop flavour. The tenderizing enzymes become active approximately 24 hours after death so a minimum of 1–2 days hanging time is required (see p. 164 for hanging times). Older birds will require a longer hanging time than young birds. Birds should be hung by the neck in a cold, well-ventilated area, this does not need to be refrigerated.

Marinating

Some furred game such as venison will require marinating in wine to make it more tender and moist.

Larding and barding

The chef needs to compensate for the low fat content of game by either inserting fat into the meat (larding) or by covering the breasts of birds with fat (barding). Barding is applied mainly to game but may be used on meat and poultry that has not been larded. As with larding, its purpose is to prevent the item becoming dry during cooking. Slices of pork fat or fatty bacon are used to cover mostly the breast of the bird and are tied in place with string.

Classification

Game is divided into two categories:

Furred game – Venison, hare, wild rabbit, wild boar.
Feathered game – Pheasant, partridge, grouse, wild duck, wood pigeon, woodcock, snipe, teal, plover.

Quality

Furred game

Venison

This is the term given to the flesh of deer and includes roebuck (*le chevreuil*) – the most popular – red and fallow deer. The venison season is July to March, but with modern deer farming it is now generally available all year round. It is available fresh, chilled or frozen. Venison is becoming increasingly popular with the diet conscious as it has the lowest fat content of any red meat. The best all-round venison comes from three to four-year-old animals. Younger deer are more tender but older animals have more flavour. The flesh should be deep red almost black on the outside. There should be small flecks of fat in the flesh with some thin layers of fat on some parts of the carcass – the more fat the better the quality. The flesh of the buck (male) is considered superior to that of the doe (female). Venison will have a strong meaty smell, but not a rancid or rotten smell.

Wild boar (sanglier)

Wild boar is jointed as for pork. It should be less than twelve months old to be at its best, this is called marcassin (young boar). Wild boar between one and two years old will require marinating prior to cooking. Joints and cuts such as saddle and cutlets may be prepared as for venison, the saddle may also be presented cold as can the head. Young boar is not larded as it is quite fatty. Boars over two years old should not be used.

Rabbit and hare

Wild rabbits are traditionally eaten only when there is an 'R' in the month (when the breeding season is over). Rabbit has a shorter body, ears and feet than a hare. Hares are in season August to March. A male hare (buck) is tender up to one year old, a female (doe) up to eighteen months. Young hares are used for sauté, older ones for civet or jugged hare. Hares are at their best at $7-8$ months, weighing approximately $2^{1}/2-3$ kg $(5-6$ lb). Wild rabbit is at its best at $3-4$ months old.

1. The ears of a young hare or rabbit should tear easily and the claws on the feet should break easily.
2. The harelip is not as pronounced on a young animal; older hares have a very prominent harelip and grey-tinged fur.
3. If the bones under the rabbit's jaw break easily under pressure this means that it is a young rabbit.
4. Neither hares nor rabbits should have too strong a smell. They should be plump and well fleshed and the hind legs should be well developed.

Feathered game

1. The beak should be pliable and break easily.
2. The breastbone at the vent end should be pliable.
3. The feathers on the breast should be soft and downy, and quill feathers should be round not pointed.
4. Any spurs on the legs should be short and the legs smooth.
5. The breast should be plump.
6. The birds should be as intact as possible with a minimum of 'shot' damage.

Storage of game

1. Game should be hung to allow it to become tender and flavoursome in a well-ventilated, cold room at $5-6$°C.
2. Old birds or venison will require more hanging time than young ones.
3. Feathered game is hung without being plucked or drawn.
4. Furred game (apart from hare) should be drawn but not skinned prior to hanging. Following skinning/drawing/plucking, game should be kept under refrigeration at 2°C.
5. Once processed, venison may be held in a cold room, covered in its marinade for up to ten days.

Hanging times

The list of hanging times listed below is a guide only; hanging time will depend on such factors as the type, condition, age and storage temperature of the item. Great care should be taken with water birds such as teal and wild duck as they soon develop a rancid/oily taint.

Grouse	2 days maximum		Wild duck	1 – 2 days
Woodcock	3 – 4 days maximum		Wood pigeon	2 – 3 days
Quail	1 day maximum		Venison	7 – 14 days
Pheasant	7 – 14 days		Wild rabbit	2 – 3 days
Partridge	4 – 7 days		Hare	5 – 6 days

To skin

Furred game

Venison

1. First, make a cut through the skin and around the tops of the legs, then cut down the inside of the legs towards the middle of the belly.
2. Next, cut a shallow incision down the centre of the belly, this should not be necessary if the animal has already been drawn, as there will already be a cut down the belly.
3. Separate the flesh from the skin (using the point of a small knife) by easing the skin outwards from the belly and over the back legs until the skin can be pulled upwards from the lower back towards the breast.
4. Separate the flesh from the skin around the front legs, breast and neck until the skin can be pulled from the neck towards the lower back, remove the skin completely. Remove the hooves at the first joint.

Rabbits and hares

1. Lay the animal on its back and make a cut on the inside of the front and back legs from thigh to paw. Separate the skin from the flesh using the tip of a small knife. Pull the rear legs through and out, cut off the feet and tail and turn the animal over. Separate the skin from the flesh at the rump of the animal, pull the skin towards the head.
2. Pull the front legs through the cut in the skin and up over the shoulders, cut off the paws. Continue to pull the skin over the head, until the neck is exposed; cut through the neck and discard head and skin. The head may be skinned and used in the preparation of game stock/soup.

Evisceration (the removal of the internal organs)

Furred game

Most furred game, apart from hare will normally be drawn immediately after killing (field dressed), this means that the chef will have to undertake this task only occasionally.

Venison

1. Cut off the head and discard. Hang the deer up by its front legs and make a shallow incision from the collarbone through the breast and along the belly to just above the hind legs.

2. Pull the cut open and apart and remove the intestines, making a large round cut at the anal opening. Leaving the kidneys in place, remove the liver, heart and lungs. (The offal is often used for stocks, gravies, etc. so place them in a separate container, for later use.)
3. Cut upwards through the middle of the ribs/breast and on through the centre of the neck. Completely remove the windpipe.
4. Thoroughly clean out the inside of the carcass with absorbent kitchen paper until no trace of moisture is left.
5. Clean down and thoroughly sterilize the area.

Hare

1. Taking care not to perforate the intestines, make a shallow cut along the belly from the vent between the back legs to just below the ribcage (covering the bottom of the ribcage is a thin membrane called the diaphragm, this retains the blood in the chest cavity and should not be punctured until the hare is to be jointed and cooked).
2. Taking care not to rupture the diaphragm, open out the cut between the back legs and belly. Split the pelvic bone and remove the intestines, making a round cut to clean the anal opening.
3. Discard the intestines, clean down and thoroughly sterilize the area.

Cuts of hare/rabbit (stews (civet), sauté, pies, etc.)

1. Before cutting a hare into joints the blood from the diaphragm must be removed and saved along with the lungs, liver and heart. To make this easier nature has provided the chef with a convenient channel along the length of the backbone.
2. Spread the back legs well apart, then hold the hare over a basin with the head end held uppermost and the hind legs in the basin. Puncture the thin membrane over the rib cavity allowing the blood to run down the channel, along the backbone and between the hind legs into the basin.
3. Still holding the hare over the bowl, remove the lungs, liver and heart into the basin. Reserve the liver and heart but discard the lungs. (If the blood is not to be used immediately then a drop of vinegar will need to be added as this will assist in keeping the blood fluid and the basin should be sealed with cling film to prevent evaporation.)

Civet

The term 'civet' particularly applies to ragout (brown stews) of furred game which are moistened with red wine and garnished with button onions, mushrooms and lardons of bacon and combined with the blood of the animal. This liaison (thickening) with blood is essential to the dish. The name comes from the word 'cive' meaning 'green onion', this is because the dish is flavoured with onions (chives). The most famous civet uses hare and is called jugged hare in English. Only hare can be used for jugged hare, but civets can be made from just about any game – venison or feathered game.

Rabbits and hares are cut as follows:

1. Remove the hind legs where they join the pelvis, and cut each into two. Remove the pelvis by cutting square across the base of the saddle (reserve the bones for stock).
2. Remove the forelegs and cut into two or leave whole depending on the size of the animal.
3. Trim along each side of the forequarter/saddle to remove the breast flaps and excess rib bones.
4. Remove the sinew along the back by placing the point of a small knife underneath the sinew and drawing it horizontally along the back, taking approximately 1cm (^{1}/$_2$ in) at a time.
5. Cut across the trunk of the animal into two, just behind the rib cage, to give the forequarter and saddle. The forequarter is then cut into two and the saddle into two, three, or four depending on the size of the animal.

To prepare for roasting

1. Remove the fore legs by cutting across just behind the legs.
2. Trim along each side of the forequarter/saddle to remove the breast flaps and excess rib bones.
3. Remove the sinew along the back by placing the point of a small knife underneath the sinew and drawing it horizontally along the back taking approximately 1 cm (^{1}/$_2$ in) wide strip at a time.
4. Cut through the middle of the pelvis and press the legs outwards to lie flat.
5. Using a larding needle, place strips of pork back fat along the back and through the legs.

To prepare a saddle for roasting

Prepare as for roasting but remove the hind legs as for stewing, then lard with strips of pork fat along the saddle. (A long saddle is the forequarter and the saddle, providing two portions; the more traditional saddle is cut just below the rib cage and is served as a portion.)

Fillet of hare and rabbit

These are the two strips of flesh running the length of a long saddle. Prepare a long saddle as described then carefully bone out. Fillets may be cut into collops and sautéed or left whole and used for the centre of a pâté en croute or a game terrine. They can also be flattened and rolled for paupiettes, or, in the case of rabbit, used as escalopes.

Joints/cuts of venison

Venison is cut in the same way as for lamb, except that the best-end is not separated from the saddle (venison has a long saddle as opposed to lamb which has a best-end and saddle). Venison is normally purchased as a carcass, forequarter or haunch. Other cuts can be purchased such as saddle, leg or loin.

Forequarter – both shoulder plus middle neck etc.
Haunch – legs.

Dissection of a venison carcass

1. **Remove the legs** (haunch) by cutting with a large knife 5–8 cm (2–3 in) from the round of the aitchbone (depending on the size of animal), then saw through the bones.
2. **Remove the breasts** by cutting from just below the elbow at the shoulder, finishing by sawing through the rib bones.
3. **Remove the forequarter** by cutting just below the elbow of the shoulders and finishing with a saw.
4. **Remove the shoulders** by cutting the forequarter on either side of the backbone and cutting down over the ribs to separate the shoulders from the middle neck.
5. **Split the legs** (haunch) by cutting through the meat and cartilage, then sawing through the aitchbone.

The above will give you the main joints from a carcass, i.e. haunches (legs), a long saddle and shoulders. The breast, middle neck and trimmings are used for stews (ragouts, civets), pâtés, terrines and, along with the bones, for stocks and soups. The joints may be further divided/cut into leg steaks and loin chops.

Marinating

All venison and some other furred game requires marinating for a period before cooking; this will assist in tenderization, and help to enhance the flavour and moistness of the meat. The time in the marinade will depend on various factors such as the sex and age of the animal and size of the joint/cut to be marinated. Small cuts such as steaks and chops from a two-year-old animal will require only an hour marinating in olive oil, salt and pepper, whereas large joints from old animals may need several days. In some continental countries the venison, once hung, is divided into the main large joints and marinated for up to four days.

Hare for a civet may be marinated in a little brandy and aromats as an alternative to a standard marinade.

Red wine marinade

1/2 litre (1pt) oil	1 kg (2 lb) sliced carrots
1 kg (2 lb) sliced onions	2 bottles red wine
6 cloves garlic (crushed)	250 g (8 oz) chopped celery
50 g (2 oz) parsley stalks	30 peppercorns
1/4 litre (1/2 pt) vinegar	6 bay leaves
(preferably red wine)	3–4 sprigs of thyme

The marinade should be made just prior to use in a container that is non-tainting: the wine and vinegar can be tainted by aluminium or copper, so stainless steel or plastic containers are ideal. The vegetables, herbs and spices are placed in a large container; the meat is placed on top and completely covered with the liquid. Cover with a sheet of greaseproof paper and put in a cool place. The meat should be turned two or three times a day, each time placing the vegetables/herb mixture on top of the meat.

Feathered game

Due to the fact that feathered game is hunted, rather than farmed under controlled conditions it is impossible to give precise specifications in the way that one can for poultry or other meats. I have therefore given general descriptions, approximate weights and portions for the most commonly used birds.

Grouse

Description: A small (300 g/12 oz) but highly-prized game bird, at its best when young and tender (1 – 1¹/₂ years old). Young birds have pointed wings and small spurs. Grouse is easily identified by its grey plumage and furry legs.

Season: The grouse season is relatively short, beginning on the 'glorious twelfth' August and finishing on 20 December.

Portions: One to two.

Uses: Roasting, pot-roasting (poêle); older birds: terrines, pies, braising, salmis of game.

Woodcock

Description: Woodcock have long legs and a long thin beak and weigh 250–300 g (8–12 oz). They are usually hung 'well' with the head left on and are un-drawn, apart from the gizzard which is removed by making a hole just behind the leg of the bird and removing it with the point of a trussing needle. The eyes should be removed and the bird 'trussed' with its own beak. This is done by inserting the pointed beak through the legs in the same place as if it was a trussing needle. Snipe is also prepared in this fashion.

Season: October to February.

Portions: One.

Uses: Roasting, pot-roasting (poêle), braising, grilling.

Quail

Description: A very small bird (50g/2oz) with a rounded shape (plump) and quite fatty. This bird is normally raised on farms but has retained its game status.

Season: Available all year round.

Portions: A minimum of one bird per portion but often two are given as a portion.

Uses: Roasting, pot-roasting (poêle), stuffed and braised, grilling.

Pheasant

Description: The most well-known out of all the game birds, pheasant is often sold as a brace (one cock bird plus one hen bird). The hen is considered to be the most tender but the cock is usually larger. Younger birds have a pliable beak, flexible tip to the breastbone and short spurs on the legs. Weight is $1^{1}/_2 - 2$ kg (2 – 4 lb).

Season: October to February.

Portions: Three to four.

Uses: Roasting, pot-roasting (poêle), suprêmes may be sautéed, salmis, braising.

Partridge

Description: The two most common types are the 'grey legged' and the 'red legged': the grey legged is considered superior. Weight is $250 - 500$ g ($^{1}/_2 - 1$ lb).

Season: September/October to February.

Portions: One to two.

Uses: Roasting, pot-roasting (poêle), salmis, casseroles, grilled; older birds: braising.

Wild duck

Description: Various species of wild duck are used but the most common is the mallard; widgeon and teal are also served as wild duck. It is most important that water birds are served when in season and fresh, as they can develop a fishy taste when old or out of season. Weight is $1 - 1^{1}/_2$ kg (2 – 3 lb).

Season: Mallard/widgeon – August to March; teal – October to February.

Portions: Mallard, two; widgeon/teal, one.

Uses: Roasting, pot-roasting (poêle), salmis, braised.

Pigeon

Description: Both wild and tame pigeons may be eaten; indeed, pigeon was once considered excellent fare, but older birds can be tough and stringy. Young birds (squabs) can be superb. Weight is 500 g (1 lb).

Season: Wood pigeon – August to March; pigeon – all year.

Portions: One to two. Available also as individual, vacuum-packed/frozen breasts.

Uses: Roasting (when young), braising, pies, breasts may be sautéed.

Many game birds are now available out of season due to freezing; it should be remembered, however, that game can be an expensive commodity and customers who order game are usually quite discerning. If the quality is not first class or the chef does not take into account the drying effect of freezing, the result may not be up to standard.

Preparation of game prior to cooking

Furred game: All furred game will benefit from marinating prior to roasting, and because of its low fat content it will require the addition of fat to prevent the meat from becoming dry during roasting: strips of pork fat are inserted into the flesh with a larding needle. Small cuts prior to cooking will also benefit from larding.

Feathered game: This will also require the addition of fat prior to roasting, but the process is different: slices of pork fat are placed over the breasts of game birds and tied in place, this is called barding.

Stuffed game birds

Certain game birds may be boned and stuffed or pressed; for larger birds follow the instructions for boning a bird given in the recipe for chicken galantine (see p. 156). Small game birds may be boned with the fingers with the help of a small knife.

Salmis

A salmis of game is a dish prepared from feathered game such as partridge, wild duck and pheasant. It is made from game which is two-thirds cooked. The roasted meat is often finished at the table in a sauce made of red or white wine, mushrooms and truffles. It is moistened with demi-glace and served with heart-shaped croutons spread with game farce. Poultry such as duck, pigeon or guinea fowl may also be used.

French Terms

Grouse	La Grouse		Wood pigeon	Le Ramier
Woodcock	Le Bécasse		Venison/roebuck	La Venaison/chevreuil
Quail	La Caille		Wild rabbit	Le Lapin de garenne
Pheasant	Le Faisan		Hare/young hare	Le Lièvre/levraut
Partridge	Le Perdreau		Teal	La Sarcelle
Wild duck	Le Canard savage		Snipe	La Bécassine

Joints/Cuts

Venison

Saddle	La selle
Legs, haunch	Le gigot
Shoulders	L'epaule
Loin	La longe
Best-end	Le carré

Other cuts of venison such as: chops/cutlets (côtelettes), medallions (médaillons) and noisettes are all cut as for lamb.

Rabbit / hare	
Saddle	râble
Legs	Le cuisse
Fillet	Le filet

Offal

Most of the offal that comes from game is used in pâtés or terrines, or in the case of feathered game, the liver is used for the farce which accompanies roast game birds. Other parts such as the heart, lungs and head are used for soups, stocks and sauces.

Venison heart, liver and kidneys may be cooked as for lamb; the liver and kidneys will need to be soaked in cold water for 3–4 hours to remove any traces of stale blood or urine.

Game farce

500 g (1 lb 2 oz) game or chicken livers	2 bay leaves
141 g (5 oz) finely-diced onion	sprig of fresh thyme
250 g (9 oz) butter	salt and mignonette pepper

1. Melt 100 g/4 oz of butter in a sauté pan; add the onions, bay leaves and thyme and fry until softened and lightly coloured.
2. Add the well-drained livers and seal on the outside leaving them slightly pink inside.
3. Pass through a fine sieve and leave to cool, beat in the remainder of the softened butter on a machine or in a food processor.
4. Check the seasoning and use immediately or cover with cling film.

SEVEN

Preparations, Sauces, Dressings and Cold Soups

Preparations

Fish

Mousse of salmon (ten portions)

Uses: Cornets of smoked salmon, cold buffets, Carolines, Duchesses.

Reduce to a paste 500 g (1 lb) of cooked smoked salmon in a mortar and pestle, or use a food processor. Season with cayenne and a few drops of anchovy essence. If to be served cold, add 150 ml (1/3 pint) half-whipped cream (making sure it is very cold). Colour with red colouring, add some melted aspic or softened melted gelatine and pour into a mould and allow to set. Turn out and finish with fish aspic.

Mousseline

Follow the instructions for mousse of salmon above with the addition of two egg whites, then place the mix over a bowl of ice and water and gradually beat in up to 500 ml (1 pint) of half-whipped double cream. Omit the aspic and gelatine. This mix may then be poached as quenelles or used to fill barquettes or tartlettes.

These two recipes are suitable for use with other fish and shellfish, for example smoked trout, mackerel, lobster, prawn or crab. It may be difficult to spoon mould the quenelles (the mix may be too flimsy) in which case poach instead.

Smoked fish mousse (ten portions)

350 g (12 oz) smoked mackerel, trout, eel, salmon or similar fish	seasoning a few drops of lemon juice
125 ml (1/4 pint) double cream	

1. Remove all skin and bones from the fish.
2. Place the flesh into a food processor or liquidizer, add the seasoning and lemon juice.

3. In a separate bowl, three-quarters whip the cream until the marks of the whisk are just visible.
4. Gently fold the cream into the fish mixture and adjust the seasoning.
5. Fill ten individual ramekin dishes with the mixture.

The top surface may be decorated with blanched tomato flesh, cucumber, fresh herbs (dill, parsley, tarragon, etc.) and sealed with a little melted aspic. Serve accompanied with buttered toast or a selection of wholemeal/granary breads and butter.

Court bouillon (for oily fish)

To every 4 litres (gallon) of cold water add the following:

2 large onions (sliced)	20 white peppercorns
4 bay leaves	250 ml ($^1/2$ pint) vinegar
4 carrots (sliced)	250ml ($^1/2$ pint) white wine
25 g parsley stalks	a little oil (light vegetable)

Court bouillon (for white fish makes 4 litres)

2 litres white wine	bouquet garni
2 litres water	50 g (1$^1/2$ oz) sea salt
250 g (8 oz) shredded onions	12 white peppercorns

Court bouillon (red wine)

As for white fish but replacing the white wine with 1$^1/2$ litres of red wine and increase water to 2$^1/2$ litres. Add 250 g of sliced carrots.

All the above *court bouillons* are simmered for 30 minutes, strained through muslin, and allowed to cool before using.

Shellfish mousse (ten portions)

600 g (1$^1/4$ lb) cooked shellfish (scallops, prawns, lobster, scampi, etc.)	250 ml ($^1/2$ pint) double cream
200 ml (8 fl oz) fish velouté	carmine red colouring
200 ml (8 fl oz) aspic jelly	seasoning

1. Pass the cooked fish twice through the fine plate of a mincer.
2. Place in a food processor or pass through a sieve.
3. Heat the velouté in a saucepan, add the fish and the aspic jelly, season and colour if necessary. Bring to the boil, then transfer to a cold mixing bowl.
4. Fill another bowl with ice, place the bowl containing the fish mixture on top and stir slowly but continuously until the mixture begins to thicken/set.
5. Remove from the ice and fold in the half-whipped double cream; adjust the seasoning and colour.

The above may be served in individual portions as for smoked fish mousse, or for presentation on cold buffets poured into moulds that have previously been lined with a layer of aspic jelly and decorated with truffle (garnishing paste), blanched leek leaf, cucumber skin, lemon rind, tomato flesh, red and green peppers, all cut into small shapes either by hand or with aspic cutters.

Gravalax (20–30 portions)

1 × 4–5 kg (8–10 lb) fresh salmon	100 g (4 oz) fresh dill (including stalks)
1 kg (2 lb) sea salt	1 lemon
1 level tsp saltpetre	mignonette pepper

1. Scale, remove the head and fillet the fish into two halves.
2. Remove all the bones from across each fillet.
3. Place one fillet onto a stainless-steel tray, flesh facing upwards; squeeze over half the lemon juice, and then sprinkle with the combined salts. Gently rub in the coarsely chopped dill stems and leaves. Do the same to the other fillet.
4. Place one fillet on top of the other with the flesh facing each other. Wrap in cling film and tinfoil and place in the fridge. Leave to marinate for twelve hours, turn over once, then continue to turn at twelve-hour intervals until four turns have been completed. The gravalax is then ready to serve.

To serve: gently remove any remaining salt, dill, etc. and carve on the slant into thin slices, allowing three to four slices per portion. Garnish with salad, watercress and lemon. Accompany with brown/granary bread and butter and serve with sauce for gravalax (see following recipe).

The fish should be re-wrapped after each service to prevent the flesh from drying out.

Sauce for gravalax (ten portions)

5 tbsp dill mustard (or Dijon mustard with chopped fresh dill)	500 ml (1 pint) olive oil
	15 g (1/2 oz) sugar
5 ml (2 fl oz) wine vinegar	seasoning
juice of half a lemon	

1. Place the mustard, lemon juice and vinegar in a bowl and whisk well.
2. Gradually add the oil, whisking continuously. Adjust the seasoning.

Marinade for mackerel and herring (ten portions)

1 litre (2 pints) dry white wine	1 sprig of thyme
600 ml (1 pint) wine vinegar	4 bay leaves
5 small carrots (peeled, canalled and thinly sliced)	6 parsley stalks
	16 peppercorns
10 button onions (peeled and sliced into rings)	salt

1. Place all the above ingredients into a stainless-steel pan, bring to the boil and simmer gently for ten minutes.
2. Lay small cleaned mackerel or herring (fillets may be used) into a buttered tray and cover with the hot marinade.
3. Allow to poach gently: 5 minutes for fillets, 10 – 15 minutes for a whole fish.
4. Allow to cool in the liquor and then chill in the refrigerator.
5. Serve with a little of the cooking liquor and vegetables and garnish with lemon and parsley.

Crèmes pour hors-d'œuvre

Various fish such as smoked salmon, caviar, tuna, cooked prawns and smoked trout may be passed through a food processor or pounded to a puree and combined with double cream to produce crèmes or 'creams' for filling cold barquettes, bouchées, tartlets, etc. They may also be used to produce a variety of small moulds. This is done by adding a little melted aspic prior to the cream and filling lightly-oiled moulds, such as petits four moulds or barquettes. The mixture is allowed to set in the fridge, then demoulded by dipping the mould in hot water for no more than a second or two. Turn out and garnish.

Uses: As petit hors-d'œuvre; fillings for cold barquettes; hollowed out, poached vegetables; spreads and stuffings for the preparation of hors-d'œuvre; canapés, finger buffets, etc.

The glazed moulded creams may be used to garnish fish dishes for presentation on cold buffets.

Crème au saumon fumé (ten portions)

225 g (8 oz) smoked salmon
50 ml (2 fl oz) double cream
    (unwhipped)
small pinch of cayenne pepper

few drops of lemon juice
150 ml (6 fl oz) stiffly whipped
    double cream

1. Pass the smoked salmon through a food processor or pound to a fine, smooth paste.
2. Stir in the liquid cream, adding a little at a time. Season with cayenne pepper and lemon juice. Fold in the whipped cream and adjust the seasoning.

The above recipe may be set with the addition of 50 – 70 ml (2 – 3 fl oz) of fish aspic or plain aspic, then used to fill decorated and chemised moulds, for use on decorated buffets, etc.

Marinades for fish prior to deep-frying

Fish is marinated prior to deep-frying, not only to add flavour, but to moisten, preserve the colour and soften the connective tissue – this is done by the acid in the lemon juice.

Marinade for fish à l'Orly (ten portions)

juice of two lemons	75 – 100ml (3 – 4 fl oz) oil
25 g (1 oz) chopped parsley	salt and pepper

Place the washed and dried fish on a tray and sprinkle with the lemon juice, parsley and oil, season with salt and pepper. Allow to marinate for approximately 30 minutes before use.

General marinade for deep-fried fish (ten portions)

125 ml (¹/4 pint) oil	2 bay leaves
juice of 1 small lemon	25 g (1 oz) chopped parsley
125 ml (¹/4 pint) dry white wine	salt and pepper

Mix the above ingredients and pour over the washed and dried fish. Allow to marinate for approximately 30 minutes prior to deep-frying.

Pastes

Pâte pour barquettes et tartelettes (pastry for barquettes and tartelettes)

500 g (1 lb) flour	water to bind
250 g (8 oz) butter	salt and mignonette pepper
2 eggs	dried mixed herbs (optional)
4 egg yolks	

1. Melt the butter and allow to cool.
2. Sift together the flour, salt and pepper, add the butter, herbs, eggs, egg yolks and water.
3. Quickly combine into a ball, mixing as little as possible, then place onto the worktop and with the heel of the hand knead away small pieces of paste, to combine the ingredients. Repeat, forming a ball of paste each time.
4. Wrap the paste in clingfilm and place in the refrigerator for two to three hours before using.

To prepare barquettes and tartlettes

1. Prepare the above paste (pâté).
2. Grease the moulds (preferably with a proprietary non-stick agent such as 'vegelene') or any salt-free fat or oil.
3. Roll out the pastry and line the moulds. Prick well with a fork and allow to rest for at least half an hour in the refrigerator.
4. Line the inside of the pastry with tinfoil or greaseproof paper.
5. Fill the lined moulds with baking beans and bake blind in a moderate oven gas mark 6/200°C/400°F for 10 – 15 minutes, or until light brown.
6. Empty the moulds of beans and lining paper, and return to the oven for a few minutes to dry out the base.

Savoury short paste

1 kg (2¹/₄ lb) soft flour	3 eggs
250 g (9 oz) butter or margarine	salt
250 g (9 oz) lard	water to bind

1. Sift the flour and salt into a mixing bowl.
2. Cut the cold fats into 1 cm (¹/₂ in) cubes and rub into the flour.
3. Beat the eggs and make a well in the mix.
4. Gradually incorporate the eggs, adding a little cold water to bind to a smooth paste.
5. Roll into a ball and allow to rest in a refrigerator for at least half an hour before use.

This pastry can be used to prepare savoury flans or pies, or as an alternative to barquette and tartlette paste.

Note: For a vegetarian short paste, replace the lard with a hard vegetable fat such as Trex or Purra, and use free-range eggs.

Vegetarian shortcrust pastry

160 g (6 oz) wholewheat flour	1 tsp soft brown sugar
40 g (1¹/₂ oz) butter/margarine	pinch of salt
40 g (1¹/₂ oz) hard white fat	1¹/₂ tbsp sunflower oil
(Trex, Purra, etc.)	2 – 3 tbsp water
1 tsp baking powder	

1. Sieve the flour and salt.
2. Cut the fat into small cubes and rub into the flour.
3. Dissolve the sugar in the water and add the oil.
4. Make a well in the flour and add the water, cut the water in with a palette knife (do not stint on the amount of water).
5. Combine the mix with your hands to form a very wet ball; wrap in cling film and place in the refrigerator to relax for approximately 30 minutes.
6. When rolling out, roll in one direction only, and move the pastry half a rotation after each roll to prevent the wet paste from sticking.

Vegetarian hot water pastry (amount for a 1 kg / 2 lb loaf tin)

350 g (12 oz) wholewheat flour	150 ml (6 fl oz) water
1 tsp baking powder	salt
100 g (4 oz) hard white vegetable	1 egg to glaze
fat (for example, Purra)	

1. Melt the fat in the water.
2. Mix the salt with the flour; make a well and add the water and fat and mix into the flour with a spatula or palette knife.
3. Place on a table and knead until smooth. Cut into two-thirds and one-third sized portions. Use the larger portion for lining the sides of the tin and reserve the smaller

for the lid. (This paste must be kept warm while being used. A bowl placed over a container of hot water will assist in keeping the paste at the correct temperature as long as it is kept covered with a cloth.)

Note: To make the pastry suitable for a vegans, glaze with substitute egg mix).

Pastry for samosas (makes 10 – 16, depending on size)

250 g (8 oz) wholewheat flour	4 tbsp vegetable oil
^{1}/2 tsp salt	4 tbsp water

1. Sieve the flour and salt into a mixing bowl.
2. Gradually dribble the oil over the flour, and slowly add the water while mixing (the mix needs to be more wet than dry). Mix and knead for approximately 5 minutes; rest in a warm place (room temperature) for 30 minutes.
3. The paste must be made warm and pliable prior to rolling by kneading in the hands.
4. Roll one way only, giving the paste one-eighth of a turn each time to prevent sticking.

Suet paste

1 kg (2^1/4 lb) flour	500 – 600 ml (1 – 1^1/4 pint) water
500 g (18 oz) shredded beef suet	good pinch of salt
40 g (1^1/2 oz) baking powder	

1. Sift the flour, baking powder and salt into a mixing bowl.
2. Add the suet and mix.
3. Make a bay and gradually add the cold water to make a firm paste.

Uses: Savoury steamed puddings and dumplings.

Pâté à choux (choux paste)

1 litre (2 pints) water	16 – 18 eggs
500 g (1 lb) margarine	pinch of salt
500 g (18 oz) strong flour	

1. Using a wide shallow pan, melt the margarine in the water.
2. Remove from heat and add the flour, which has previously been sieved with the salt onto a sheet of greaseproof paper.
3. Beat to a smooth paste with a spatula.
4. Return to the heat and cook until the mixture leaves the sides of the pan.
5. Remove from the heat and allow to cool.
6. Add the eggs – initially two at a time – while the paste is still warm, beating them in quickly and thoroughly.
7. Towards the end, add the eggs one at a time, until the mix is of a dropping

consistency. (A dropping consistency is when the paste raised up on the wooden spoon/spatula drops off of its own accord.)

The paste can be used immediately or stored in a bowl in the fridge covered with a greased greaseproof paper to prevent the surface drying out.

Uses: Carolines, duchesses, savoury profiteroles.

Hot water paste

500 g (1 lb) medium-strength flour   150 g (5 oz) lard
250 ml (1/2 pint) water   1 tsp salt

1. Sift the flour and salt into a mixing bowl.
2. Rub in 50 g (2 oz) of the fat into the flour.
3. Place the remaining lard in a pan with the water and bring to the boil. Remove from the heat and allow to cool for a few minutes.
4. Make a well in the flour and pour in the water and lard; mix immediately with a wooden spoon/spatula.
5. When cool enough to handle, knead until smooth.
6. Use immediately or place in a bowl above a bowl of hot water and cover with a damp cloth to keep warm.
7. Keeping the remaining paste warm, remove the required amount and reserve one-third for a lid. Roll out the paste to a thickness of 1/2 cm (1/4 in).

The paste should be used while still warm, when it is easy to mould and shape.

Uses: Raised pies, pork pies.

Puff pastry (2 kg / 4 lb)

1 kg (2 lb) strong flour   approximately 1 litre (2 pints) of
1 kg (2 lb) butter or pastry margarine   very cold water mixed with
salt   a little vinegar or lemon juice

1. Mix the salt, flour and enough water to make a fairly firm dough. Roll the dough into a ball.
2. Cut a cross into the ball of dough to make a star shape; pull down the 'points' of the star and roll out to half the thickness of the centre.
3. Add the block of fat, which has been kneaded to the same texture as the dough.
4. Fold over the sides, press to flatten, then roll out to a rectangle. Fold into three, sealing the sides.
5. Rest the dough for 20 minutes, then do a double turn; rest 20 minutes and do a single turn; rest another 20 minutes, then do a double turn, rest and use.

Panades (panadas)

Panadas are binding mixes which are used to cohere forcemeats and stuffings; they range from the simple potato panada used for the binding of fish cakes to a frangipane panada which is used in the finest fish and meat forcemeats. All panadas should be cold before using.

Panade à la farine (flour panada) (500 g / 1 lb)

50 g (2 oz) butter   500 ml (1/2 pint) water
125 g (5 oz) flour   salt and pepper

1. Sieve the flour onto a sheet of greaseproof paper.
2. Place the water, butter and seasoning into a wide shallow pan and bring to the boil.
3. Remove from the heat and rain in the flour, stirring continuously with a spatula.
4. Return to the heat and stir until the mixture is smooth and leaves the sides of the pan (approximately 5 minutes).
5. Spread evenly onto a shallow buttered tray and cover with a buttered cartouche.

Panade à la pommes de terre (potato panada)

500 g (1 lb) cooked   50 g (2 oz) butter
   mashed potatoes   salt and pepper
125 ml (1/4 pint) milk

1. Place the milk and seasoning into a wide shallow pan, bring to the boil and gradually mix in the potato.
2. Add the butter; cook gently on the side of the stove, stirring constantly until the texture becomes fairly dry.
3. Spread onto a buttered tray to cool covered with a buttered cartouche.

Uses: Fish cakes, meat and potato cakes (fricadelles).

Panade à la frangipane (frangipane panada)

100 g (4 oz) flour   75 g (3 oz) butter (melted)
4 egg yolks   250 ml (1/2 pint) milk
salt and pepper

1. Place the egg yolks, flour and seasoning into a mixing bowl; gradually add the melted butter and the hot (boiled) milk, beating well.
2. Pass through a strainer into a wide shallow pan and cook out on the side of the stove, stirring constantly to the boil.
3. Remove from the heat and spread onto a buttered tray and cover with a buttered cartouche. Allow to cool before use.

Uses: Forcemeats of fish, meat, poultry and game.

Panade au pain (bread panada)

225 g (8 oz) white breadcrumbs   250ml (^{1}/2 pint) milk
salt and white pepper

1. Place the milk and seasoning into a wide shallow pan and bring to the boil.
2. Remove from the heat and gradually rain in the breadcrumbs, stirring constantly.
3. Return to the stove and cook quickly, stirring with a spatula until the mixture leaves the sides of the pan.
4. Spread onto a buttered tray and cover with a buttered cartouche.

Uses: White forcemeats (chicken, veal, fish, etc.).

Seasonings

Seasoning is often a matter of preference; whether you prefer the flavour of spice to that of herbs, or indeed a combination of both, is of little consequence, but the ratio of seasoning to meat is important and is often left to guesswork. An experienced larder chef will be able to gauge the required amount by taste, but this is not always the case when it comes to less experienced members of the team. The following guides should be of assistance.

Salt and pepper mix

This is the most commonly used seasoning:

500 g (1 lb) salt to 175 g (7 oz) pepper.

Uses: All general seasoning.

Salt and spice seasoning

500 g (1 lb) salt   15 g (^{1}/2 oz) mace
150 g (6 oz) pepper   7 g (^{1}/4 oz) cayenne pepper
7 g (^{1}/4 oz) ground ginger

Uses: Pork pies, sausage rolls, etc.

Salt, spice and herb seasoning

500 g (1 lb) salt   7 g (^{1}/4 oz) ground ginger
150 g (6 oz) pepper   7 g (^{1}/4 oz) mace
7 g (^{1}/4 oz) cayenne pepper   10 g (^{1}/3 oz) rubbed sage

Uses: Pork pies, sausage rolls, etc.

Veal and ham pie seasoning

500 g (1 lb) salt   pinch of rubbed thyme
200 g (8 oz) pepper   7 g (^{1}/4 oz) parsley
10 g (^{1}/3 oz) mace

Uses: Veal and ham pies.

Steak pie seasoning

500 g (1 lb) salt   pinch of cayenne pepper
150 g (6 oz) pepper   small pinch of ground cloves

Uses: Steak pies, steak and kidney pies, cornish pasties.

Ratio of seasoning to meat

The amount of seasoning required is:

30 g (1 oz) for every 1.5 kg (3 lb) of meat for large pies, etc.
   or
15 g (¹/₂ oz) for each 500 g (1 lb) of meat for smaller pies, pasties, etc.

Basic sausage seasoning

500 g (1 lb) salt   7 g (¹/₄ oz) cayenne pepper
50 g (2 oz) white pepper   7 g (¹/₄ oz) ground ginger
50 g (2 oz) black pepper   7 g (¹/₄ oz) mace
25 g (1 oz) nutmeg   25 g (1 oz) rubbed sage

Uses: Pork sausages.

Ratio: 25 g (1 oz) for every 500 g (1 lb) of meat.

Herb sausage seasoning

500 g (1 lb) salt   7 g (¹/₄ oz) ground ginger
50 g (2 oz) white pepper   7 g (¹/₄ oz) mace
50 g (2 oz) black pepper   50 g (2 oz) rubbed sage
25 g (1oz) nutmeg   50 g (2 oz) rubbed thyme
7 g (¹/₄ oz) cayenne pepper

Uses: Pork and herb sausages, beef sausages, pork and beef sausages.

Ratio: 25 g (1 oz) for every 500 g (1 lb) of meat.

Stuffings

Parsley and thyme stuffing (1 kg / 2 lb)

500 g (1 lb) white breadcrumbs   250 g (10 oz) diced onion
300 g (10 oz) suet   50 g (2 oz) butter
10 g (¹/₃ oz) chopped parsley   4 eggs
10 g (¹/₃ oz) rubbed thyme   nutmeg, salt and pepper
grated rind of half a lemon

1. Sweat the onion and thyme in the butter until the onion is soft.
2. Place the rest of the ingredients, except the eggs, in a mixing bowl.
3. Add the onion and butter mix and combine.
4. Lightly beat the eggs and add, season with salt, pepper and a pinch of nutmeg.

Uses: Chicken/poultry, lamb and veal.

Sage and onion stuffing (1 kg/2 lb)

200 g (8 oz) dripping	200 g (8 oz) pork sausagemeat
300 g (12 oz) diced onions	2 eggs
500 g (1 lb) white breadcrumbs	10 g (^{1}/$_3$ oz) chopped parsley
25 g (1 oz) rubbed sage	salt and pepper

1. Melt the dripping in a pan and gently cook the onions, then add the sage and cook a further 2 minutes. Allow to cool.
2. Place the rest of the ingredients, apart from the eggs, into a mixing bowl.
3. Add the onion mixture and combine. Lightly beat the eggs and add to the mix. Season with salt and pepper.

Uses: Pork, goose and rabbit.

The texture of both the above stuffings may be modified with the addition of any of the following: milk, brown stock, jus/gravy.

Chestnut stuffing (*farce de marrons*) (1½ kg/2 lb 8 oz)

500 g (1 lb) pork sausagemeat	2–3 eggs
50 g (2 oz) chopped suet	nutmeg, salt and pepper
500 g (1 lb) white breadcrumbs	Jus lie to moisten
200 g (8 oz) dried chestnuts (soaked overnight and roughly chopped)*	

1. Soak the peeled dried chestnuts overnight in water.
2. Mix together the rest of the ingredients, except the eggs and jus.
3. Lightly beat the eggs and add to the mixture; moisten with the jus and season with salt, pepper and nutmeg.

Uses: Used mainly for turkey, but may be used with other fowls.

* I have stated using dried chestnuts in this recipe as they are readily available, of good quality and do not require the time-consuming preparation of the fresh variety. If using fresh chestnuts, they must be split, baked, peeled and chopped prior to use.

Veal stuffing (1 kg / 2 lb)

500 g (1 lb) chopped beef suet
500 g (1 lb) white breadcrumbs
250 g (10 oz) cooked ham (diced)
50 g (2 oz) chopped parsley
25 g (1 oz) mixed herbs

grated rind of 2 lemons
3–4 eggs
pinch of nutmeg
salt and pepper
white stock to moisten

1. Combine all the ingredients apart from the eggs and stock.
2. Lightly beat the eggs and add to the mixture.
3. Season with salt, pepper and nutmeg and moisten if required with white stock.

Farce au gratin (game farce) (1 kg / 2 lb)

750 g (1½ lb) chicken livers
250 g (10 oz) fat bacon
100 g (4 oz) diced onions
2 bay leaves

a sprig of thyme
120 g (5 oz) butter
salt and pepper

1. Dice the bacon and cook gently in the butter with the herbs.
2. Add the onions and cook until lightly browned.
3. Add the chicken livers and fry quickly.
4. Season with salt and freshly-ground black pepper.
5. Pass through a fine sieve and allow to cool.
6. Cover the surface with a layer of melted butter and a paper lid. Store in the refrigerator for later use.

The chicken livers must be well drained before use or the mix will be sloppy in texture.

Spare ribs

Spare ribs – thanks to the influence of Chinese restaurants – have become increasingly popular. The marinade outlined below will give an authentic flavour to ribs, which are to be served hot or cold. The marinade is also suitable for marinating pork prior to stir-frying (see Stir-fried rice, p. 187). For ten portions, 4–5 kg (8–10 lb) of belly pork is cut along the ribs into strips approximately 3–5 cm (½–1 in) wide.

Spare ribs marinade (ten portions)

2 bottles soy sauce
4 bay leaves (crushed)
2 Demi-tasse cups of brown sugar
  (Coca-Cola may be used in place
  of sugar, or for a low sugar
  version, diet cola)

2 demi-tasse cups of vinegar
a good pinch of Chinese five spice
  powder
8 cloves of garlic (crushed)
a few drops of red colouring
salt to taste

1. Crush the garlic and mix with the rest of the ingredients, ensuring that the sugar is fully dissolved.

2. For a light flavour, marinate for 1 hour, for a stronger flavour marinate overnight.
3. Remove the ribs and place in a roasting tray with a little oil.
4. Cook for 1 – 2 hours, depending on the quality, preferably with steam at 180° C / 350° F for 30 minutes, then at150° C / 300° F for the remainder of the cooking time. (The steam assists in keeping the ribs moist and reduces shrinkage.)

Stir-fried rice (ten portions)

750 g (1¹/₂ lb) long-grain rice (patna)
250 g (8 oz) spring onions
250 g (8 oz) shredded chicken
50 g (2 oz) king prawns
250 g (8 oz) diced marinated roast
   shoulder/hand of pork
half a red/green pepper (diced)

50 g (2 oz) root ginger
50 ml (2 fl oz) vegetable oil
dash of sesame oil
3 eggs
100 g (4 oz) broccoli
4 cloves garlic

1. Marinate the pork overnight, then roast.
2. Rinse the rice several times in cold water.
3. Place the rice into a pan and add approximately twice the amount of water. Cover with a wet cartouche of greaseproof paper and a tight fitting lid.
4. Put the rice onto boil and check after 10 minutes (*Do not remove the lid until cooked*). If boiling, remove to a low heat and allow to cook slowly for a further 20 minutes, still tightly covered. Remove from heat and allow to cool.
5. Shred the chicken, dice the pork, dice the peppers, peel and slice the garlic, peel and slice the ginger, wash and slice the broccoli (including the stalks) and slice the prawns. Beat the eggs, and with a little milk cook as a thin flat omelette; roll up and shred. It is important that all ingredients are prepared in advance of cooking.
6. Heat the vegetable oil in a wok or an equivalent dish. Add a dash of sesame oil and the sliced garlic. When the garlic starts to brown add the sliced ginger, onions, peppers and broccoli and stir. Add the shredded chicken, prawns, cooked diced pork and rice, stir until heated through. If necessary, moisten with clear chicken stock. Add the egg pancake and stir until heated through.

Tikka marinade (ten portions)

2 tsp coriander seeds
2 tsp cumin seeds
1 tbsp chilli powder
¹/₄ jar tikka paste
juice of 2 lemons

50 g 2 oz tomato puree
¹/₂ litre (1 pint) natural live yoghurt
50 g (2 oz) fresh ginger
¹/₂ head of garlic

1. Grind the seeds, peel and grate the ginger and crush the garlic.
2. Add the rest of the ingredients. Marinate the meat (chicken, turkey, lamb, etc.) for a minimum of 3 hours. Place on skewers and cook brushed with a little oil at as hot a temperature as possible (a tandoor or char-grill is ideal for this purpose). When charred on the outside serve accompanied by sliced browned onions; mint and cucumber raita should be offered separately.

Mint and cucumber raita (ten portions)

1 litre (1³/4 pint) natural yoghurt   30 g (1 oz) chopped fresh mint
1 cucumber (grated)

1. Mix the mint into the yoghurt.
2. Prior to serving, grate the cucumber and add to the yoghurt. Season and serve chilled.

Pork sausage (2 kg / 4 lb)

1¹/2 kg (3 lb) lean pork (shoulder)   200 g (8 oz) onions
¹/2 kg (1 lb) fat pork (belly)   200 g (8 oz) breadcrumbs
30 g (1 oz) salt, spice and herb seasoning   water to moisten

1. Mince the meat and breadcrumbs.
2. Dice and sweat the onions without colour, add the seasoning and cook gently for
   1 –2 minutes.
3. Allow onions to cool then combine with the meat mixture.
4. Moisten with a little water.

Use for pork sausagemeat or pass through a sausage funnel into prepared casings and tie
off into 8 cm (3 in) lengths.

Tortillas (8 – 10 tortillas)

50 g (2 oz) course-ground cornmeal   75 g (3 oz) wholemeal flour
150 ml (6 fl oz) water   20 g (³/4 oz) butter or margarine

1. Bring the water and half the fat to the boil. Rain in the cornmeal, stirring constantly;
   cover and simmer gently for 4 –5 minutes. Remove from the heat and beat in the
   remaining fat.
2. Place the flour and salt in a separate bowl and add the cornmeal mix; work together
   by hand, kneading until smooth.
3. Roll into a cylinder shape and wrap in clingfilm.
4. Cut into 3 cm (1 in) slices, keeping the remaining mix wrapped so that it stays warm.
5. Roll out in one direction (dusting with ground cornmeal) turning each time, until it
   is the size and shape of a side plate.
6. Cook in a hot, dry frying/omelette pan until light brown and hot.
7. Shape while still warm by moulding around a thin rolling pin.
8. This mix is also suitable for enchiladas and tacos, the only difference being the
   shape required.

Refritos (re-fried bean filling for tortillas)

500 g (1 lb) cooked beans (black-eyed
    beans or pinto; black or red kidney
    beans may also be used)
2 tbsp olive oil
2 cloves crushed garlic
1 diced onion
1/2 tsp ground coriander

1 tsp ground cumin
1/2 tsp garam masala
1 green pepper (diced)
1 green chilli (chopped)
pinch of chilli powder
squeeze of lemon juice
salt and pepper

1. Fry the onion and garlic in a little oil, seasoned with salt.
2. Heat a separate frying pan and dry fry the spices, add to the onion.
3. Finely chop the chilli and add along with the diced pepper to the rest of the mix; cook gently for 4 – 5 minutes.
4. Mash the beans with a potato masher and add to the mix. Heat through, then add the lemon juice.

Mexican tomato sauce (makes approximately 1/2 litre / 1 pint)

1 tsp sunflower/olive oil
1 onion (finely diced)
1 clove of garlic (crushed)
pinch of chilli powder

1/2 lemon (quartered)
2 cloves
1 bay leaf
1 × 450 g (14 oz) tin of tomatoes

1. Heat the oil and fry the onion and garlic; add the chilli, lemon, cloves, bay leaf and tomatoes. Bring to the boil and simmer for 10 – 15 minutes.
2. Remove the bay leaf, cloves and lemon and liquidize until smooth.

Egg replacement for vegetarian / vegan dishes

One tablespoon of water and two tablespoons of soya flour is a suitable replacement for an egg in most preparations.

Sauces

A sauce is a liquid that has been thickened by one or more of the following:

Melted butter and flour (roux)
Starch, e.g. fecule, arrowroot or
    cornflour (diluted)
Egg yolks
Butter and flour kneaded to a
    paste (beurre manié).

Butter stirred, shaken or whisked into
    a liquid, e.g. beurre blanc.
Pureed vegetables or fruit (coulis).
The addition of such ingredients as
    fromage frais or yoghurt reduced to
    a liquor.

It can also be any liquid or thickened liquid that complements or provides contrast to a dish. Sauces play an important part in aiding the digestion of food, for example meats with a high fat content can be counteracted by the use of astringent herbs or acid- or fruit-based sauces.

Storage: stocks, sauces, soups, gravies and glazes

All these items are 'high risk' foods; this means that they are highly susceptible to bacterial infection. If storing these items, rapid cooking and correct temperature control must be carried out to prevent the risk of food poisoning. The product for storage should be placed in a clean pot, bucket or container, it should then be cooled down as quickly as possible. The cooling down process should take no longer than 90 minutes before refrigeration. Once cold the product must be covered and labelled with the contents and the date when it was produced. These items should be kept in a refrigerator away from uncooked foods, and if possible stored separately at a temperature below 5°C, or if frozen, −18°C. If stored together with raw food, they should be kept on a higher shelf to prevent any drips from the uncooked food contaminating them. Never forget that bacteria will grow rapidly between 5°C and 63°C, and food should always be kept above or below these temperatures. Never reheat more than once, and boil for at least 2 minutes before use.

Dressings

Vinaigrette

3 parts olive oil   salt and mignonette pepper
1 part vinegar (malt, white
   wine or cider)

Place the vinegar and seasoning in a bowl and whisk thoroughly. While continuing to whisk, gradually add the oil.

Vinaigrette (for vegetable hors-d'œuvre, ten portions)

1 litre (2 pints) olive oil   2 hard-boiled eggs
300 ml (2/3 pint) white wine vinegar   mixed herbs (parsley, chives,
2 tbsp French mustard   chervil or tarragon)
5 gherkins   seasoning

Mix together the mustard and vinegar. Gradually add the oil, whisking constantly.
Finely chop all the remaining ingredients and combine with the oil and vinegar. Season.

French dressing

As for vinaigrette but with the addition of French mustard to the vinegar.

Dijon dressing

As for vinaigrette but add Dijon mustard to the vinegar.

English dressing

As above but replace the Dijon mustard with English mustard, preferably whole-grain.

Lemon dressing

As for vinaigrette but replace the vinegar with lemon juice.

Garlic dressing

As for vinaigrette with the addition of one clove of crushed garlic and one tablespoon of chopped parsley to 500 ml (1 pint) of dressing, added with the vinegar.

Anchovy dressing

As for vinaigrette with the addition of one teaspoon of anchovy essence to the vinegar.

Thousand island dressing

Add 50 g (2 oz) of brunoise of peeled red and green peppers to 500 ml (1 pint) of mayonnaise. Season with paprika and chilli/tabasco. (See also Salads, p. 242.)

Dill dressing

Add 15 g (1/2 oz) of chopped dill and a pinch of sugar to vinaigrette at stage 1.

Black Forest dressing

1 litre (2 pints) oil	1 dessertspoon of English mustard
200 ml (8 fl oz) vinegar	100 ml (4 fl oz) water
2 egg yolks	seasoning and sugar

1. Whisk together the egg yolks, mustard, seasoning and a quarter of the vinegar and water. Whisk over a *bain-marie* until it reaches the 'ribbon' stage.
2. Remove from the *bain-marie* and slowly but steadily add the oil.
3. Correct the consistency with the remaining vinegar and water.
4. Adjust seasoning and add sugar to taste.

Acidulated cream (soured cream dressing) (1 litre / 2 pints)

750 ml (27 fl oz) fresh cream	seasoning
250 ml lemon juice	

Whisk together all the ingredients and serve with fruit-based salads.

Sauce vert, 1 (green sauce) (ten portions)

1/4 litre (1/2 pint) mayonnaise	50 g (2 oz) mixed herbs (e.g. parsley, chervil, tarragon, chives)

Stir the very finely chopped herbs into the mayonnaise and season to taste.

This version of *sauce vert* is more of a dressing than a sauce; the more substantial version is given later (see p. 195).

Honey and lemon dressing (1 litre / 2 pints)

750 ml (27 fl oz) oil   10 g (¹/₄ oz) salt
250 ml (8 fl oz) lemon juice   mignonette pepper
warmed/melted honey to taste

Place the salt, pepper and lemon juice into a stainless-steel bowl and mix well. Add the oil a little at a time, whisking continuously, then add the liquid honey to taste.

Blue cheese dressing (1 litre / 2 pints)

150 – 250 g (5 – 8 oz) blue cheese   750 ml (27 fl oz) vinaigrette
   (depending on the strength of   dressing
   cheese used)

Remove any rind or discoloured parts from the cheese and pass through a fine sieve. Gradually mix in the vinaigrette and season to taste.

Roquefort is the type of cheese most used in this dressing, but other suitable cheeses include gorgonzola, mycella, Danish blue, stilton and Bavarian blue.

Healthy eating dressings

Yoghurt dressing (1 litre / 2 pints)

800 ml natural yoghurt   200 ml lemon juice or white wine
salt and white pepper   vinegar

Blend together all the ingredients and season to taste.

Tofu and walnut dressing (ten portions)

¹/₂ packet soft silken tofu   2 tbsp lemon juice
3 tbsp walnut oil   grated rind of 1 lemon
4 tbsp orange juice   salt and pepper

Blend together all the ingredients and season.

Fruit vinaigrette (ten portions)

50 ml sunflower oil   ¹/₂ tsp English mustard powder
1 tsp honey   ¹/₂ tsp celery seeds
2 tbsp fresh orange juice   2 tsp shoyu
2 tbsp fresh lemon juice

Mix all the ingredients and chill well.

Shoyu dressing (ten portions)

4 tbsp sunflower oil
3 tbsp shoyu
2 tbsp cider vinegar
1 tbsp dry sherry

50 mm (2 in) root ginger (peeled,
   grated and squeezed, only
   the juice is used)
seasoning

Mix all the ingredients and season to taste.

Shoyu and tamari

Shoyu is pure 'soya' sauce as opposed to soy sauce, it is made by fermenting soya beans, salt and barley (or wheat) in oak barrels. It has a rich soy flavour and can be quite salty. Tamari is similar to soy sauce but with a richer flavour; pure tamari is wheat-free making it suitable for use in gluten-free recipes and in place of shoyu.

Cold Sauces

Mayonnaise (1 litre / 2 pints; can be made either by hand or by machine)

8 egg yolks
25 ml (1 fl oz) vinegar
2 level tsp English mustard powder

1 litre (2 pints) oil (preferably olive oil)
salt and ground white pepper
25 – 50 ml (1 – 2 fl oz) hot (boiled) water

1. Separate the eggs; place the yolks into a bowl or food processor with the vinegar, mustard and seasoning, mix thoroughly with a whisk (manual).
2. Gradually add the warm oil, whisking continuously; (the oil should be at blood temperature – 37°C).
3. Modify the consistency and remove any 'oily' taste by whisking in the hot water. Adjust the seasoning.

Aïoli (1 litre / 2 pints)

50 g garlic (peeled and crushed)
6 egg yolks
1 litre (2 pints) virgin olive oil

60 ml (2 fl oz) lemon juice
30 ml (1 fl oz) boiled warm water

1. Mix together the well crushed garlic and the egg yolks and gradually add some of the oil, mixing continuously.
2. As the sauce begins to thicken, gradually add the lemon juice along with the oil.
3. Once all the oil and vinegar has been added, add the warm water and season with salt and white pepper.

Aïoli is suitable for serving with cold meats, poached fish, eggs, for enriching fish/broth soups and as a dip for crudités or on cold buffets.

Quick whole mayonnaise (1 litre / 2 pints; mechanical emulsion)

4 whole eggs	1 litre (2 pints) olive oil
50 ml (2 fl oz) vinegar	salt and ground white pepper
2 tsp English mustard	hot boiled water

Place whole eggs, mustard, vinegar and seasoning in a food processor. Turn on full speed and gradually add the oil. Modify the consistency with the hot water.

Mayonnaise will curdle/split if (a) the oil is too cold; (b) the oil is added too quickly. (This is minimized if prepared in a food mixer or processor as the whisking is much faster.); or (c) the eggs are stale or too much oil is added in relation to the egg yolks. Curdled mayonnaise may be recovered or 'brought back' by placing one or two egg yolks and a little vinegar into a bowl and gradually adding the curdled mayonnaise, whisking continuously.

Fresh mayonnaise must be kept cold as it is a 'high risk' food: it must be kept covered and refrigerated when not in use, and must not be allowed to stand in ambient temperatures for more than one hour. It is recommended using pasteurized eggs when making mayonnaise. Lemon juice may be used instead of vinegar, especially for service with fish and shellfish.

Derivatives of mayonnaise

Cambridge sauce (1 litre / 2 pints)

6 hard boiled eggs or yolks	20 g (¹/₂ oz) capers
25 g (1 oz) anchovy fillets	10 g (¹/₄ oz) chopped parsley
20 g (¹/₂ oz) *fines herbes* (chervil, French tarragon, chives)	1 litre (2 pints) mayonnaise

1. Blanch and refresh the *fines herbes*, then chop finely.
2. Rinse the capers in hot water to remove the stale vinegar.
3. Place the eggs/yolks in a mortar or bowl and pound to a paste, together with the capers, anchovies, *fines herbes*.
4. Pass the paste through a fine sieve and add to the mayonnaise.
5. Finish with the chopped parsley.

Gloucester sauce (1 litre / 2 pints)

1 litre (2 pints) mayonnaise	15 g (¹/₂ oz) chopped fennel
250 ml (¹/₂ pint) sour cream	

1. Add the finely-diced fennel to the mayonnaise and modify the texture with the cream, and season.
2. Serve with 'fatty' cold meats such as pork, duck or goose.

Sauce bretonne (ten portions)

$1/4$ litre ($1/2$ pint) mayonnaise
5 medium-sized tomatoes
(concasse)

25 g (1 oz) tomato puree
pinch cayenne pepper
15g ($1/2$ oz) tarragon

Finely chop the tomato flesh. Blend the tomato puree, mayonnaise and tarragon. Stir in the tomato concasse and season to taste with cayenne.

Sauce vert, 2 (green sauce; 10 portions)

1 litre (2 pints) mayonnaise
75 g (3 oz) blanched spinach
and watercress leaves

50 g (2 oz) fresh mixed herbs,
e.g. parsley, chervil, tarragon, chives.

Blanch the spinach and watercress for one minute, drain and squeeze out the water. Pass through a fine sieve. Stir the spinach and watercress puree and the finely chopped herbs into the mayonnaise and season to taste.

Both sauce Bretonne and sauce vert (2) may be served with cold vegetables, for example globe artichokes, or with cold fish such as trout, salmon and shellfish.

Sauce remoulade (1 litre / 2 pints)

1 litre (2 pints) mayonnaise
25 g (1 oz) chopped gherkins
25 g (1 oz) chopped capers

10 g ($1/2$ oz) chopped *fines herbes*
15 ml (1 tbsp) anchovy essence

Rinse the capers under hot water and drain well. Add chopped ingredients to the mayonnaise and mix throughly.
Sauce remoulade can be used for cold egg dishes, fried fish or grilled meats.

Sauce tartare (1 litre / 2 pints)

As for sauce remoulade but omit the anchovy essence.

Sauce Marie Rose (Cocktail sauce for fish and shellfish; 1 litre /2 pints)

700 ml (1 pint) mayonnaise
300 ml ($1/2$ pint) good tomato ketchup
100 ml ($3^1/2$ fl oz) horseradish sauce
juice of 1 lemon

Worcester sauce
salt and pepper
pinch of cayenne

Combine all the ingredients and mix well. Lightly whipped cream may also be added.

Sauce tyrolienne (1 litre / 2 pints)

1 litre (2 pints) mayonnaise
50 g (2 oz) shallots, finely chopped
350 g (12 oz) tomato concasse
$1/2$ clove of garlic, crushed

1 bay leaf
15 g ($1/2$ oz) *fines herbes*, chopped
12 ml ($1/2$ fl oz) oil

1. Sweat the shallots and garlic in the oil, without colouring.
2. Add the tomato concasse and the bay leaf. Cook gently to dry out, then pass through a fine sieve or liquidize.
3. Allow to cool, then add to the mayonnaise with the *fines herbes*.

This may be served with fried fish and cold meats.

Cumberland sauce

1 kg (2 lb) redcurrant jelly	¹/₂ litre (1 pint) port
50 g (2 oz) finely-chopped shallots	1 tsp English mustard powder
juice of 1 lemon	zest of 2 oranges, cut julienne
juice of 2 oranges	

1. Warm and melt the redcurrant jelly with the port wine, allow to cool.
2. Blanch and refresh the shallots and add to the mixture.
3. Peel the oranges thinly, cut the zest into julienne; blanch and refresh and put to one side.
4. Squeeze the lemon and oranges and strain the juice into the redcurrant jelly mixture.
5. Dilute the mustard powder with a little water and add to the mixture.
6. Add the julienne of orange to finish.

Sauce Vincent (1 litre / 2 pints)

¹/₂ litre (16 fl oz) sauce vert	¹/₂ litre (16 fl oz) sauce tartare

Mix together the two sauces. This sauce may be used for cold or fried fish dishes. (See also Thousand Island dressing and Marie Rose sauce, p. 195.)

Oxford sauce

Prepare as for Cumberland sauce but substitute the julienne of orange zest with chopped blanched orange and lemon zest.

Horseradish sauce (Sauce Raifort; 1 litre / 2 pints)

700 ml (1 pint) cream	white vinegar
200 g (6¹/₂ oz) horseradish	cayenne pepper
150 g (5 oz) white breadcrumbs,	salt
soaked in milk	sugar

1. Finely grate the horseradish.
2. Whip the cream, taking care not to over-whip.
3. Squeeze the milk from the breadcrumbs, which should be soft in texture.
4. Combine the above ingredients and modify the texture with the vinegar.
5. Season with salt and cayenne pepper and add the sugar to remove any trace of bitterness.

This sauce can be used for smoked fish, roast/boiled beef, chicken Maryland.

Pesto (1 litre / 2 pints)

250 g (8 oz) basil leaves
1 head of garlic
150 g (5 oz) pine kernels
20 g (1 oz) chopped parsley

700 ml (1$1/3$ pint) olive oil
150 g (5 oz) grated Parmesan
salt and ground black pepper

1. Place all the ingredients except the oil in a food processor and blend to a paste. Gradually add the olive oil and season to taste.

Pesto can be used as a dip, but it is usually served as a dressing for pasta.

Mint sauce (sauce menthe, 1) (1 litre / 2 pints)

300 g (9$1/2$ oz) mint leaves
100 g (3$1/2$ oz) brown sugar

700 ml (1$1/3$ pint) vinegar
pinch of salt

1. Place the mint leaves on a board, sprinkle with the salt and brown sugar and chop finely.
2. Slightly warm the vinegar and combine with mint mixture. Allow to stand/cool for one hour before serving.

Mint sauce (sauce menthe, 2) (1 litre / 2 pints)

300 g (9$1/2$ oz) mint leaves
150 g (5 oz) brown sugar

700 ml (1$1/3$ pint) vinegar
300 ml ($1/2$ pint) water

1. Place the mint leaves on a board, sprinkle with the salt and brown sugar and chop finely.
2. Boil the water and add to the mint; add the vinegar. Allow to stand/cool for one hour before serving.

Vegetarian tomato sauce (Unthickened; ten portions)

100 ml (3$1/2$ fl oz) olive oil
1 onion, finely diced
4 cloves of garlic
pinch of chilli powder
2 × 450 g (14 oz) tins of tomatoes

2 tsp chopped fresh oregano
2 tsp chopped fresh basil
2 tbsp tomato puree
seasoning

1. Heat the oil gently and sweat the onion without colour.
2. Add the tomato puree and cook out for 2 minutes.
3. Add the tomatoes and the strained juice.
4. Simmer for 10 minutes, add the oregano and liquidize.
5. At the last moment add the chopped basil and season.

This sauce may be served hot or cold and is excellent with vegetables such as mushrooms and leeks.

Chaud-froid

Chaud-froid literally means 'hot-cold'; they are sauces which are prepared hot and served cold. They are used on all manner of cold buffet items: from glazing hams and chicken gallantines to collops of lobster. Chaud-froids are prepared from a range of sauces depending on what is to be glazed, i.e. for a chicken gallantine, the base sauce would be chicken velouté; fish is glazed with fish velouté; and meats, such as lamb and game, are glazed with brown chaud-froids made from demi-glace. Delicate food or ones which do not have an appropriate sauce, such as ham, may be glazed with a béchamel sauce-based chaud-froid. Chaud-froid sauces need to set when cold so aspic jelly or gelatine is added while the sauce is still hot. There are three main colours for chaud-froid: white, pink and brown; green chaud-froid is also used but is not as common.

White chaud-froid sauce, 1 (chaud-froid blanc) (1 litre / 2 pints)

1 litre (2 pints) béchamel or velouté (chicken, fish, etc.)	250 ml ($^1/_2$ pint) cream
	few drops of brandy or sherry
50 g (2 oz) leaf gelatine	

1. Soak the gelatine and add to the hot sauce.
2. Modify the colour and consistency of the sauce with the cream.
3. Add the brandy or sherry for flavour.

This sauce should be pure white, something which is achieved by the addition of the cream; however, it may not be necessary to add all the cream if using a pale-coloured sauce or béchamel.

If aspic is used in the preparation of a buffet, it can be combined with the appropriate white sauce and the chaud-froid made up as follows:

White chaud-froid sauce, 2 (chaud-froid blanc) (1 litre / 2 pints)

1 litre (2 pints) sauce (velouté, béchamel)	125 ml ($^1/_4$ pint) cream
$^1/_2$ litre (1 pint) aspic jelly	few drops of brandy or sherry

1. Place the sauce in a wide thick-bottomed pan on the stove and reduce by boiling.
2. Add the aspic and the cream a little at a time.
3. Reduce to a coating consistency (approximately 1 litre / 2 pints).
4. Season and add the brandy or sherry. Strain and cool before use.

An alternative to the above that has gained in popularity is to use a mixture of mayonnaise and aspic jelly to coat the fish, etc. instead of the chaud-froid. This mix can also be used to bind vegetable or Russian salads.

Mayonnaise colée (1 litre / 2 pints)

750 ml (1½ pint) mayonnaise
350 ml (¾ pint) aspic jelly

Mix the melted but cool aspic with the mayonnaise.

Pink chaud-froid (*chaud-froid à l'aurore*) (1 litre / 2 pints)

1 litre (2 pints) white chaud-froid
125 ml (¼ pint) dry sieved fresh tomato pulp/puree

1. Combine the sauce and tomato while the sauce is still hot.
2. Pass through a fine strainer or muslin or liquidize.

The colour should be a pale delicate pink, and the sauce may be used to coat fish, shellfish
or chicken.

Brown chaud-froid (*chaud-froid brun*) (1 litre / 2 pints)

1 litre (2 pints) demi-glace   50 g (2 oz) leaf gelatine
125 ml (¼ pint) Madeira

1. Place the sauce and the Madeira on the stove in a wide thick-bottomed pan and
   reduce by boiling.
2. Remove from the heat and add the soaked, drained gelatine, stir until dissolved.
3. Allow to cool before use.

Brown chaud-froid may be made by substituting the gelatine with ½ litre (1 pint) of aspic
jelly. In this case the aspic is added a little at a time while the sauce is reducing until a
quantity of approximately 1 litre (2 pints) is achieved. Truffle essence can also be used to
flavour the sauce.

Cold soups

The repertoire of cold soups is constantly being extended: the recipes here are two of the
best-known 'classic' examples, but fruit soups are also typical.

Gazpacho andalouse (1 litre / 2 pints)

6 cloves of garlic   200 g (6½ oz) peeled cucumber
100 g (3½ oz) sliced bread   50 g (2 oz) green pepper
100 ml (3½ fl oz) olive oil   50 g (2 oz) red pepper
2 × 450 g (14 oz) tins of tomatoes   100 ml (3½ fl oz) vinegar
   (drained, strained and the juice reserved)   10 g (¼ oz) cumin seeds

1. Peel and crush the garlic. Dice the bread and add to the crushed garlic.
2. Gradually mix the oil into the bread mix, season with salt and allow to stand for 10 minutes.
3. Drain, de-seed and chop the tomatoes. Peel and chop the cucumber. De-seed the peppers and chop. Add to the bread.
4. Moisten with a little of the strained tomato juice and allow to stand covered in a fridge for approximately 1 hour.
5. Crush the cumin seeds and add.
6. Liquidize and chill well. Modify the texture if necessary with a little of the strained tomato juice. Garnish with chopped herbs such as parsley and basil.

Accompaniments: Gazpacho should be served with sauceboats of the following, all of which should be finely diced.

Croutons	Cucumber	Red/green pepper
Onion	Tomato concasse	

Vichyssoise (chilled leek and potato soup) (1 litre / 2 pints)

30 g (1 oz) butter	$^1/_2$ litre (1 pint) milk
200 g (6$^1/_2$ oz) white of leek	200 g (6$^1/_2$ oz) sliced potatoes
50 g (1$^1/_2$ oz) onion	100 ml (3 fl oz) cream
1 litre (2 pints) chicken stock	chopped chives

1. Melt the butter and sweat the chopped leek and onion until soft.
2. Add the stock and milk. Bring to the boil and skim.
3. Add the sliced potatoes, season and simmer gently until tender, approximately 1 hour.
4. Liquidize and pass through a fine strainer. Re-boil in a clean pan. Chill thoroughly and adjust the seasoning. The consistency can be altered by the addition of cream. Garnish with chopped chives.

Fruit soups

Fruit soups are served cold and can be prepared from most fruits that can be pureed, e.g. apples, melons, peaches and cherries. Some types of fruit require cooking in syrup or liqueur prior to being pureed and cooled. The main requirement with fruit soups is that they are palatable and that the right balance is struck between sweet and savoury. Sweetness may be modified with lemon juice, spices or alcohol (wines, fortified wines and kirsch).

EIGHT

Hors-d'œuvre

Introduction

Hors-d'œuvre is the term used to describe a wide range of items served as the opening course of a meal. The word comes from the French 'hors-de l'œuvre' or 'outside the work' meaning 'work's over, so let's eat'! Most hors-d'œuvre are prepared from spare or excess commodities found in any busy kitchen. They are also known as starters, appetisers, zakouskis and antipasto.

The quality of the hors-d'œuvre depends on the flair, imagination and experience of the chef. The chef must balance colours, flavours and seasonings to make a range of individual delights which together produce an overture to the meal that is both pleasing to the eye and to the palate. Most hors-d'œuvre are made up on the spot from what is available on that particular day, this means mainly cooked food items such as vegetables, cold meats, fish and shellfish. The making of hors-d'œuvre is a true test of a chef's ability, and requires an understanding of how foods blend together with regard to flavour, texture and presentation.

Classification

Classic hors-d'œuvre are divided into two main categories. These are:

Hors-d'œuvre A selection of dishes presented either plated or individually, and sometimes presented on a trolley (though this is a rare sight nowadays). Approximately a dozen items of food are arranged together and served ice cold: these can include almost anything that may be offered cold. A high degree of expertise is required by the chef who prepares the hors-d'œuvre (hors d'oeuvrier), as he or she is often required to produce something extraordinary from left-overs.

Single hors-d'œuvre These are items of food that are prepared and served as a dish in their own right (for example, 'melon slices') or when several items are combined to form an individual dish. Many items prepared as single hors-d'œuvre can also be presented as part of an hors-d'œuvre *variés*.

Other classifications of hors-d'œuvre

Hot hors-d'œuvre: Hot starters prepared from the kitchen.

Hors-d'œuvre Moscovite: A classic-style presentation displayed on a cold buffet (see hors-d'œuvre Moscovite, p. 204).

Canapés: A selection of items served usually prior to a meal and presented on toasted breads, puff pastry or savoury biscuits. May be served plain or glazed with aspic.

The function of hors-d'œuvre

The main function of hors-d'œuvre, as its alternative name 'appetizers' suggests is to:

(a) stimulate the gastric juices which in turn stimulates the appetite;
(b) cleanse the mouth/palate.

When to serve hors-d'œuvre

Various: Cold hors-d'œuvre *variés* are mainly served at lunchtime, before the soup course or as part of a cold buffet selection.

Single: De luxe hors-d'œuvre, like caviar, tend to be served only for dinner, but single hors-d'œuvre prepared from less expensive items are served at both lunch and dinner.

Hot hors-d'œuvre: Served mainly at lunchtimes.

Hors-d'œuvre Moscovite: Presented on cold buffets and for occasions such as cocktail parties and reception buffets.

Hygiene and preparing and serving hors-d'œuvre

It is essential that a high degree of hygiene is maintained during the preparation of hors-d'œuvre. Outlined below are some general points to consider when preparing and serving hors-d'œuvre.

- Most items are pre-cooked and thus must be kept cold at all times.
- Because both raw and cooked commodities are used, separation during preparation is vital to prevent cross-contamination.
- Fish, meats, pâtés and sausage all carry a high risk of cross-contamination.
- Hors-d'œuvre often require a great deal of handling during preparation and tend to be presented during the warmer months making contamination more likely.
- Hors-d'œuvre are often presented on cold buffets where the room temperature is high; this means they must be very well chilled beforehand and not presented until required.
- Hors-d'œuvre should not be held without refrigeration in a 'hot' room for more than one hour, after which time they should be removed and replaced with fresh pre-chilled items.
- All precautions should be taken to prevent contamination, including the use of separate sinks, boards and knives for fish, meat and vegetables and cooked and raw items.

- All mechanical equipment such as mincers, liquidizers, bowl choppers, etc. should be stripped down and sterilized between operations.

Examples for hors-d'œuvre selection (hors-d'œuvre variés)

The following is a guide to the types of commodities that can be used when compiling a hors-d'œuvre variés.

Fish- or shellfish-based: Tuna, prawns, mussels, oysters, crab, shrimps, lobster, sardines, anchovies, rollmop/bismarck herrings, smoked trout, mackerel, trout, salmon, eel.

Meat-based: Charcuteir, pâtés, terrines, smoked hams, beef, turkey, chicken, mortadella, rillet/rillons, galantines.

Egg-based: Egg mayonnaise, stuffed eggs, hard-boiled eggs (with curried mayonnaise), pickled eggs, scotch eggs, jellied eggs, various quiches.

Vegetable-based: Pasta or rice dishes – made with asparagus, artichokes, peppers, etc. (see also Vegetable hors-d'œuvre, p. 229). Pasta salads, rice moulds/salads, ravioli.

Fruit-based: Various types of melon, mangoes, pawpaw, stuffed apples, olives, grapes, pineapple, kiwi fruit, figs, grapefruit, pears, bananas, etc.

Single/simple salads: Tomato, cucumber, asparagus, beetroot, potato, red cabbage, bean, sweetcorn.

Compound salads: (See also Salads, p. 242) Any salad which will complement the other items to be presented, for example Niçoise, Waldorf, bagatelle, Italian.

Speciality dressings: Vegetables à la grecque, à la portugaise.

Convenience items: Any pre-prepared or cooked items, such as beetroot, pickles, tinned or frozen fish or shellfish, artichoke bottoms, pre-cooked meats (pastrami, hams, etc.).

Vegetarian/wholefood items: Vegetarian pâtés, various wholefoods with suitable dressings, vegan preparations.

Single hors-d'œuvre examples

Oysters, foie gras, dressed crab, smoked salmon, avocado pear, melon, caviar, smoked meats/sausages/hams (e.g., Parma ham), potted shrimps, smoked trout, smoked eel, snails, asparagus tips, half a grapefruit, fruit juices.

Combinations served as single hors-d'œuvre:

Cocktails fruit, seafood.

Platters seafood/shellfish, continental sausages/meats (e. g. salami, mortadella, garlic or liver sausage, pastrami).

Stuffed or filled items tomatoes, eggs, avocado with prawns.

Other items egg mayonnaise/harlequin, melon and Parma ham, compound salads.

Hors-d'œuvre Moscovite

This is a classic-style presentation of certain types of hors-d'œuvre, which could otherwise be described as a 'cocktail finger buffet' since the items are normally presented as *petits* hors-d'œuvre. 'Moscovite' refers to the manner of presentation, which must be followed if the term is used.

Presentation

Set a layer of clear aspic jelly on a large round silver flat and fill the centre with Russian salad that has been previously set in aspic (an ice cream bombe mould is often used for this purpose). Surround with small versions of the following:

Stuffed eggs

Stuffed tomatoes

Barquettes (boat-shaped pastry cases) filled with caviar or lumpfish/salmon roe; prawns, sardines, anchovies, smoked eel, mackerel, etc.

Tartlets (round pastry cases) filled with chicken, game, cheese, ham, etc.

Cornets of ham/smoked salmon

Bouchées (small puff pastry cases) filled with any type of filling

Carolines (small choux pastry eclairs) filled with savoury fillings or mousses of fish, meat, poultry or game, masked with chaud-froid sauce and glazed with aspic jelly

Duchesses (walnut-sized choux paste profiteroles) filled as for carolines, glazed with aspic and decorated with nuts, preferably pistachios

The variety of items on offer should be of various colours, flavours, and textures.

Single hors-d'œuvre

Oysters (see also Chapter 4, Fish & Shellfish, p. 70)

Quality:
1. Purchase alive in tightly-closed shells.
2. Oysters should have a fresh smell.
3. Purchase on the day of use.
4. The best variety are English, and are available when there is an 'R' in the month, i.e. September to April.

Storage: In a cold room; keep moist by covering with damp sacks.

Uses:

(a) Raw in half-shells served on crushed ice
(b) Seafood/shellfish platters
(c) Seafood stir-fries
(d) As part of an hors-d'œuvre *variés*

Caviar

Types: Beluga, sevruga, salmon caviar (red), mock caviar (lumpfish roe).

Storage: At 0°C in the original container.

Uses:

(a) As a single hors-d'œuvre on crushed ice, served with blinis (buckwheat pancakes, see recipe below), or with hot thick buttered toast. Approximately 15 g ($^1/2$ oz) is enough for one portion. Caviar should be presented accompanied by lemon, the sieved white and yolk of a hard-boiled egg and perhaps a little chopped onion.

(b) As an hors-d'œuvre, served between two blinis – sour cream may be offered separately.

(c) As an hors-d'œuvre, served on crushed ice with lemon and toast.

(d) As a garnish for canapés.

(e) As a filling for duchesses, etc.

(f) As part of an hors-d'œuvre *variés*.

Blinis

Prepare a pancake batter by sifting together equal parts flour and buckwheat flour. Season with a pinch of salt, and beat in enough milk to produce a creamy consistency. Add an egg yolk and allow to stand for about one hour. Heat a small crêpe or pancake pan and coat with oil; add enough batter to make a pancake which measures approximately 5 – 8 cm (2 – 3 in).

Pâté

Types:

- Foie gras (goose liver)
- Liver pâté (*pâté de foie*): Chicken, goose, duck, pork, calf's liver
- *Pâté maison* (Homemade pâté)

Storage: Pâté must be kept chilled at all times at a temperature of approximately 1°C. It should be stored away from other foods and wrapped well to prevent it becoming discoloured and drying out.

Uses:

(a) Plated with salad and with hot buttered toast served separately.

(b) Garnishing of canapés.

(c) As a filling for carolines.

(d) As part of an *assiette charcuterie*.

(e) As part of an hors-d'œuvre *variés*.

(f) As part of a cold buffet.

Saucisson

Ready made sausages.

Charcuterie

Continental/smoked meats and pâté.

Uses:

(a) Saucisson (a selection, plated and garnished).
(b) *Assiette* (a selection of cooked meats and salad, garnished with olives and gherkins).
(c) Both a and b may be offered on cold buffets and as a part of an hors-d'œuvre *variés*.

Ham

Types:

  – Parma, prosciutto (Italian hams and the best-known)
  – Jambon de Bayonne (French)
  – Jambon de Westphalia (German)

Uses:

(a) As an hors-d'œuvre, served in very thin slices with lemon; brown bread and butter and freshly ground black pepper should be offered separately.
(b) As an hors-d'œuvre with melon or figs.
(c) As part of an hors-d'œuvre *variés*.
(d) Garnishing canapés.
(e) As part of a cold buffet.

Service:

  – Plated as a single hors-d'œuvre or with other items as part of a selection.
  – In ravier dishes as part of a selection.
  – On silver flats for service on a cold buffet.

Potted shrimps/fish

Uses: Plated as a single hors-d'œuvre, garnished with salad and lemon. Hot buttered toast and/or brown bread and butter should be offered separately.

Preparation: May be prepared in-house or bought in frozen.

Method: Bind picked cooked shrimps with half their weight of cooled melted unsalted butter. Season with salt, mace, nutmeg and freshly ground white pepper. Press firmly into small pots or ramekins and top up with fresh melted butter to which a small pinch of cayenne pepper has been added. Refrigerate until set. This recipe may be used to prepare potted fish using salmon, smoked trout, eel, haddock, etc.

Grapefruit and melons (See Fruit hors-d'œuvre, p. 212)

Fruit juices

Serve freshly squeezed if possible. Serve very well chilled.

Avocado pears (See Fruit hors-d'œuvre, p. 212)

Asparagus tips (See Vegetable hors-d'œuvre, p. 229)

Herrings: rollmop, bismarck, smoked (See Fish hors-d'œuvre, p. 209)

Snails (See Fish hors-d'œuvre, p. 209)

Dressed crab

$^{1}/_{2}$ – 1 kg (1 – 2 lb) crab	white breadcrumbs lightly
150 ml ($^{1}/_{4}$ pint) mayonnaise	soaked in milk
tomatoes	lobster coral
anchovies	vinaigrette dressing
hard-boiled egg	lettuce
capers	Worcester sauce
olives	

Cook crab in a *court bouillon* (see p. 71) for 20 – 30 minutes, and allow to cool in the cooking liquor. Rinse and brush to remove any white scum.

To dress:

1. Remove legs and claws; crack the shells with a pair of nutcrackers or lay flat on a chopping board and crack with a cutlet bat.
2. Remove the flesh, including the flesh from the joints, using the blunt end of a trussing needle. Place in a clean basin.
3. Remove the under-shell/soft shell by levering it away from the hard upper-shell, starting at the tail and taking care not to break the hard shell.
4. Remove and discard the gills ('dead man's fingers') and sac (located behind the eyes).
5. Scrape out the brown meat from inside the shell and pass through a sieve. Place in a separate basin from the white claw meat. Split the soft shell in two down the middle and remove the meat.
6. Season the brown meat with Worcester sauce, mayonnaise, salt and pepper and bind with fresh breadcrumbs that have previously been soaked in milk and squeezed dry.
7. Shred the white meat with the fingertips, taking great care to remove any hard pieces of shell. Season with vinaigrette dressing and salt and pepper.
8. Clean and dry the shell thoroughly, then press around the natural line to break it. Polish the outside of the shell with a finger dipped in oil.

9. Fill the centre of the shell with the brown meat and smooth with a small palette knife.
10. Tuck the white meat into the sides of the shell, keeping it separate from the brown meat.
11. Decorate the borders between light and dark meat with lines of the sieved hard-boiled white and yolk of an egg and finely chopped parsley.
12. Form a lattice pattern with trimmed fillets of anchovies; garnish with sliced rounds of stuffed olives, capers and sprinkle with lobster coral.
13. Dress on lettuce leaves garnished with salad and the crab legs. Serve vinaigrette/mayonnaise separately.

Dressed crab may be used for presentation both as an hors-d'œuvre and as a salad. An alternative presentation for service as an hors-d'œuvre *variés* is to prepare as above but instead of presenting the whole crab in its shell, the crabmeat is arranged and garnished in a small white rectangular ravier dish, or as part of a plated selection.

Eggs

Oeuf mayonnaise (egg mayonnaise) served plated as single hors-d'œuvre.

Oeuf farcie (stuffed egg) served plated as single hors-d'œuvre.

Oeuf harlequin (egg harlequin) served plated as single hors-d'œuvre.

Egg mayonnaise

Halves of hard-boiled eggs are dressed on lettuce leaves (rounded-sides uppermost), coated with mayonnaise and garnished with strips of anchovy fillets, arranged trellis-fashion. Sprinkle with rinsed and squeezed capers and a pinch of cayenne pepper, finish by garnishing with salad. (To achieve the correct consistency, mayonnaise will often require diluting with hot water. Capers should be rinsed of pickling vinegar and squeezed dry to minimize any traces of bitterness.)

Stuffed eggs

Halve the hard-boiled eggs lengthways and remove the yolks. Add a little softened butter and flavour as you fancy with, for example, mayonnaise, tomato ketchup, anchovy essence, pounded and sieved shrimps or prawns. Season and pipe neatly with a star tube into the holes left in the whites. Present dressed on lettuce leaves with salad garnish.

Stuffed eggs are presented rounded-side down: to prevent the eggs rolling to one side, a thin slice should be cut from the rounded-side allowing the eggs to stand upright.

Egg Harlequin

Prepare as for egg mayonnaise except one half of the egg is coated with Marie Rose sauce to give a red contrast to the white of the mayonnaise.

All the above can be used as single hors-d'œuvre, quartered eggs presented in ravier dishes, or as part of a plated selection for hors-d'œuvre *variés*.

Smoked fish

Smoked salmon, mackerel, trout, eel, etc. can be served as single hors-d'œuvre, and are prepared in the same way as for hors-d'œuvre *variés*. Present plated on lettuce leaves with salad and quarters of lemon; brown bread and butter is offered separately. Creamed horseradish sauce is served with all smoked fish except for smoked salmon (its flavour is too strong for salmon).

Fish / shellfish cocktails

Cocktails prepared from shrimps, prawns, crab, lobster, tuna or a combination of shellfish or cooked fish and shellfish may all be served as single hors-d'œuvre or as hors-d'œuvre *variés*.

Allow 50 g (2 oz) of fish /   71 ml (2½ fl oz) Marie Rose sauce
   shellfish per portion   lemon quarter
3 – 4 lettuce leaves   seasoning

1. Wash and dry the lettuce and shred finely.
2. Place a spoonful of sauce into the base of a glass cocktail dish or metal coupe dish.
3. Place the shredded lettuce on top of the sauce and top with drained and seasoned fish/shellfish.
4. Coat with a layer of sauce.
5. Sprinkle the surface of the sauce with a small pinch of cayenne pepper and garnish with shellfish or fresh herbs such as parsley, mint or dill.
6. Slice between the rind and flesh of a lemon wedge and hook over the rim of the dish with the rind facing outwards.

The most simple and well known of dishes can suffer from complacency when preparing them; for instance, the flavour of frozen shellfish is greatly diminished by the water which is produced during thawing. This must be squeezed out of the shellfish before using. In addition, seasoning brings out the true flavour of seafood, a fact that most chefs seem to ignore.

Canapés

Even though canapés are a classic preparation in their own right, they perform the same function as hors-d'œuvre, so I feel that it is justified to include them in this chapter. Cocktail canapés (*canapés à la russe*) are dainty, savoury appetizers made from a wide variety of ingredients. Canapés are most often prepared on toasted white or brown bread, but may also include the following:

– Savoury biscuits such as Ritz crackers.
– Untoasted continental breads such as rye, pumpernickel, etc.
– Bases of puff pastry.
– Small bouchées, tartlets, barquettes, beignets soufflé.
– Stuffed cucumber, celery, mushrooms, etc.
– Shellfish such as prawns or small pieces of meat, breadcrumbed and deep-fried.

Uses:

(a) Served prior to a meal with pre-meal drinks (usually before being seated at the table).
(b) At receptions or cocktail parties.
(c) As part of a finger buffet.

Preparation: Gently toast both sides of a slice of bread (a long, sliced sandwich loaf is ideal for this purpose). While still warm, lightly flatten. When cool (but not cold), spread with butter.

Thinly-sliced items such as ham, salamis, hard cheeses, etc. may be placed on top of the toast prior to being cut into shapes. For other items, the toast can be stamped out using cutters or cut into various shapes before topping and garnishing.

Glazing, decorating and garnishing

Once the canapés are prepared, place on wire cooling racks over the top of a tray with raised sides. Then chill as they need to be very cold for glazing, otherwise the aspic jelly will not stick. The aspic (fresh or convenience) must be on the point of setting, so that when it comes in contact with the ice-cold canapés it sets. This should leave a thin coat (glaze) with any surplus running off into the tray below. Return the canapés to the fridge to set the aspic. This process may require repeating so as to achieve a quality glaze.

Once the canapés have been glazed, they are ready for decorating. All items used to decorate the canapés (except sprigs of parsley) must be passed beforehand through liquid aspic jelly. Hold the item on the tip of a cocktail stick and pass it through the aspic; use another cocktail stick to position the item on the canapé.

Once the canapés have been decorated, they should be returned to the fridge to ensure that the garnish firmly adheres. The canapés are then given a final coat of glaze. If the garnish is not firmly stuck to the canapé then it will be washed off when the final coat of aspic is applied. The garnish must be enclosed in the glaze as it will dry and curl if left unglazed.

It may seem like a lot of time and effort is needed to prepare canapés, but if the fridge is cold, the gap between each application of aspic (glaze) should be no more than 10 – 15 minutes.

General rules for glazing with aspic
(for hygiene guidelines on the use of aspic see p. 267)

1. The canapés/items must be cold.
2. The aspic must be the correct consistency.
3. The aspic must be on the point of setting – this is achieved by allowing the aspic to cool naturally, then immersing the pan containing the aspic in a bowl of iced water.
4. The aspic must be stirred gently but constantly to prevent it setting on the sides of the pan, and becoming lumpy.
5. The aspic must not be stirred too vigorously as air bubbles will form, spoiling the appearance of the finished product.
6. The aspic will become thicker as it nears setting point; the pan must then be removed from the iced water and used immediately and quickly. Once it begins to

set, glazing must stop and the aspic re-melted by the application of gentle heat. The aspic is then cooled once more to the point of setting.

7. The canapés/items should be supported by a wire cooling rack with a tray placed underneath. After a coat of aspic has been applied, the wire rack and canapés/items must be placed over a clean tray.

8. The remaining aspic in the base of the original tray should be melted and strained into a clean pan, cooled and used again. Discard the aspic if it becomes discoloured or clouded in any way – it must be kept crystal clear at all times, otherwise the finished product will be impaired. Any air bubbles that appear can be removed by pricking with the point of a warm pin.

Recipes for aspic jellies

Aspic is only as good as the stock that it is prepared from; a weak stock or one which is cloudy will impair the finished product.

Basic aspic jelly (*gelée ordinaire*) (2 litres / 3 pints)

3 – 4 egg whites	1 bouquet garni
700 g (1½ lb) minced shin of beef	4 peppercorns
100 g (4 oz) onions	2½ litre (5 pints)of good beef or veal stock
100 g (4 oz) carrots	15 g (½ oz) salt
100 g (4 oz) leeks	100 – 150 g (4 – 6 oz) gelatine (depending
100 g (4 oz) celery	on the temperature. i.e. more in the
1 bay leaf	summer, less in the winter)

1. Place ½ litre (1 pint) of cold stock in a pan, add the egg whites and whisk together.
2. Add the minced shin, finely-diced vegetables and salt and mix well.
3. Allow to stand 15 – 30 minutes. While the meat is soaking, soak the leaf gelatine in cold water.
4. Add the rest of the stock to the meat mixture and mix well; add the soaked gelatine.
5. Bring to the boil, stirring occasionally.
6. As the mixture comes to the boil, stir one last time (do not stir once boiling).
7. Simmer gently for 2 – 3 hours, then strain through a double muslin. Remove all traces of fat and correct seasoning with salt only. If cloudy clarify with more egg whites.

Note: Check the setting quality by placing a little of the aspic in the fridge; it should set quite firm, if not add extra soaked gelatine.

Chicken aspic (*gelée de volaille*)

Prepare as for ordinary aspic but with the addition of 250 g (½ lb) of chicken giblets and carcasses at stage 2.

Fish aspic (*gelée de poisson*)

3 – 4 eggs whites	1 bouquet garni
700 g (1½ lb) minced white fish (sole or whiting)	1 bay leaf
	4 peppercorns
100 g (4 oz) onion	100 – 150 g (4 – 6 oz) leaf gelatine
100 g (4 oz) leeks	5 g (¼ oz) salt

Prepare as for ordinary aspic with the addition of the fish at stage 2.

Game aspic (*gelée de gibier*)

Prepare as for ordinary aspic with the addition of 250 g (½ lb) of game giblets and carcass at stage 2.

Convenience aspic (granules)

This product is fine for everyday use, though as with most convenience products, it tends to be salty. The aspic granules are whisked into hot water until dissolved, at a ratio of 50 g to 1 litre or 1 oz to the pint. The aspic must be allowed to stand to allow any air bubbles to disperse. It can then be used in the normal way.

Alternative glaze for vegetarians

This uses a substance called 'agar-agar', which is the Malayan word for jelly. It is made from a variety of seaweeds, and is usually manufactured in Japan. Agar-agar is a natural, unflavoured vegetable gelatine and is a good alternative to animal gelatine. It is available in both powder and flake form and is sold under such proprietary names as 'Gelozone'. It is readily available from most health food stores.

Method:

As a replacement for gelatine-firm set: add 1 tablespoon of agar-agar to ½ litre (1 pint) of cold liquid, gently bring to the boil and simmer for 5 minutes. Agar-agar must be boiled to set. Lemon juice helps agar-agar set, as opposed to egg whites which seem to reduce its setting strength.

As a replacement for aspic-light set: add 1 – 2 teaspoons to ½ litre (1 pint) of cold water, then boil for 5 minutes. This mix may be coloured with yeast extract if a dark glaze is required.

Fruit hors-d'œuvre – types

Citrus fruit

Limes, grapefruit, oranges, kumquats, tangerines, ugli fruit, etc.

Melons

Honeydew, gallia, cantaloupe, ogen, charantaise, watermelon.

Tropical fruits

Guava, passion fruit, papaya/pawpaw, mango, kiwifruit, pineapple, fig, avocado pears.

Citrus fruits

These are normally combined in cocktails (see cocktail nouveau Florida, p. 216) or, as in the case of grapefruit, halved and served as a single hors-d'œuvre.

They may also be served plated as an assortment, or as part of an hors-d'œuvre *variés*. Citrus fruit also feature in compound salads, such as mimosa or Japonnaise, which may be presented either as a single hors-d'œuvre or *variés*.

Melons

Melons, apart from the ogen melon, are cut into sections, the seeds are removed and the flesh is separated from the skin with a knife. It is then cut into bite-size pieces, rearranged on the skin/rind and served garnished on crushed ice.

Ogen melons, and occasionally cantaloupe melons are served whole, flavoured with fortified wines such as port, Madeira or Marsala. These are prepared by cutting out a round section around the stalk, remove but retain this 'plug'. Remove the seeds with a spoon and fill with approximately 140 ml (¹/₄ pint)of fortified wine.

The 'plug' is replaced and the melon is chilled for 2 – 3 hours. The ogen melon is traditionally served whole on crushed ice – a long-handled spoon is helpful to the customer in this instance. Cantaloupe melon may be prepared in the same way but it is generally too large to be served as a single portion; in this case the flesh is scooped out with a spoon, preferably at the table, and served with a little of the juice and the wine. Along with other melons, cantaloupe may also be served in roundels (cut with a melon or Parisienne scoop) with any of the above mentioned fortified wines. It is then presented in a coupe dish or similar dish.

A modern preparation, which has become popular in recent years, is diced or roundels of melon in a light curried mayonnaise or natural yoghurt with chopped or sieved mango chutney. This makes an excellent fruit item on an hors-d'œuvre *variés* or as part of the salads selection on a cold buffet.

Tropical fruits

These may be served plated as an assortment (*assiette de fruit*) or in cocktails. A fashionable way of presentation is to accompany the fruit with a fruit coulis. This is a natural or sweetened fruit puree, used either to line the plate or as an accompanying sauce for cocktails.

Coulis de fruit (1 litre/2 pints)

700 g (1½ lb) fresh fruit (raspberries,   200 ml (8 fl oz) sugar syrup
blackcurrants, pawpaw, etc.)   lemon juice

1. If necessary, peel and de-seed the fruit. Place in a blender with sugar syrup and lemon juice.
2. Liquidize to a puree and pass through a sieve. Chill and use as required.

The coulis can be further enhanced by the addition of fruit vinegars and liqueurs.

Grapefruit (*pamplemousse*)

There are two kinds of grapefruit: white and pink, or blood grapefruit. The pink is the sweeter of the two.

Uses:

Half (as single hot hors-d'œuvre) grilled with fortified wine and brown sugar.

Segments
- Grapefruit cocktail (single hors-d'œuvre)
- Grapefruit and orange cocktail – Florida cocktail (pineapple optional; single hors-d'œuvre)
- Dressed in ravier dishes with orange segments (hors-d'œuvre *variés*)

Preparation:

Half grapefruit
1. Cut in half horizontally, remove pips and white core.
2. Loosen each segment with a grapefruit or paring knife, leaving the surrounding pith in place.
3. Chill well and garnish with a cherry.

Segments
1. Remove the skin from the top and bottom, remove the skin and pith from the sides with a sharp knife, turning the grapefruit clockwise so as to follow the line of the skin from the previous cut.
2. Hold the grapefruit in the palm of one hand and cut away each segment of fruit from the pith. When all segments have been removed, squeeze out the remaining juice over the segments and chill well.

Avocado pear (*avocat*)

The avocado pear has become a firm favourite as a fruit hors-d'œuvre, it is in season all year round and has several applications. There are two types, red and green, the green is considered superior to the red.

Quality points:

(a) Green: smooth skin, soft when ripe.

(b) Red: rough, pebbly skin – green when unripe, purple and black when ripe.

(c) The flesh should be soft, oily, pale green and have a buttery texture.

(d) To test for ripeness, gently squeeze the pointed end, this should give easily if ripe.

Uses:

Normally eaten as a savoury, either as a starter or in salads, often served with fillings such as crabmeat or prawns. In some tropical countries avocados are used in sweet dishes. Avocado is often combined with fish, either as a stuffing or incorporated in a farce, and particularly complements hot fish dishes. It is also the main ingredient of guacamole (see 'Modern Trends', p. 216).

Avocado vinaigrette 1

Cut pear in half from top to bottom; remove the stone and criss-cross the flesh with the point of a knife. Dress with vinaigrette dressing and garnish with salad.

If the avocado is not to be served in an avocado dish, then a thin slice taken from skin of the base will assist in keeping the pear upright and stable.

Avocado vinaigrette 2

Cut pear in half from top to bottom; remove the stone and peel off the skin. Cut the pear across into thin slices and fan out onto a plate. Finish as for avocado vinaigrette 1.

Filled / stuffed avocado

Prepare as above but omit the dressing; fill the hole left by the stone with lobster meat, crabmeat, prawns, etc. Coat the fish with Marie Rose sauce; sprinkle with a small pinch of cayenne pepper. Place a collop of lobster meat or a prawn on top of the sauce and sprinkle with chopped parsley.

Serve garnished with salad and accompanied with quarters of lemon.

Fruit compound salads

Uses:

Single hors-d'œuvre

A salad such as Japonaise, usually plated and garnished.

Hors-d'œuvre *variés*

(a) dressed in ravier dishes, garnished and offered as part of a selection (*variés*).

(b) as part of a plated assortment (*variés*).

Preparation: (see Salads, p. 247)

Note: Orange-based compound salads may be offered as an accompaniment to roast duck or duckling served as a main course.

Fruit cocktails / platters

Most fruits can be combined to produce fruit cocktails or platters; one popular example is given here:

Cocktail nouveau (*cocktail de fruit nouveau*)
or Fruit platter (*assiette de fruit nouveau*)

Use a mixture of the following:

Fresh limes   Fresh pineapple
Orange segments   Kiwi fruit
Pink grapefruit segments

1. Dice or segment the fruit neatly.
2. Dress in coupes or on plates and top with fruit sorbet.

A fruit coulis may be served with the fruit platter, or add a little sweet sparkling white wine to the fruit cocktail.

Modern trends and healthy eating

The trend towards a healthier lifestyle and diet means that it is necessary to provide healthier options on menus. Two major government health reports – NACNE and COMA – have highlighted the need to adapt our diet to improve our health; both reports recommend we eat less fat, sugar and salt but increase our fibre intake. Another reason for including vegetarian or healthier options on menus is the rapidly growing number of vegetarians and 'semi-vegetarians', who now make up approximately 10 per cent of the population in the UK. With this in mind, I have included some vegetarian and healthier types of hors-d'œuvres in this section.

Guacamole (ten portions)

2 large or 3 small, very ripe   juice of 1 lemon
   avocados (peeled and mashed)   pinch of cayenne pepper
5 tomatoes (blanched, peeled,   salt and black pepper
   de-seeded and chopped)
25 g (1 oz) fresh coriander leaves
   (chopped)

Garnish:

4 tomatoes   10 sprigs of coriander
10 lemon wedges   tortilla chips

1. Mix avocado, tomato concasse, coriander, lemon juice and seasoning to a smooth puree.
2. Either place the mix in the centre of a plate and decorate with the tip of a small

knife, or place the mix in a small bowl and place this in the centre of a plate.
3. Sprinkle the top with a small pinch of cayenne.
4. Garnish with tomato, lemon and coriander, and surround with tortilla/corn chips.

Crudités

Crudités, or raw vegetables, have gained in popularity. There are several options when it comes to serving crudités, and the method of presentation will influence the choice of vegetables. The most common presentation is to cut vegetable and salad items into convenient shapes, then provide a range of dips to accompany them. Some typical examples of vegetables for crudités include:

Batons of carrots	Whole small radish with the
Florets of cauliflower	stalk (about $^1/_2$ in) attached
Strips of celery	(to allow for holding)
Button mushrooms (quartered)	Strips of fennel
Diamonds of red/green pimentos	Leaves of chicory
Tomatoes (quartered)	Spring onions
Thick slices/half-moons of	Broccoli florets
cucumber	

Some dips include:

Marie Rose sauce	Chutney
Garlic mayonnaise	Greek dip
Mayonnaise (flavoured with	Chilli sauce
curry paste and mango)	Pesto

Crudités may also be presented in ravier dishes, for presentation on a cold buffet or as part of an hors-d'œuvre *variés*. In this case, several of the vegetables are served shredded or grated, for example:

Grated red cabbage	Quartered, peeled tomatoes
Grated carrot	Radish
Grated white cabbage	Canalayed sliced cucumber
Shredded celeriac	

The above vegetables may be presented in ravier dishes or glass or wooden bowls; garnish with lettuce and sliced lemon and accompany with various sauces and dressings. Some examples of suitable sauces and dressings include:

Vinaigrette dressing	French dressing
Mayonnaise	Marie Rose sauce
Garlic dressing	Lemon dressing
Shoyu dressing	Yoghurt and mint dressing (low-fat)
Vegan mayonnaise	

Savoury dips

Garlic mayonnaise (ten portions)

4 cloves of garlic (crushed)   squeeze of lemon juice
1/2 litre (1 pint) mayonnaise   salt and mignonette pepper

Mayonnaise and curry dip (ten portions)

2 tbsp curry paste   2 tbsp chopped mango chutney
1/2 litre (1 pint) mayonnaise   salt and mignonette pepper

Chilli dip (ten portions)

1 onion (diced)   1 tsp sugar
3 red chillies (chopped)   25 g (1 oz) paprika
25 g (1 oz) tomato puree   1 × 350 g (14 oz) tin of tomatoes
65 ml (2 fl oz) white vinegar   lemon juice

1. Place the onions and vinegar in a pan and reduce by half. Add paprika and chillies and simmer gently for 2 minutes.
2. Add the tomato puree and sugar, cook for a further minute, then add the diced tomatoes and enough of the juice to make a thick sauce.
3. Cook for a further 5 minutes, season and finish with lemon juice.
4. Allow to cool before use.

Note: Proprietary taco sauces may be used as an alternative to the chilli dip.

Greek dip (ten portions)

100 ml (4 fl oz) light tahini   pinch of ground caraway seeds
4 tbsp water   50 ml (2 fl oz) olive oil
75 ml (3 fl oz) tamari   seasoning
juice of 2 lemons

Mix all the ingredients in a food processor or whisk vigorously to combine.
Season and allow time for the mix to chill well and develop its flavour in a refrigerator.

'Vegan mayonnaise' (alternative, egg-free 'mayonnaise') (ten portions)

200 ml (8 fl oz) soya milk   4 tbsp fresh mixed herbs
  (unsweetened)   400–600 ml (14–22 fl oz) soya oil
8 tbsp lemon juice   salt and pepper
4 tbsp English mustard powder

1. Place all the ingredients apart from the herbs and soya oil in a blender.

2. Blend ingredients together and gradually add the oil until the desired consistency is obtained.
3. Add the chopped herbs and blend briefly to incorporate.
4. Adjust the seasoning.

Storage: The mayonnaise mix can be stored in an air-tight container in the refrigerator for 4 – 5 days.

Uses: As for mayonnaise.

Vegetarian/healthy eating alternatives

Layered vegetable terrine (ten portions)

65 ml (2¹/2 fl oz) sunflower oil	200 g (8 oz) carrots
16 large spinach leaves	200 g (8 oz) asparagus tips
568 ml (1 pint) skimmed milk	2 medium-sized leeks
50 g (2 oz) wholemeal flour	2 red peppers
1 onion	25 – 50g (2–3 oz) creamed horseradish
2 large eggs	340 g (12 oz) quark or curd cheese
2 bay leaves	Gamashio (see note p. 220)
200 g (8 oz) mangetout	grated nutmeg

1. Blanch, refresh and drain spinach leaves.
2. Place milk, onion and bay leaves on the heat to infuse for 10 minutes.
3. Place oil into a warm saucepan, add the flour and cook out for 3 – 4 minutes, stirring constantly.
4. Allow to cool, then gradually add the hot, strained milk; bring to the boil stirring constantly.
5. Season with nutmeg, gamashio and black pepper, allow to cook for a further 5 minutes.
6. When cool, add the quark or curd cheese, eggs and horseradish.
7. Halve the red peppers and place skin-side uppermost under the salamander until the skins bubble. Allow to cool then remove the skins.
8. Lightly steam the remaining vegetables, refresh and drain well. Peel the mangetout, half the leeks lengthways, and cut the carrots and peppers into long batons.
9. Line a terrine or loaf-tin with some of the spinach leaves, retaining some for the top.
10. Place 1 cm (¹/2 in) of the sauce in the base of the tin, then alternate with a layer of vegetables, then more sauce, then another layer of vegetables, finishing with a layer of sauce.
11. Fold over the spinach to enclose the mix and seal with the remaining leaves.
12. Place in an oven in a *bain-marie* and cook for 1–1¹/2 hours at gas mark 3–4/170°C/ 350°F until firm to the touch.
13. Allow to chill completely, preferably overnight, prior to turning out and slicing.

The colours in this dish may be modified by using other varieties of vegetable such as sweetcorn, tomatoes, green peppers, etc. The layers may also be coloured by using tomato or spinach puree in the sauce.

Gamashio (sesame salt): Gamashio is a perfect way to allow people to cut down on salt without them realizing it. It should be placed on the table in place of salt, people may then season with their normal amount but their salt intake will be reduced, depending on the ratio of sesame seed to salt. Gamashio can be bought commercially, but it is easy to make yourself by grinding ten parts sesame seeds to one part sea salt. Use as for sea salt.

Melon tomato and pineapple salad (ten portions)

1 large honeydew melon	30 ml (1 fl oz) olive oil
1/2 a fresh pineapple	300 g (10 oz) tomatoes (blanched,
25 g (1 oz) chives (chopped)	de-seeded and diced)
juice of 1 lemon	30 whole mint leaves for garnish
15 g (1/2 oz) fresh mint (finely chopped)	lettuce

1. Cut the melon into slices, then dice over a bowl to retain the juice.
2. Peel then dice the pineapple in a similar manner.
3. Add the tomatoes, mint and chives.
4. Mix together the oil and lemon juice and add to the fruit.
5. Lightly toss the fruit in the dressing and season to taste.
6. Allow to chill in the refrigerator.
7. Dress on lettuce (preferably of two different colours/types and garnish with mint leaves.

Black olive pâté (ten portions)

1 × 350g (14 oz) tin of black olives	
or equivalent (stoned)	2 cloves of garlic (crushed)
8 spring onions (diced)	200 ml (8 fl oz) red wine
6 medium-sized tomatoes (blanched,	15 g (1/2 oz) tomato puree
peeled, de-seeded and diced)	50 g (2 oz) fromage frais or curd cheese
75 ml (3 fl oz) olive oil	7 g (1/4 oz) fresh basil

1. Drain, rinse and dice the olives.
2. Heat the oil in a saucepan and gently cook the onions until soft; add the garlic, tomato puree and tomatoes, and cook to a pulp.
3. Add the red wine and olives. Season and reduce by boiling to a thick consistency.
4. Cool, then gently mix in the cheese.

Serve well chilled, garnished with salad and accompanied with toasted wholemeal bread, crispbread or warm pieces of pitta bread.

Humus

Below are two sets of quantities for humus; one is for a pâté and one for a dip, both are for four portions. As humus can become dry quite quickly, it is best served as fresh as possible. The 'dip' is the most authentic presentation, whereas the pâté is the more convenient for the customer to eat.

Pâté

100 g (4 oz) chickpeas (uncooked weight)	1/2 tsp salt
juice of 1 lemon	1 tbsp olive oil
50 ml (2 fl oz) water (cooking liquor)	3 tbsp light tahini
2 cloves garlic	freshly ground black pepper
	pinch of paprika

Accompaniments:

lemon quarters	shredded lettuce
picked parsley	watercress
wholemeal pitta bread	black olives

1. Soak peas overnight; drain and rinse, then cover with fresh water, bring to the boil and simmer gently for approximately 45 minutes.
2. Drain the peas, saving the cooking liquor.
3. Grind the peas in a food processor or coffee grinder.
4. Place the peas in a bowl, add the required amount of cooking liquor, tahini, lemon juice, paprika, olive oil and mix well.
5. To present: Line a plate with the shredded lettuce, portion the humus with an ice cream scoop and place in the middle of the lettuce. Decorate with lemon, paprika, olives, parsley, watercress and strips of toasted pitta bread.

Humus dip

Prepare as for pâté but adjust the ingredients as follows:

125 ml (1/4 pint) water (cooking liquor)	juice of 1 1/2 lemons
4 tsp light tahini	2 tbsp olive oil

1. Add the ingredients to the cooked, ground peas. Place dip in the centre of a plate and decorate the top with a fluted pattern, using a palette knife. Moisten the surface of the humus with olive oil to prevent it drying out.
2. Garnish with lemon, paprika, olives and strips of toasted pitta bread.

This may also be offered on cold buffets, in which case it is best presented in a dish or bowl surrounded by toasted pitta bread.

Tzatziki (ten portions)

1 kg strained Greek yoghurt	approximately 250 ml (¹/2 pint) olive oil
2 cucumbers (grated)	125 ml (¹/4 pint) vinegar
10 cloves of garlic (crushed)	salt and pepper

1. Grate the cucumbers and allow to drain of all excess liquid.
2. Mix together the cucumber, garlic and yoghurt.
3. Add the oil and vinegar alternately until the correct consistency is acquired – not too liquid, but not too firm.
4. Season, chill well and serve accompanied with toasted pitta bread. This may be served as a dip or as a starter.

Taramasalata (ten portions)

2 kg potatoes	juice of 4 lemons
200 g (8 oz) fish roe	1 small onion (finely chopped)
500 – 750 ml (1 – 1¹/2 pint) olive oil	

1. Wash the potatoes and boil them in their skins; drain, and when cool enough to handle, peel and mash.
2. Place in a liquidizer/food processor and add the roe and onion. Blend for approximately 10 minutes, adding the oil and lemon juice alternately drop by drop.
3. When the correct consistency is acquired, season and chill.

This may be served as a starter, garnished with salad and accompanied by toasted pitta bread, or served as a side dish to accompany vegetarian meals, especially ones based on beans or lentils.

Fish and shellfish hors-d'œuvre

Fish, and especially shellfish, can provide a wide and varied range of hors-d'œuvre, which is limited by only the imagination and creativity of the chef. The numerous species of fish and fish offal (such as caviar and roe) that are available, the different preservation methods (smoking, salting, etc.) and ways of cooking seafood (with sauces, in mousses, moulds, and so on), mean that the chef should have no trouble in the production of fish hors-d'œuvre.

In this section, I give a sample of what can be achieved using seafood; it goes without saying that the range of possibilities is almost endless. For further ideas and recipes see single hors-d'œuvre (p. 44) and Chapter 4 on Fish and Shellfish (pp. 68–77).

Herring (*hareng*)

Uses: Hors-d'œuvre, buffets, canapés, mousses, pâtés. soused (rollmops, bismarck, maatjes).

Rollmops (whole or in fillets) (ten portions)

10 small (whole) or 5 medium-sized herrings (fillets)

1. Wash, scale and remove the bones. Place under cold running water for several minutes to open the pores, then dry thoroughly with a cloth.
2. Fill the centre with shredded onion or quartered dill pickle, then roll up and hold in place with a cocktail stick.
3. Cover with the pickling mixture (see below), seal in a large glass jar or similar vessel and allow to stand for a minimum of 3 – 4 days (if possible, leave for one week before using).

Pickle for rollmops / Bismarck / maatjes (ten portions)

125 ml (¹/4 pint) vinegar	2 bay leaves
60 ml (2¹/2 fl oz) white wine	sprig of thyme
16 peppercorns	parsley stalks
100 g (4 oz) carrots (canalled	6 cloves
and sliced in rings)	juice of 2 lemons
2 onions	salt

1. Shred the onions, peel and slice the carrots.
2. Place the rest of the ingredients into a saucepan with a little water and bring to the boil. Remove from the heat and allow to cool.
3. Pour over the prepared herrings.

Bismarck

Prepare as for rollmops but serve flat.

Maatjes

Prepare as for bismarck but flavour with extra spices such as chillies, mustard and dill seeds.

Smoked herring fillets

Available in tins, packed in oil. Serve in ravier dishes garnished with sliced onions.

Mackerel (*maquereau*)

Fresh mackerel may be soused (pickled) as for rollmop herrings. Smoked mackerel fillets are often served as an hors-d'œuvre: with crushed peppercorns and serve garnished with salad. Horseradish cream is offered separately.

The quality of smoked mackerel varies considerably and can have a soft, pasty texture if not top quality.

Horseradish makes oily commodities easier to digest, it should therefore accompany most oily fish and those pickled in oil.

Smoked mackerel mousse (ten portions)

350 g (14 oz) smoked mackerel fillets   50 ml (2 fl oz) aspic jelly
100 g (4 oz) tomato concasse   125 ml (¹/₄ pint) double cream
15 g (¹/₂ oz) fresh chervil and   (lightly whipped)
   parsley (chopped)   seasoning

1. Remove all skin and bones from the fillets.
2. Pass the fish through a sieve or place in a food processor.
3. Add seasoning, aspic, tomato and herbs.
4. Fold in the cream and correct the seasoning.

Serve garnished with salad and accompanied by hot buttered toast.

Salmon – fresh (see also Gravalax, p. 176)

There are many applications for cooked, fresh salmon including salads, stir-fries, cocktails, tartlettes, barquettes, canapés and mousses.

Salmon – smoked

Use smoked salmon as you would for fresh salmon. Smoked salmon is one of the most popular hors-d'œuvre and is excellent in sandwiches and for buffet use. The fresh salmon is prepared by being split into two fillets/sides, then lightly salted and smoked.

Preparation:

The side of salmon is trimmed to remove any dry or bony parts. All the bones are removed (remove small bones with tweezers or pliers) and the surface is lightly rubbed with oil. The salmon is then sliced very thinly, at an angle, with a thin flexible knife (a special knife is often reserved or purchased for this purpose).

Storage:

Sides of smoked salmon should be stored in a fridge away from other foods, especially strong smelling ones as it can quickly pick up other flavours. Sides should be kept wrapped in oiled greaseproof paper to prevent drying out; sliced salmon should be tightly wrapped in clear plastic film.

Smoked salmon can be purchased ready sliced, but does not keep well and should be used as soon as possible.

Service:

Single hors-d'œuvre: Usually plated, garnished with salad and lemon and accompanied with brown bread and butter.

Hors-d'œuvre *variés*: Presented in raviers dishes, often shaped into cornets, dressed on lettuce, garnished with lemon and parsley.

Mousse of salmon

The following recipe can be used as fillings for cornets of smoked salmon, carolines, duchesses, buffets, hors-d'œuvre:

Mousse of salmon (cold)

500 g (1 lb) cooked smoked salmon
175 ml (¹/₃ pint) half-whipped
    double cream (very cold)
50 ml (2 fl oz) aspic or 15 g (¹/₂ oz)
    softened gelatine

red colouring
anchovy essence
cayenne pepper

1. Pass the fish through a sieve or place in a food processor and reduce to a fine paste.
2. Season with cayenne pepper and a few drops of anchovy essence.
3. Gently fold in the lightly whipped cream and colour with red colouring if necessary, taking care not to use too much.
4. Add some melted aspic or softened gelatine.
5. Pour into moulds and allow to set. The moulds can be lined with aspic and decorated, or turn out and finish with fish aspic.

Mousseline (hot)

Follow the instructions for mousse of salmon but omit the aspic/gelatine, and add two lightly beaten egg whites. Place the mixture over a bowl of iced water to chill thoroughly. Gradually beat in up to 500 ml (1 pint) of half-whipped double cream.

The mousseline mixture may be poached as quenelles or used to fill barquettes or tartlettes, prior to cooking.

Both recipes are suitable for other kinds of fish and shellfish, such as smoked trout, mackerel, lobster, prawns or crab. However, with some types of seafood it may be difficult to spoon-mould the quenelles as the mix may be too soft; in this case, poach in well-buttered dariole or quenelle moulds or add some breadcrumbs that have previously been soaked in milk (bread panade) and squeeze out before adding to the mixture. Poach in a *bain-marie* in a moderate oven until firm.

Smoked eel

Smoked eel is in my opinion superior in taste and texture to both smoked trout and smoked mackerel, although the name tends to put some people off.

Uses: Single and hors-d'œuvre *variés*, buffets, canapés, barquettes and tartlettes.

Preparation and Service: The whole eel is skinned, cut into sections and the bones are removed. It is presented in the same manner as for smoked trout/mackerel.

Smoked fish products

There are several other smoked fish products which are available in tins, these include smoked herrings, mussels, fish roe and sprats. These make an acceptable addition to an hors-d'œuvre *variés*.

Tuna / tunny fish (*le thon*)

Uses: Compound salads, hors-d'œuvre *variés*, stuffed tomatoes, canapés, tartlettes, barquettes, sandwiches.

Preparation and service: The cooked fish (usually tinned) is drained, shredded and seasoned with lemon juice, vinaigrette or mayonnaise.

Tuna, especially tinned tuna, has a soft texture and will benefit from the addition of diced onions and peppers which will give it a more pleasing crunchy texture.

Smoked trout (*truite fumé*)

Uses: Single and hors-d'œuvre *variés*, mousses, mousselines, carolines, duchesses.

Preparation and service:

Whole fish (single hors-d'œuvre) Gently remove the skin from the presentation side; remove both the lateral and dorsal bones. Present re-formed, accompanied by salad and lemon. Horseradish cream and brown bread and butter should be offered separately.

Fillets (hors-d'œuvre *variés*) Lightly oiled and dressed on lettuce, accompanied by peeled lemon slices, horseradish cream and parsley.

Fish and shellfish cocktails

Uses: Single and hors-d'œuvre *variés*, cold buffets.

Some examples include:

> **Prawn** *Cocktail de crevettes rose*
> **Crab** *Cocktail de crabe*
> **Shrimp** *Cocktail de crevettes*
> **Crayfish / Lobster** *Cocktail de homard*
> **Seafood** *Cocktail de fruits de mer*

Ingredients for fish / shellfish cocktail (makes one portion)

50 g (2 oz) cooked fish or shellfish	¼ peeled tomato
50–75 ml (2–3 fl oz) Marie Rose sauce	sprig of parsley
⅛ of an iceberg lettuce	small pinch of cayenne pepper
⅙ of a lemon	

Mix the fish/shellfish with the sauce and serve on a bed of lettuce and decorate.

Service: As a single hors-d'œuvre, plated or served in ravier dishes.

Mussels (*moules*)

Uses: Hot hors-d'œuvre (*moules marinière*; breadcrumbed and deep-fried); single hors-d'œuvre (seafood platters/cocktails); hors-d'œuvre *variés* (canapés; salads).

Preparation: See Chapter 4, Shellfish, p. 70.

Service: Mussels should be drained well, dressed with vinaigrette dressing and garnished with finely chopped onion and parsley.

Pickled mussels (convenience) Drain off the vinegar, rinse with cold water. Dress as for fresh mussels.

Smoked Mussels see Smoked Fish, p. 209–26.

Cockles (*les clocisses*)

Uses: Single hors-d'œuvre (seafood/shellfish platters/cocktails); hors-d'œuvre *variés* (canapés; salads).

Preparation and Service: Fresh cockles must be cleaned of all sand and grit by soaking in clean water for 24 hours. Prepare as for mussels, but extend the cooking time to 8 – 10 minutes.

Shrimps (*crevettes*)

Uses: Single hors-d'œuvre (seafood/shellfish platters/cocktails); hors-d'œuvre *variés* (potted shrimps).

Cooking: Plunge into boiling salted water and cook for 5 – 6 minutes (do not over cook); when the shrimps turn bright pink, drain and then remove the shells.

Potted shrimps

¹/₂ litre (1 pint) shrimps	pinch of cayenne pepper
100 g (4 oz) butter	pinch of nutmeg
pinch of powdered mace	

1. Melt the butter in a saucepan, add cooked shrimps and flavourings and bring almost to the boil.
2. Spoon into small tubs or ramekins.
3. Allow to cool. When cold pour over a little more melted butter to seal.

Dress on lettuce, garnish with salad and lemon quarters and serve with hot fingers of buttered toast.

Snails (*les escargots*)

Edible snails were once produced only in France, but this has changed and they are now also farmed in the UK. Snails have a small but enthusiastic following in Britain, and people either love them or hate them. Fresh snails that are large enough for consumption are first starved and then fed on flour (to clean them), they are soaked in water and vinegar, blanched and refreshed, and the tip of the tail is removed. They are then ready to be poached in white wine or a *court bouillon*. Once cooked, they are drained and replaced in their cleaned shells; the shells are sealed with garlic butter. To keep snails upright when heating they should be placed on a layer of salt.

Convenience: These are purchased as one tin of cooked snails and one bag of cleaned shells. All the chef needs to do is to replace the snails into the shells and seal them with butter prior to heating through in the oven. Convenience snails can be very tough and chewy if overcooked or reheated on too high a temperature.

Butter for snails

The traditional snail butter has always been garlic butter. It seems a shame, however, to limit them to this one flavour; thus, along with the original butter, a few alternatives are also given below.

Garlic butter for snails (*beurre d'escargots*) (makes 500 g (1 lb))

(Approximately 100 – 150 g
   (4 – 6 oz) should be sufficient for
   twelve snails, depending on shell size.)
400 g (12 oz) butter
50 g (2 oz) finely chopped shallots

15 g ($^1\!/_2$ oz) crushed garlic
25 g (1 oz) chopped parsley
pinch of finely-chopped tarragon
   and chervil
mignonette pepper

Soften butter to a smooth paste, add the rest of the ingredients and mix until smooth.

Café de Paris butter (500 g (1 lb))

400 g (12 oz) butter
25 g (1 oz) parsley
$^1\!/_4$ of a small bottle of
   Worcester sauce
$^1\!/_8$ bottle Tabasco sauce
few drops anchovy essence
2 tsp curry powder

2 tsp French mustard
10 g ($^1\!/_4$ oz) basil
10 g ($^1\!/_4$ oz) rosemary
2 bay leaves
10 g ($^1\!/_4$ oz) mixed herbs (all the herbs
   should be finely chopped)

Soften butter to a smooth paste, add the rest of the ingredients and mix until smooth.

Paprika butter (500 g (1 lb))

400 g (12 oz) softened butter
1 heaped tbsp paprika

few drops of white wine vinegar

Soften butter. Mix paprika and vinegar and blend well with the butter.

Vegetable hors-d'œuvre

Vegetable hors-d'œuvre can be used:

(a) As a single hors-d'œuvre
(b) As part of an hors-d'œuvre *variés*
(c) As a hot hors-d'œuvre

Single vegetable hors-d'œuvre

These are vegetables which are served alone with a sauce or dressing, for example globe artichokes or asparagus tips.

Hors-d'œuvres *variés*

Many vegetables can be served as part of an hors-d'œuvre *variés*; the choice depends on what is in season and striking a balance between items, for example, preparing a colour scheme that is complementary.

Asparagus tips (*asperges*)

Types: White and green.

Season: Spring through to summer.

Convenience: Frozen or tinned.

Uses:

Hot with melted butter, sauce hollandaise or maltaise, mousseline

Cold with vinaigrette, French dressing or mayonnaise.

Quality and purchasing:
1. Look for fresh, firm shoots, with closed compact tips. Spreading tips indicate older asparagus and flat angular stalks tend to be woody and tough.
2. Avoid asparagus with thin, woody, dry or dirty stems.
3. Asparagus is sold loose or in bundles and graded according to the thickness of the stem and plumpness of the buds.

Storage: Asparagus should be stored in a cool, well-ventilated room.

Preparation:
1. Scrape or peel the stem with a small knife.
2. Wash well under cold running water.
3. Tie into bundles prior to boiling. Special asparagus pans are available which raise the points (the most delicate parts) out of the water, this means that the tougher stems are boiled and the tips are lightly steamed.

Cooking:

Boil in salted water 10–15 minutes.

Steam 'atmospheric', 10–15 minutes, not tied in bundles.

Steam 'half bar', 2 – 8 minutes.

The times given here are only a rough guide: thinner or better quality asparagus (points) will require less cooking than the sprew/sprucetips or thicker, older asparagus. To test if cooked: squeeze the stem between the thumb and finger, this should give under light pressure. Take great care not to over cook.

Asparagus for serving cold should be refreshed under cold running water until cold; do not allow the asparagus to lie in the water for any length of time as the flavour will seep into the water.

Convenience asparagus:

Frozen is definitely inferior to fresh asparagus, but is far superior to tinned in both flavour and texture.

Tinned is very soft in texture and is suitable only for items that require an asparagus flavour without the texture, for example mousses, soups, quiches, barquettes and tartlettes.

Preparation and service of globe artichokes

Globe artichokes are available in the UK from July to October. They are related to the thistle family, and the part that is eaten is the unopened flower bud. Globe artichokes have no connection to Jerusalem artichokes, which are a completely different vegetable, and although similar in flavour, resemble knobbly potatoes. Globe artichokes are normally served as a first course (hors-d'œuvre).

To cook an artichoke

Allow one artichoke per person. Wash well and remove any small lower leaves. Boil the heads in salted water to which a little lemon juice or vinegar has been added (the acid in the water helps to keep the artichoke green). Cooking times will vary from 30 to 45 minutes, depending on the size of the artichoke. If cooked in a pressure cooker or steamer, the cooking time can be reduced by 5 – 7 minutes at high pressure. The artichokes are ready when a leaf comes away with a gentle pull.

To serve an artichoke

Whole artichokes are served intact with melted butter or Hollandaise sauce, however, they must be 'de-choked'. To de-choke an artichoke: gently part the inner leaves, removing the very small ones in the centre. Then scrape out the hairy 'choke' with a teaspoon. The centre of an artichoke can be filled with a thick sauce, for example a flavoured mayonnaise, or a stuffing. Special artichoke plates may be used for the service of whole artichokes, these have one section for the sauce and one for the discarded leaves. Otherwise, serve artichokes on a medium-sized plate with a side plate for the discarded leaves.

To serve artichoke hearts

Remove all the leaves and the choke from a cooked artichoke and trim the heart into a neat round with a sharp knife.

Convenience artichokes

Both artichoke hearts and bottoms are available tinned. The hearts are drained and dressed with vinaigrette and used as part of an hors-d'œuvre *variés*. Artichoke bottoms have long been prized by chefs and gourmets; these are normally filled and garnished to resemble tartlettes. Many classical garnishes associated with hot preparations include artichoke bottoms, but they are also ideal for garnishing cold buffet items and as part of an hors-d'œuvre *variés*.

Sauces for artichokes

Hot artichokes are delicious served plain with melted butter, to which a squeeze of lemon juice and a pinch of black pepper has been added. Three sauces suitable for serving with cold artichokes are: sauce brettone, sauce vert and vinaigrette (see Chapter 7, Sauces and Dressings, p. 195).

A la grecque / portugaise

These are really vegetable marinades: the vegetables are cooked in a flavoured liquid and left to cool in the cooking liquid. The vegetables are presented ice cold in the unstrained cooking liquor. All manner of vegetables can be prepared in this way – button onions, leeks and celery are some examples, but cauliflower and button mushrooms are the most frequently used. The vegetables may be offered as hors-d'œuvre or on cold buffets.

A la grecque (1 litre / 2 pints)

750 ml (1 1/2 pint) water	sprig of thyme
250 ml (8 fl oz) olive oil	20 white peppercorns
juice of 4 lemons	20 coriander seeds
4 bay leaves	salt

Place all the ingredients into a stainless steel pan and bring to the boil; skim and simmer for 10 minutes. Add the vegetables and cook until *al dente* (the vegetables must still retain a good texture after cooling in the liquor). Allow to cool and chill thoroughly.

A la portugaise (1 litre / 2 pints)

2 finely chopped onions	250 ml (8 fl oz) dry white wine
100 ml (3 fl oz) olive oil	4 bay leaves
500 g (1 lb) tomato concasse	sprig of thyme
(or equivalent of tinned	6 cloves of garlic (crushed)
plum tomatoes)	20 g (3/4 oz) chopped parsley
100 g (3 1/2 oz) tomato puree	salt and pepper

Sweat the onions and garlic in the oil until soft. Add the white wine, bring to the boil, and add the remaining ingredients apart from the parsley; simmer for 10 – 15 minutes. Add the chopped parsley and vegetables and simmer in the cooking liquor as for *à la grecque*.

Note: Tinned tomatoes should be used in this dish (unless fresh ripe plum tomatoes are available) as they give a richer flavour than salad tomatoes.

Sweet peppers (*poivrons*)

Sweet peppers along with hot peppers or chillies, are members of the capsicum family. Sweet peppers are also known as pimentos.

Season: This used to be in the autumn, September – November, but now available all year round.

Quality: Should be smooth with a glossy brightness, have a taught skin and no sign of blemishes.

Colours: Peppers may be green, yellow or red. Green peppers are the most common; they are unripe in this state and not as sweet or soft in texture as when they are red or yellow.

Size and shape: They can be up to 25 cm (10 in) long and vary in shape, from long and narrow to almost round.

Storage: Store in the salad compartment of a refrigerator, where they will keep up to five days. Red peppers are riper and therefore more perishable; green peppers are less ripe and have a longer shelf-life.

Uses: Hors-d'œuvre (for example, stuffed); in speciality dressing (*à la grecque* or *portugaise*; garnishing, canapés, crudités.

Convenience: Pimentos may be obtained tinned or frozen: the tinned variety are pre-cooked, the frozen are blanched (half-cooked). Both have a superb colour and are excellent for garnishing. Air-dried pimentos are produced on the Continent and have a superb flavour.

Fennel (*fenouil*)

The flavour of fennel is similar to that of anise (aniseed), but it lacks the pungency of anise and is more sweet and aromatic.

Uses: In salads (raw); suitable for use with speciality liquors such as *à la grecque* or *portugaise*; cooked and served as part of an hors-d'œuvre *variés*, served with a suitable dressing.

Preparation:
1. Trim the fennel bulb, stalks and leaves.
2. Boil or steam for approximately 10 – 20 minutes (depending on size), take care not to overcook.
3. Drain well and cut into quarters lengthways. Dress in entrée dishes with a suitable dressing.

Storage: On racks in a cool, well-ventilated room.

Fennel fronds, which are the top fern-like part of the plant, are excellent for garnishing and decoration of hors-d'œuvre, salads and buffet pieces, especially fish.

Sweetcorn (maize)

Uses: Whole as a hot hors-d'œuvre (corn on the cob); in kernels as part of an hors-d'œuvre *variés*.

Preparation: Cooked sweetcorn kernels are dressed with vinaigrette and garnished with diced red and green peppers.

Baby sweetcorn

This is a first-class product that has gained in popularity. It has a delicate flavour, superb crunchy texture and a bright colour which will enhance the appearance of any selection of single salads or hors-d'œuvre *variés*.

Preparation: Wash well, then lightly steam or boil (never overcook). Drain well then dress on lettuce leaves with a light dressing.

If using sweetcorn kernels, I would advise against the tinned variety as this has little texture and leaves a bitter aftertaste. The first choice should be freshly cooked corn on the cob, with the kernels removed after refreshing. However, frozen sweetcorn is an acceptable alternative.

Mangetout

This is a vegetable that has also become more popular in recent years. 'Mange tout' literally means 'eat all', and as the name implies, the small underdeveloped pea pods are cooked and eaten intact. Other varieties include sugar peas and sugar snap peas.

Uses: As part of a vegetable stir-fry (hot hors-d'œuvre); as a garnish for salads; as a salad served on its own; as part of an hors-d'œuvre *variés*.

Mangetout must never be overcooked. It is topped and tailed to remove any remaining stalk and flower, it is then lightly steamed, stir-fried or boiled. When cooked correctly it has a crisp texture, excellent flavour and is deep green.

Button onions

Uses: Fresh button onions are best prepared with a speciality liquor such as *à la grecque* or *portugaise*. They are lightly steamed or boiled, refreshed and combined with the liquor and left to marinate. They may also be pickled.

Button mushrooms

Uses: As a single salad served on its own; as part of an hors-d'œuvre *variés*; suitable for *à la grecque* or *portugaise*; breadcumbed with chopped garlic and parsley and deep-fried; served as a hot hors-d'œuvre with mayonnaise or flavoured dips; stuffed. (See Stuffed Vegetables, p. 235)

Beetroot (*betterave*)

Season: Available all year round.

Quality:

(a) Must be clean and free from soil.
(b) Should be round and firm.
(c) Free from cuts and spade marks.

Uses: Salads (mixed or single); as part of an hors-d'œuvre *variés*.

Storage: On racks in a cool, well-ventilated room. Never leave in sacks or boxes as it has a tendency to go mouldy.

Preparation: Wash well and steam or boil until tender. When cooked the skin should come away with gentle rubbing. Allow to cool or refresh and peel. Slice or dice and dress with finely diced onion, vinegar or dressings such as vinaigrette, mayonnaise or natural yoghurt.

French beans (*haricot vert*)

Season: June to December.

Quality:

(a) The beans must be bright green and firm, not wilted.
(b) They should be medium-sized and not stringy.
(c) They should be absolutely fresh, clean and unmarked.

Storage: In a cool, dry place, on well-ventilated racks.

Uses: As a single salad; as part of an hors-d'œuvre *variés*; as an ingredient in salads such as *salad niçoise*.

Note: A recent introduction that has been of great benefit to the chef (especially in the winter months), has been the appearance of 'Kenya beans': these are perfect in size and have a superbly crunchy texture when cooked correctly. Although the price may at times be prohibitive, they are an excellent addition to the chef's repertoire of foods.

Cauliflower (*choufleur*)

Season: At its best in late summer, but available for most of the year.

Quality:

(a) Ensure that there is no discoloration on the florets.
(b) The florets should be firm.
(c) The stem should be hard and white.
(d) The leaves should not be limp.

Storage: Cool, well-ventilated storeroom.

Uses: For service *à la grecque* or *portugaise*, crudités, single salad.

Stuffed vegetables (*legumes farcis*)

Uses: Hot or cold hors-d'œuvre; as a single hors-d'œuvre or as part of an hors-d'œuvre *variés*; buffets.

Types: Tomatoes, peppers, mushrooms, aubergines.

Recipes for hot stuffed vegetables can be found in most cookbooks. 'Beef tomatoes' are a relatively recent product: these are large tomatoes which are halved and filled as for regular tomatoes.

Sweet peppers

All colours of pepper may be used for cold hors-d'œuvre service.

Preparation:
1. First, remove the skins. This is done by halving the peppers lengthways, removing the seeds and white pith, and placing the peppers under the salamander (grill) skin-side uppermost until the skin bubbles and darkens. Allow the peppers to cool slightly and carefully peel off the skin (a portion of the stalk is usually left on to keep the pepper's shape).
2. The peppers are marinated in olive oil and garlic and stuffed with a suitable filling such as rice salad or ratatouille; dress with olive oil and chopped fresh basil leaves.

Mushrooms

These are often filled with a mushroom duxelle that has been bound with breadcrumbs. (Note that the lack of correct seasoning is often a problem with this filling.) Additions to this classic filling are limitless. Examples include: smoked ham, cheese, anchovies, chicken and crabmeat. The texture of the filling should be fine enough to allow it to be piped into upturned mushroom cups in a decorative whirl.

Aubergines

Aubergines make an excellent stuffed vegetable and the dark purple colour of their skin will enhance any presentation.

To prepare for stuffing:
1. First, cut the aubergines into two lengthways.
2. Criss-cross the flesh with a small knife.
3. Lightly fry or grill with a little oil.
4. Remove the flesh with a spoon, taking care not to damage the skin.
4. Dice the flesh and combine with the filling of your choice, such as tomatoes, garlic and parsley, tuna, crabmeat or prawns.
5. Dress with an oil-based dressing, preferably with chopped fresh basil leaves (basil leaves can also be used as a garnish).

Stuffed tomatoes (*tomates farcis*)

Tomatoes make an excellent addition to any hors-d'œuvre. The choice of fillings limited only by the chef's imagination. An old favourite recipe is as follows:

Tomatoes à *la* monegasque (ten portions)

20 small tomatoes   salt and mill pepper
5 tbsp of olive oil   20 sprigs of parsley
3 tbsp white wine vinegar

Filling:

100 g (3^1/$_2$ oz) drained, cooked   2 small onions (peeled and
   tuna (finely chopped)   finely chopped)
4 hard-boiled eggs (shelled   3 tbsp of chopped mixed fresh herbs:
   and finely chopped)   parsley, tarragon and chervil
                                           4 tbsp of mayonnaise

1. Cut off the top of the tomatoes at the rounded end and remove the pips with a spoon.
2. Sprinkle the insides of the tomatoes with a mixture of oil, vinegar, salt and pepper and allow to marinate for approximately 40 minutes.
3. Meanwhile, prepare the stuffing by combining all the ingredients, mixing well and lightly season.
4. Pile the filling into the tomatoes, replace the tops at an angle and garnish with picked parsley.

Convenience vegetables

In some instances frozen vegetables can be used as a substitute for fresh ones, and certain tinned or pickled varieties are ideal for serving on an hors-d'œuvre *variés*. For example:

- Frozen cauliflower florets – for use in *à la grecque* or *portugaise*.
- Tinned ratatouille – as part of an hors-d'œuvre selection or filling.
- Pickled red cabbage/beetroot/mixed pickles/onions/gherkins and tinned red pimentos – for use in salads and for garnishing canapés.
- Tinned tomatoes – for use in the preparation of *à la portugaise*, ratatouille and compound salads.
- Tinned new potatoes – for use dressed as a single salad or sliced and used in salad Niçoise, or combined with onion, vinaigrette, mayonnaise for a potato salad.
- Dehydrated mushroom duxelle mix – for use in stuffings.
- Frozen peas – for use in various salads.
- Pickled capers – for use as a garnish.
- Frozen asparagus tips – used in place of fresh asparagus.
- Various tinned beans – for use in salads.
- Frozen whole green beans – for use in salads like salad Niçoise.
- Tinned water chestnuts – for use in stir-fries.

Rice and pasta dishes

Rice

Although rice is often served as a part of an hors-d'œuvre selection, there are not that many recipes which cover this area. Thus it is up to the experience and imagination of the chef to come up with suitable rice-based dishes.

Hot rice preparations such as risotto may, of course, be served as a hot hors-d'œuvre. Kedgeree is not seen as often as it once was on breakfast menus, but it has found a new use as a hot hors-d'œuvre. Many rice preparations are suited to an hors-d'œuvre selection and certain compound salads may be offered as single hors-d'œuvre, for example such salads as Andalouse, Egyptienne, Mikado and Carmen. Any rice which is left over from service with entrees can be featured cold; it is usually enhanced with colourful additions such as green peas and diced red peppers. Rice that has been prepared as a pilaff can be flavoured with curry and garnished with sultanas, pineapple and coconut. Left-over risotto or paella can be pressed into saverin or dariole moulds, chilled, turned out and garnished. Chicken livers, previously sautéed in butter, can be diced and combined with rice and vegetables.

Pasta

Pasta is often served as a hot hors-d'œuvre, but it may also be presented cold, in which case the smaller pasta shapes are used, such as macaroni, shells and ravioli. Stuffed tortellini is an excellent dish, especially when filled with a fish or seafood mixture of salmon or prawn.

Rice salad (ten portions)

500 g (1 lb) of rice (boiled)	4 cloves of garlic (crushed)
2 red peppers (peeled or tinned)	150 g (6 oz) peas (cooked)
6 tomatoes (blanched, peeled,	125 ml (1/4 pint) vinaigrette dressing
de-seeded and diced)	Worcestershire sauce (few shakes)

1. Slice the red peppers lengthways into 1/2 cm (1/4 in) strips.
2. Combine the rest of the ingredients.
3. Garnish with chopped parsley.

This salad will benefit from being allowed to marinate for a few hours or overnight.

Pasta salads

Small cooked pasta can be prepared as for rice salad. Also, cooked shells or macaroni can be combined with other ingredients, for example seafood, chicken breasts, tomatoes, olives, and so on, and dressed with a suitable sauce, such as a light Marie Rose sauce for seafood. Fresh pasta such as ravioli or small cannelloni may also be used, especially with various fillings, for example smoked salmon and spinach puree.

Convenience products

Most pasta can be purchased pre-prepared, ready for cooking. Ravioli is available pre-prepared in a sauce. Proprietary brands of pasta sauce and pesto are also available ready-made.

Meat hors-d'œuvre

Many types of meat can be used for hors-d'œuvre. Pre-prepared items include: continental sausages, salami, liver sausage, garlic sausage, mortadella, pâté, terrines, galantines, rillets and rillons of pork, ham, smoked ham, smoked beef (pastrami), turkey breast, air-dried beef. Left-over cooked meats can be made into salads or mousses.

Most of the above may be served plated as single hors-d'œuvre or dressed in raviers or on flats and garnished with salad. Meat-based compound salads also make an excellent hors-d'œuvre.

Pâté maison 1

2¹/₂ kg (5 lb) chicken livers	50 g (2 oz) dried mixed herbs
1 kg (2 lb) onions	or 100g (4 oz) of fresh herbs
1 kg (2 lb) stewing veal	8 – 10 eggs
500 g (1 lb) green bacon	¹/₂ litre (1 pint) cream
500 g (1 lb) shoulder of pork	¹/₄ bottle red wine
2 heads garlic	¹/₄ bottle brandy
25 g (1oz) mixed spice	200 g (8 oz) butter

1. Gently fry the diced pork, veal, onions and crushed garlic in the butter with the herbs until semi-cooked.
2. Add the drained chicken livers and diced bacon.
3. Gently fry the livers until sealed and half-cooked, taking care not to overcook (they should still be pink in the centre).
4. Add the red wine and boil for a few minutes to reduce.
5. Pass the mixture twice through the mincer.
6. Place in a mixing machine with a whisk and beat in the brandy. Add the eggs one by one. Check the seasoning.
7. Line pâté moulds or earthenware dishes with streaky bacon and add the mixture.
8. Cover with buttered tinfoil and place in a tray filled with water (*bain-marie*).
9. Cook in a moderate oven gas mark 4/150 – 180°C/300 – 350°F for 2 – 2¹/₂ hours until set. Cool overnight, then slice or portion with a spoon.

Pâté maison 2 (*terrine maison*)

1 shoulder of pork (boned)	1 kg (2 lb) streaky bacon
5 kg (10 lb) chicken livers	500 g (1 lb) brown sugar
2 kg (4 lb) onions	1 bottle of sherry
3 heads of garlic	¹/₂ bottle of brandy

50 g (2 oz) mixed spice
15 g (½ oz) nutmeg
2 litres (4 pints) single cream
200 g (8 oz) butter

75 – 100 g (3 – 4 oz) aspic
   jelly granules
18 – 20 eggs
seasoning

1. Sweat diced pork and onions for a few minutes, then add the crushed garlic.
2. Add the chicken livers and cook for a few minutes (do not overcook).
3. Add the brown sugar.
4. Mince, add the rest of the ingredients (apart from the bacon) and mix well.
5. Check the seasoning and line the moulds with the bacon.
6. Place a layer of the pâté into the mould one-third of the way up.
7. Add some diced turkey breast, pork fillet or kidney, add another layer of pâté mix and repeat, finishing with a layer of pâté.
8. Cook as for Pâté Maison 1. When cool, cover the surface with melted butter or lard.

Pâtés and terrines

The term 'terrine' refers to the earthenware terrine dish in which it is served. Terrines tend to be more course in texture than pâté, although this is not always the case.

Pâté en croute

This traditional French pâté en croute is more like a pork pie than a pâté in pastry.

350 g (12 oz) lean pork
   (minced twice)
150 g (6 oz) fat pork
   (minced once)
1 pork fillet (marinated
   overnight in brandy)

50 g (2 oz) pistachio nuts
500 g (1 lb) pork fat
diced truffle
3 egg yolks
500 g (1 lb) pâté pastry (see below)

1. Cut the pork into strips and season with salt, black pepper, mixed spice and nutmeg.
2. Mince, then chill until very cold.
3. Working the mix over a bowl of ice, add the nuts and truffle.
4. Line the mould with the pastry, followed by the thinly sliced pork fat.
5. Place a layer of pâté into the base of the mould; wrap the pork fillet in fat and lace down the centre of the mould. Cover with the rest of the mix.
6. Top with the remaining pastry and decorate.
7. Glaze with beaten egg yolks and bake for one hour at gas mark 4/140°C/270°F.

Pâté pastry

500 g (1 lb) soft flour
200 g (8 oz) lard

good pinch of salt
cold water to bind

1. Rub the lard into the sieved flour and salt.
2. Gradually incorporate the water to make a paste.

Hot or warm meat salads (salades chaudes et tièdes de viands)

One of the latest trends in cooking is 'hot' or warm salads. These consist of hot or warm items served on a base of chilled salad. When prepared correctly, hot salads are delicious and are particularly popular with the health conscious diner. Once the principles of how to prepare a hot salad are grasped, it is well worth the time and trouble to experiment and create new examples.

Rules for preparing hot salads

1. The salad ingredients should be as fresh and as crisp as possible.
2. The salad items should be very well chilled so as to contrast sharply with the hot items.
3. The salads should be lightly dressed at the last minute to retain crispness.
4. The hot items should be cooked to order and only added to the salad immediately prior to service.

Salade chaude provençale (ten portions)

350 g (12 oz) lambs liver	50 g (2 oz) chopped parsley
(or chicken livers)	100 g (4 oz) butter
4 cloves of garlic	200 g (8 oz) bacon (*lardons*)

Garnish/Salad:

10 stuffed olives	50 g (2 oz) grated horseradish
lemon wedges	8 tomatoes (blanched, peeled
1 iceberg lettuce	and quartered)
4 potatoes (cooked and diced)	125 ml (¹/4 pint) olive oil

1. Remove the membrane from the liver, slice very thinly and bat out gently.
2. Place garnish (salad) ingredients in a bowl and lightly dress with the horseradish and oil beaten together.
3. Heat up a heavy frying pan and add the butter; as the butter starts to foam (take care it does not burn), add the liver.
4. Cook for 1 – 2 minutes each side until the blood starts to show through. Remove from pan and keep warm.
5. Add bacon and chopped garlic to the pan and cook until the garlic just starts to colour (approximately 1 minute). Add the chopped parsley and pour over the livers.
6. Arrange the salad around the edge of a fish plate.
7. Cut the liver into strips and place in the centre of the salad, pour over a little of the butter, bacon and garlic.
8. Garnish with an olive in the centre, wedges of lemon and extra chopped parsley.

Salade chaude tikka (ten portions)

For the tikka marinade:

4 tsp coriander seeds
2 tsp cumin seeds
2 tsp chilli powder
1/2 jar tikka paste
juice of 4 lemons
50 g (2 oz) tomato puree
1/2 litre (16 fl oz) natural strained
   yoghurt

50 g (2 oz) root ginger
1 head of garlic
3 × 1 1/2 kg (3 1/4 lb) chickens
1 sliced onion (fried quickly in
   a little oil until brown)

Salad:

1/2 a curly endive or frisée lettuce
1/2 a radiccio lettuce (shredded)
2 heads of chicory (chopped)
10 medium-sized spinach leaves
mint leaves to garnish

Mint and cucumber raita:

1/2 litre (1 pint) natural yoghurt
25 g (1 oz) chopped fresh mint
1 cucumber (grated)

1. Grind the seeds, then combine with the crushed garlic, grated ginger, lemon juice, tikka paste and yoghurt.
2. Bone out the chickens and place in marinade for a minimum of 3 hours. Then place on oiled skewers.
3. Cook the chicken, brushed with a little oil, at as hot a temperature as possible in a tandoor or on a char-grill. (The ideal texture for the chicken is to be charred on the outside but soft and moist in the centre.)
4. Combine the salad ingredients; arrange and place the cooked chicken in the centre, accompanied by the browned onions.
5. The mint and cucumber raita should be offered separately.

Pepperoni, apple and pepper salad (ten portions)

200 ml (1/2 pint) olive oil
300 g (10 oz) sliced pepperoni
6 red peppers (de-seeded and
   cut into strips)
6 yellow peppers (de-seeded
   and cut into strips)
5 cloves of garlic, thinly sliced

125 ml (1/4 pint) balsamic vinegar
mixed leaves: radiccio, frisée,
   lamb's lettuce, oak leaf, etc.
2 eating apples, peeled and finely
   chopped
seasoning

1. Heat the oil to a high temperature in a frying pan or sauté pan; add the peppers and cook until they start to char.
2. Add the garlic, cook until lightly browned, then add the pepperoni and balsamic vinegar. Cook on a high heat until most of the vinegar has evaporated.
3. Place the washed and drained mixed leaves in a bowl and dress with the pepperoni and peppers. Garnish with the chopped apple.

NINE

Salads

There are 'now' three types of salads; I say now because of the recent popularity of 'hot salads' (*Salades chaudes*) (see Hors-d'œuvre, p. 240). Other than hot salads, salads fall into two main groups:

(a) 'simple' or single/plain salads, and;
(b) 'compound' salads.

Single salads

The simple or single salads are further divided into:

1. Single salads, containing one main ingredient such as cucumber, tomato, lettuce, potato, beetroot, pimento, vegetables (*salade russe*), coleslaw or rice.
2. Mixed salads, containing a mixture of 'salad' ingredients, for example green salad (*salade vert*) is a mixture of different types of lettuce, plus watercress, sorrel, Belgian endive, spring onions, etc. Mixed salad (*salade panachée*) ia a mixture of prepared single salads such as tomatoes, cucumber, watercress, radishes, spring onions, arranged into a selection. French salad (*salade française*) has a base of lettuce, tomato and cucumber with quartered hard-boiled egg. These are just some suggestions; other salad items may be added for variety. French dressing is offered separately.

Single salads are often served dressed with vinaigrette as part of an hors-d'œuvre selection. Potatoes, vegetables and coleslaw may be dressed with vinaigrette or mayonnaise, and quite often both are used. Mixed salads may be served on buffets or to accompany a main course, in which case French dressing is offered separately in sauceboats. Salads may be presented in bowls (wood, glass, etc.), 'crescents' or ravier dishes (for buffets and hors-d'œuvre selections).

Points for consideration when preparing salad items

1. Always use the freshest possible ingredients.

2. Wash thoroughly in cold water; ice in the water will assist in keeping items like lettuce crisp.
3. Check for damage, insects, discolouration, rot, etc.
4. Remove any tough parts such as the thick skin on cucumbers, tomatoes and peppers, and any course centres of the leaves of lettuces and cabbages.
5. Drain the items thoroughly in a salad basket or colander, taking care to avoid bruising. Lay onto a clean tea towel and gently pat dry.
6. Keep cold until required.
7. Tear rather than cut lettuce if possible as this will lessen the damage to the cells within the leaves and it will retain more of its nutritive value. If, as in the case of a chiffonade, a knife must be used, it should be a stainless steel one as this will not react with the plants juices (a carbon steel knife may taint or impart a bitter flavour).
8. Prepare and dress as close to service as possible to ensure crispness and to preserve the vitamin C content.
9. Store all salad ingredients separately in a covered section of a refrigerator or in a separate fridge away from meats or fish. Salad ingredients must not be allowed to contaminate or be contaminated by other ingredients, either cooked or raw.

Potato salad (*salade de pommes de terre*) (ten portions)

850 g (2 lb) potatoes	parsley/chives
50 g (2 oz) onions	125 ml (1/4 pint) vinaigrette
500 ml (1 pint) mayonnaise	seasoning

1. Wash and scrub the potatoes – do not peel. Steam, boil or bake in their jackets. Allow to cool, then peel and dice. Peel and finely dice the onions and add to the potatoes.
2. Toss the potatoes and onions in the vinaigrette and season. Cohere with mayonnaise and garnish with chopped chives or parsley.

Note: The potatoes benefit from being slightly warm when the vinaigrette is added, this is because more of the dressing tends to be absorbed giving a better flavour than when dressed cold.

New potato salad (*salade de pommes de terre nouvelle*) (ten portions)

1 kg (2¼ lb) small new potatoes	parsley/fresh mint
50 g (2 oz) onions	125 ml (1/4 pint) vinaigrette
500 ml (1 pint) mayonnaise	seasoning

1. Wash and scrub the potatoes, but do not peel them. Steam or boil the potatoes, peel and finely dice the onions and add to the potatoes. Toss the potatoes and onions in the vinaigrette and season.
2. Cohere with mayonnaise and garnish with chopped or whole fresh mint leaves or parsley.

Various ingredients may be added to potato salads, for instance, for German potato salad (*salade de pommes de terre allemande*) sliced or diced apples is added. Other variations include the addition of sliced continental sausages such as frankfurters or strips of garlic sausage. Dressings for potato salads may be flavoured with chopped garlic or herbs such as mint or chervil; watercress leaves may also be added to make a *salade cressoniere*. Curry paste and chopped mango chutney can be used to flavour mayonnaise. A small pinch of cayenne pepper sprinkled on top of the mayonnaise will enhance the flavour of potato salads. Other vegetables that may be presented as single salads include:

Red peppers (*salade de piment*) Cut off both ends of the peppers, cut through the side, open out and remove the seeds. Grill until the skin bubbles then remove the skin. Cut into batons or julienne. Dress with vinaigrette and season, garnish with sliced onion.

Radishes (*salade de radis*) Trim the stalk to 1 cm in length and cut off the roots. Place in iced water to crisp up. Dress with vinaigrette.

Artichoke bottoms (*salade d'artichauts*) Cut the cooked artichoke bottoms into juliennes and dress with lemon-flavoured vinaigrette.

Asparagus (*salade d'asperges*) Cook the asparagus until it is just done. Refresh and drain well. Cut into approximately 3 cm (1 in) lozenges (diamonds), discarding any tough stalks and reserving the points for the top. Dress with lemon dressing and garnish with blanched and refreshed lemon zest.

Bean salads Soaked and cooked beans such a haricot, red kidney, flageolets and black-eyed, may be served dressed with vinaigrette, either alone as with haricot bean salad (*salade d'haricot blancs*) and flageolets bean salad (*salade de flageolets*), or in combination as a mixed bean salad. Sprouted beans have become increasingly popular for use in salads.

Rice salad (*salade de riz*) (ten portions)

250 g (10 oz) cooked long-grain rice	200 g (8 oz) cooked peas
5 tomatoes	seasoning
1 small onion (diced)	French dressing with a few drops
1/4 lettuce	of Worcester sauce added

Remove the eyes, blanch, peel and dice the tomatoes. Combine with the other ingredients. Dress on crisp leaves of lettuce.

Coleslaw (ten portions)

500 ml (1 pint) mayonnaise	2 medium onions (shredded)
750 g (1 1/2 lb) white cabbage	seasoning
200 g (8 oz) carrot	

1. Remove the outside leaves of the cabbage, wash and drain well. Cut into quarters, remove the stalk and shred finely, removing any course leaf ribs.

2. The carrot may be grated, cut into fine julienne, or shredded on a mandolin or food processor.
3. Combine the cabbage, onion, and carrot, season and cohere with mayonnaise.

Coleslaw may be enhanced by the addition of such spices as cumin or coriander, or by fruit such as pineapple.

Apple and fennel coleslaw (ten portions)

200 g (8 oz) fennel	1 tsp fennel seeds
200 g (8 oz) white cabbage	seasoning
200 g (8 oz) carrot	fennel fronds or walnuts to garnish
3 green apples	

Dressing:

50 ml (2 fl oz) walnut oil	125 ml (1/4 pint) mayonnaise
25 ml (1 fl oz) cider vinegar	

1. Finely shred the cabbage and fennel. Peel and grate the carrots. Peel and core the apples, and dice finely.
2. Place the fennel seeds in a bowl and add the cabbage, apple, carrots and fennel.
3. Mix together the cider vinegar and oil and add. Toss briefly and drain. Cohere with the mayonnaise and season.

Vegetable salad (*salade russe*) (ten portions)

500 g (1 lb) carrots	100 g (4 oz) peas
200 g (8 oz) turnip	50 ml (2 fl oz) vinaigrette
200 g (8 oz) French beans	250 ml (1/2 pint) mayonnaise

1. Wash and peel the carrots and turnip; cook whole separately, refresh and dice into 1/2 cm (1/4 in) cubes.
2. Top, tail and cook the beans, and cook the peas. Cut the beans into 1 cm (1/2 in) lozenges (diamonds).
3. Combine all the well-drained vegetables, mix with the vinaigrette, season and cohere with mayonnaise.
4. Garnish with slices of beetroot and chopped hard-boiled egg.

Compound salads

Compound salads are made from a combination of ingredients which are not necessarily salad items. Most compound salads can be grouped under the following headings:

Fruit-based Fruit are the main ingredient.

Vegetable-based Vegetables are the main ingredient.

Meat-based Meat or poultry are the main ingredient.

Fish-based Fish and/or shellfish are the main ingredient.

These categories encompass most compound salads, but by no means all; other kinds of salad can be based on rice or pasta, and some may not fit readily into any group. 'Miscellaneous' salads include those made with cheese, for example cottage cheese or mozzarella, and ones which combine, say, meat and fruit or fish and fruit. The list of compound salads is almost endless, but some of the most well-known examples are included here. The points for consideration when preparing salad items are the same as for single salads.

Meat-based compound salads

Meat salad (*salade de viandes*) (ten portions)

500 g (1 lb) thinly-sliced cooked red meat	50 g (2 oz) gherkin cut into julienne
200 g (8 oz) tomatoes	chopped parsley
1 clove of garlic	English mustard-flavoured
50 g (2 oz) shredded onion	vinaigrette
200 g (8 oz) cooked French beans	seasoning

1. Blanch, refresh, peel and remove the seeds from the tomatoes. Cut the flesh into julienne.
2. Crush the garlic, cut the beans into lozenges, and cut the meat into julienne.
3. Combine all the ingredients and dress with vinaigrette.

Carmen salad (*salade carmen*) (ten portions)

8 red peppers (pimentos), grilled, skinned and diced	200 g (8 oz) cooked and refreshed long-grain rice
350 g (12 oz) diced white of chicken	fresh tarragon (French)
100 g (4 oz) cooked peas	seasoning
	French dressing

Combine the ingredients except the tarragon, and dress with the vinaigrette. Arrange on lettuce leaves and sprinkle with chopped tarragon.

This salad benefits from being allowed to stand for a few hours in the fridge; this allows the rice to take the flavour of the dressing. This salad may also be prepared with tinned pimentos.

Beatrice salad (*salade Beatrice*) (ten portions)

500 g (1lb) cooked breast of chicken	20 asparagus tips (cooked)
350 g (12 oz) cooked potatoes	250 ml (½ pint) mayonnaise (with a tbsp
25 g (1 oz) truffle	of ready-mixed English mustard added)

1. Cut the chicken, potatoes and asparagus stalks (reserving the points) into thin batons. Combine and cohere with the mustard-flavoured mayonnaise.

2. Dress on lettuce leaves and garnish with the asparagus tips and julienne of truffle (garnishing paste can be used as a cheaper alternative to truffle).

Egyptian salad (*salade egyptienne*) (ten portions)

350 g (12 oz) long-grain rice (cooked as a pilaff and cooled)
150 g (6 oz) chicken livers
100 g (4 oz) ham
100 g (4 oz) mushrooms
50 g (2 oz) peas

4 red peppers (grilled, peeled and diced)
4 tomatoes (concasse)
10 artichoke bottoms (tinned or cooked)

1. Sauté the chicken livers and mushrooms; blanch and refresh the peas.
2. Dice the cooked ham, livers and mushrooms.
3. Combine all the ingredients except the artichokes; season and dress in the artichoke bottoms.

Fruit-based compound salads

Salade mimosa (ten portions)

8 oranges
150 g (6 oz) grapes
4 bananas

200 ml (½ pint) cream
2 – 3 lettuces
juice of 1 lemon

1. Peel and segment the oranges, peel and de-pip the grapes, dice the banana into ½ cm (¼ in) cubes.
2. Marinate the fruit in the lemon juice, then drain well and add the cream.
3. Wash and drain the lettuce, separate out the hearts and use the outside leaves to line the salad container, placing the lettuce hearts in the centre. Dress the lettuce hearts with the salad.

Note: To peel grapes, place in a hot bowl or shallow pan on top of the stove, and revolve the pan continuously for approximately 2 minutes. Remove the grapes from the pan/bowl and allow to cool slightly before peeling off the skin with a small knife.

Salade japonaise (ten portions)

1 kg (2¼ lb) tomatoes (concasse)
750 g (1½ lb) pineapple
juice of 2 oranges and 1 lemon
2 – 3 lettuces

caster sugar
200 ml (½ pint) cream
seasoning

1. Peel and remove the stalk from the fresh pineapple, dice into ½ cm (¼ in) cubes.
2. Mix together the pineapple, lemon juice and sugar, allow to marinate for approximately 20 minutes.
3. Add the tomato, orange juice and seasoning, drain and cohere with the cream. Dress on lettuce hearts or in half oranges.

Waldorf salad (*salade Waldorf*) (ten portions)

1 medium celeriac or 2 small heads of celery	lemon juice
5 russet apples	1 lettuce
20 peeled walnut halves	250 ml (½ pint) mayonnaise

1. Peel the celeriac and cut into ½ cm (¼ in) cubes, or strip the celery of any tough fibres by lightly running a potato peeler along the length of the celery, then dice as for celeriac.
2. Peel and remove the core from the apples, then dice as for the celeriac. Dice half the walnuts.
3. Marinate the diced apple in lemon juice, drain and mix with the celery/celeriac and the diced walnuts.
4. Cohere with the mayonnaise, dress on lettuce leaves and garnish with the remaining walnut halves.

This salad can also be presented in hollowed-out apples.

Salade Dalila (ten portions)

5 bananas	250 ml (½ pint) mayonnaise
5 dessert apples	lemon juice
1 head of celery	1 lettuce

1. Wash and strip the celery of any tough fibres by lightly running a potato peeler along the length of the celery then cut into julienne.
2. Peel and dice the apples and bananas into ½ cm (¼ in) cubes and toss in a little lemon juice.
3. Drain and cohere with the mayonnaise. Dress on lettuce leaves.

Vegetable-based compound salads

Salade Andalouse (ten portions)

10 tomatoes	2 onions
4 red peppers	chopped parsley
250 g (8 oz) plain boiled rice	French dressing
4 cloves garlic	few drops of Worcestershire sauce

1. Blanch, refresh, and peel the tomatoes; cut into quarters and remove the seeds.
2. Grill, peel and de-seed the peppers, cut into julienne.
3. Crush the garlic and finely dice the onions.
4. Combine the dry ingredients and dress with French dressing to which a few drops of Worcester sauce has been added.

This salad will benefit from being allowed to marinate for a period of 4–6 hours in a refrigerator.

Salade Niçoise (ten portions)

500 g (1 lb) cooked French beans	350 g (12 oz) potatoes
50 g (2 oz) anchovy fillets	50 g (2 oz) black stoned olives
25 g (1 oz) capers	200 ml (½ pint) vinaigrette
10 tomatoes	seasoning

1. Roughly turn the potato to an even size; cook, refresh and slice into ½ cm (¼ in) slices.
2. Blanch, peel and de-seed the tomatoes, cut into eighths.
3. Rinse the capers and squeeze dry to remove any stale vinegar.
4. Cut two-thirds of the drained anchovy fillets into julienne, and cut the French beans into lozenges.
5. Combine all the ingredients, apart from some of the olives, anchovies and capers. Season and add the vinaigrette. Garnish with the remaining anchovies, olives and capers.

Bagatelle salad (*salade bagatelle*) (ten portions)

500 g (1 lb) carrots	200 ml (½ pint) vinaigrette
200 g (8 oz) white mushrooms	dressing
20 asparagus tips	1 lettuce

1. Wash, peel and re-wash the carrots, then cut into fine julienne on a mandolin grater or in a food processor.
2. Float the mushrooms in a bowl of cold water to clean; drain, slice thinly and cut into fine julienne.
3. Cook the asparagus until it is just done and cut the stalks into julienne, retaining the points for garnish.
4. Mix together the carrots, mushrooms and asparagus stalks, season and dress with vinaigrette.
5. Arrange on lettuce leaves and garnish with the reserved asparagus points.

American salad (*salade américaine*) (ten portions)

10 tomatoes	10 hard-boiled eggs
1 kg (2¼ lb) potatoes	200 ml (½ pint) vinaigrette dressing
½ a head of celery	1 lettuce
200 g (8 oz) onion rings	seasoning

1. Blanch, peel and slice the tomatoes; blanch and refresh the onions.
2. Roughly turn the potatoes to an even size; boil, refresh and slice into ½ cm (¼ in) slices.
3. Wash and strip the celery of any tough fibres by lightly running a potato peeler along the length of the celery, then cut into julienne.
4. Mix the tomatoes, celery, potatoes and onions, season and dress with the vinaigrette.
5. Dress on lettuce leaves and garnish with chopped hard-boiled egg.

Spanish salad (*salade espagnole*) (ten portions)

200 g (8 oz) cooked French beans   200 g (8 oz) onion rings
10 tomatoes   1 lettuce
100 g (4 oz) mushrooms   200 ml (½ pint) vinaigrette
5 red peppers (pimentos)   dressing

1. Blanch and peel the tomatoes, cut into eighths.
2. Float the mushrooms in a bowl of cold water to clean; drain and thinly slice.
3. Cut the beans into 3 cm (1 in) lozenges.
4. Grill and peel the pimentos and cut into thin batons.
5. Mix together the tomatoes, onions, mushrooms and beans, season and add the vinaigrette.
6. Dress on lettuce leaves and garnish with sliced mushrooms.

Fish-based compound salads

Fish salad (*salade de poisson*) (ten portions)

750 g (1½ lb) mixed cooked   2 onions (finely diced)
   fish   250 ml (½ pint) mayonnaise
125 ml (¼ pint) vinaigrette   1 lettuce
25 g (1 oz) fresh dill   seasoning

1. Flake the cooked fish and add the onion.
2. Wash, drain and chop half the dill and add.
3. Toss in the vinaigrette, drain and season.
4. Cohere with mayonnaise.
5. Dress on lettuce leaves and garnish with the remaining dill.

Mignon salad (*salade Mignon*) (ten portions)

500 g (1 lb) peeled and picked   75 ml (3 fl oz) cream
   shrimps   1 lettuce
10 artichoke bottoms   truffle or garnishing paste
200 ml (½ pint) mayonnaise   seasoning and cayenne pepper

1. Dice the artichoke bottoms and add to the shrimps.
2. Lightly whip the cream to the same texture as the mayonnaise.
3. Season with salt and cayenne pepper.
4. Cohere with the mayonnaise and cream.
5. Dress on lettuce leaves and garnish with julienne of truffle or paste.

Tuna salad (*salade thon*) (ten portions)

500 g (1 lb) tuna (cooked – fresh or tinned)	500 g (1 lb) cooked potato
500 g (1 lb) tomatoes	250 ml (½ pint) vinaigrette
12 spring onions	1 lettuce

1. Roughly turn the potatoes to an even size; cook, refresh and slice.
2. Flake the tuna.
3. Blanch, peel and slice the tomatoes; cut the spring onions into 3 cm (1 in) lengths.
4. Dress alternate slices of tomato, potato and tuna on lettuce leaves, coat with vinaigrette.

Salades chaudes/tièdes (hot/warm salads)
(see also Hors-d'œuvre, p. 240)

This type of salad may be served as a single hors-d'œuvre, as a main course or offered at the last minute on a buffet. The salads are prepared with leaf salad or vegetables, combined with hot items (usually meat, poultry or seafood) and warm dressings. The heat will cause some salad ingredients to lose their crispness, but this is not necessarily a bad thing. There are three ways to prepare hot salads: the first method is to place the hot items on top of a ready-prepared and dressed salad; the second method is to toss the hot items in the dressing and add to the salad; and the third way is to add the salad items to the pan used to cook the hot items along with the dressing at the last minute.

Dressings for hot salads are usually made by adding a flavoured vinegar at the last minute to the pan in which the hot items have been cooked, and mixing with the oil and juices in the pan. Alternatively, warm separately and then add. The salad is enhanced by the meat, poultry, game, fish or shellfish juices that are exuded during cooking. Lemon juice, cream and spices such as coriander, celery seeds and caraway seeds can also be used to flavour dressings.

The types of commodities suitable for hot salads include: strips of ham, bacon, poultry and game breasts, and livers; fish such as salmon, tuna and smoked salmon; shellfish such as scampi, scallops, oysters and shrimps; bread in the form of croutons, often flavoured with garlic; mushrooms such as oyster mushrooms, shitake and wild mushrooms, again often flavoured with garlic. Fillets of beef and lamb cut into batons are also popular.

Other warm salads that can be served on a bed of mixed salad leaves include:

- A selection of seafood or shellfish with a reduction of *fumet de crustaces*. Serve with salad and lemon dressing.
- Lightly sautéed breast of pigeon on salad, dressed with balsamic vinegar.
- Fillet of beef with finely-diced onion, fried in butter with lemon juice and sour cream.
- Asparagus tips with slices of fried mozzarella.
- Lardons of bacon fried with mushrooms and diced jacket potato.

Sample warm salad recipe (ten portions)

1 kg (2 lb) salad leaves – Frisée (curly endive), sorrel, swiss chard, lambs lettuce, oakleaf lettuce, lollo rosso lettuce, spinach leaves, watercress, chicory, corn salad (use either one type of salad leaf or a combination of different types)

500 g (1 lb) fish or shellfish, meat, poultry or game (cut into cubes or strips)
200 – 250 ml (8 – 10 fl oz) oil
125 – 150 ml (5 – 6 fl oz) white wine vinegar or 50 – 100 ml (2 – 4 fl oz) lemon juice

Warm mozzarella salad (ten portions)

10 – 12 tomatoes
1 kg (2 lb) mozzarella
4 cloves garlic

25 g (1 oz) fresh basil
250 ml (½ pint) olive oil

1. Wash and slice the tomatoes. Marinate in the oil with the crushed garlic for 10 – 20 minutes.
2. Lightly grill the sliced mozzarella and arrange alternately with the drained tomatoes.
3. Place the oil and garlic that was used to marinate the tomatoes in a pan to warm; add two-thirds of the basil leaves that have been chopped (reserving the other leaves whole for garnish).
4. Pour over the warmed dressing and garnish with the whole basil leaves. Serve immediately.

Fattoush (a Middle Eastern salad) (ten portions)

1 iceberg lettuce (shredded to chiffonnade)
10 quartered tomatoes
1 diced cucumber
12 spring onions, cut at an angle
24 capers

12 black olives, stoned and halved
25 g (1 oz) chopped mint
25 g (1 oz) coriander leaves
12 g (½ oz) chopped parsley
5 slices of toasted French or wholemeal bread

Dressing:
juice of 2 lemons
50 ml (2 fl oz) olive oil
50 ml (2 fl oz) herb or wholegrain mustard

12 g (½ oz) fresh chopped mint
3 cloves of garlic

1. Mix together dressing ingredients except the mint.
2. Mix salad ingredients in a bowl and pour over the dressing and toss.
3. Toast the bread, cool slightly then brush/rub with garlic, mint and olive oil on both sides. Flash under the salamander or place in the oven to reheat.
4. Remove the crusts, dice and sprinkle over the salad. Garnish with black olives.

Salamagundy salad (ten portions)

600 g (1¼ lb) chicken (shredded)
200 g (8 oz) curly endive
5 oranges (in segments)
200 g (8 oz) cooked beetroot
   (in thin batons)
100 g (4 oz) ham (in thin batons)
100 g (4 oz) grapes (blanched
   and peeled)

5 hard-boiled eggs
50 g (2 oz) nuts
125 ml (5 fl oz) sunflower oil
½ litre (1 pint) honey and lemon
   dressing (see Chapter 7,
   Dressings, p. 190)

1. Wash the endive, wash and cook the beetroot
2. Skin and bone the chicken and cut into strips.
3. Blanch and peel the grapes. Place the eggs in a pot of cold water, bring to the boil; cook for 10 minutes, refresh immediately for at least 10 minutes.
4. Prepare the salad dressing.
5. Place the endive, grapes, beetroot and orange segments in a bowl and dress with the salad dressing.
6. Heat the oil in a frying pan; add the seasoned chicken and sauté until just cooked. Add the ham and diced hard-boiled egg and heat gently.
7. Place a portion of salad in the centre of a plate, spoon over the hot items and garnish with the nuts.

Warm pigeon breast salad with wild mushrooms (ten portions)

10 pigeon breasts, trimmed
   and skinned
500 g (1 lb) mixed salad leaves
100 g (4 oz) dried wild mushrooms
   (cepes, bolets, etc.)

75 ml (3 fl oz) white wine vinegar
250 ml (8 fl oz) sunflower oil
sea salt and black pepper

1. Cover mushrooms with boiling water and allow to soak for approximately one hour, then drain (reserve the soaking liquor for other uses).
2. Heat the oil and add the seasoned pigeon breasts. Cook over a medium heat until the outsides are browned and the insides still pink; remove from the pan, drain and keep warm.
3. Add the mushrooms to the pan and allow to cook gently.
4. Wash and drain the salad leaves and place into ten piles. Carve the pigeon breast lengthways into thin slices and fan out over the salad leaves.
5. Add the white wine vinegar to the mushrooms, season, bring to the boil and spoon over the pigeon breasts and salad.

Healthy eating: government guidelines

Although salads are considered 'healthy', modifying some of the ingredients used in their preparation can provide an even healthier dish. Two reports by UK government advisory bodies (NACNE and COMA) both agree on the following recommendations:

- We need to lower our salt intake.
- We need to increase our fibre consumption.
- We need to lower our fat intake.

The British diet is far too high in salt: official figures vary, but on average we ingest three times the recommended amount. A high salt intake can contribute to high blood pressure, heart attacks and strokes. We also eat too much fat and not enough fibre. Saturated fat can lead to an increase in cholesterol levels, also causing heart problems. By increasing our fibre intake we can lower the risk of problems to do with the digestive tract, such as cancer of the colon. A healthier diet can be achieved by using monosaturated oils such as olive oil, using low fat yoghurt in place of mayonnaise, and reducing our salt intake (see Chapter 8, Gamashio, p. 220).

TEN

Buffets

Introduction

Up until the 1950s most first-class restaurants featured a cold buffet display (particularly at lunchtime in the summer months) in addition to their normal menu. Nowadays this is the exception rather than the rule, and buffet service is usually offered only on special occasions, such as Christmas or by customer request at special functions. An increasing number of speciality operations offer a 'buffet-style' service, for example salad bars and carveries: however, these are basically a form of cafeteria service and do not fall into the category of traditional buffet-style service. Types of buffet can vary from ones which offer simple finger-sized pieces (see Hors-d'œuvre Moscovite, p. 204) to the traditional, classical buffet which features a large variety of elaborately-decorated and garnished joints, fish, game, poultry, shellfish and other dishes.

Whatever the style of buffet, the main thing to remember is that as wide a variety of items as possible should be presented in an attractive, fresh manner: the display should be equally pleasing to the eye and the palate. A list of suitable dishes for buffet service is given in this chapter, but do not forget to consider dishes which are normally served hot but can successfully be offered cold, for example fricassees, curries, breaded lamb cutlets and deep-fried items such as scampi, chicken, croquettes, etc. Hot entrées, particularly during the winter months, are also a good addition, for example goulash, stroganoff, fish pie and chicken pie. If holding hot dishes on a buffet, the temperature should not drop below 63°C.

Room layout and arrangement

The quantity and layout of tabling will depend on the following factors:

- The amount of space available.
- The number of persons to be served.
- The style of service, i.e. pre-portioned and prepared for full self service, or carved and assisted service.
- The time allowed for service.

255

- Accessibility of the buffet to guests.
- Accessibility for staff to clear and replenish without causing disruption or inconvenience.

For small numbers, one table, either long, oblong, square or round, is usually the most convenient; for larger numbers, a more efficient service will be had if the buffet is divided into separate sections as follows: hors-d'œuvre/soup; main meats; fish; salads; dessert and cheeses; non-alcoholic beverages. Wines and spirits can be dispensed from a separate point. The main buffet display should, if possible, be placed in a position which will be seen by all the guests as they enter the room, giving an immediate favourable impression. Sufficient space must be allowed behind the tables for staff to serve and pass each other.

The buffet should be dressed so that all creases in the cloths, on top and at the front, are in line, the ends neatly boxed, and the front of the cloth to within $1^{1}/_{2}$ cm of the floor. A raised section in the centre of the table is an effective way to highlight a single centrepiece or a collection of decorated pieces, perhaps a salmon or boar's head or a fruit or flower arrangement. A raised section can be constructed using boxes and boards which are neatly boxed-in with tablecloths. It helps to highlight the centrepiece with a spotlight. Most of the decorated items on display should be tilted towards the customer by using upturned plates, saucers etc. The front of the table may be hung with loops of flowers, coloured ribbons and bows.

Assembly

The assembling and positioning of the dishes on the buffet is the responsibility of the restaurant staff in liaison with the chef du froid or garde manger, who is responsible for the preparation and garnishing of the dishes. The centrepiece is of course the main focal point and the other items should be arranged around it. The buffet will have greater visual impact if the different types of food are alternated along the run, e.g. fish, butcher's meats, game and poultry. For initial speed of service and to preserve the appearance of the buffet for as long as possible, whole decorated pieces should be surrounded by decorated portions which mirror the decoration of the main displayed item. This means that the main item remains intact for a good length of time, allowing the guests to enjoy the display for longer.

All items offered for self-service must be positioned in such a way so as to ensure that the customer can serve themselves comfortably, without having to reach. Sauces must be placed near or next to the item which it accompanies. Bread and butter should be laid out at various intervals so that the customer does not have to backtrack or go the whole length of the buffet unnecessarily. In addition, a sufficient number of plates of the correct sizes must be readily available on or near to the buffet, together with napkins, cutlery and a selection of appropriate condiments.

If time is short or the numbers are large, it is advisable to split the buffet into several sections, each on a separate table(s), e.g. hors-d'œuvres and starters can be positioned on two or three tables around the room so that diners do not have to queue in one line; and the same for entrées, salads and sweets, etc. Another way to handle large numbers is to have several small, complete buffets, each identical to the other, in various parts of the room. This divides the number of customers into manageable groups. The four or five buffet tables at the beginning of the service can be amalgamated into one or two tables as the pressure of numbers becomes less.

Service

The type of service necessary will depend on the style of buffet, for example a finger buffet will usually only require assistance by the restaurant staff in clearing and replenishment of items. Carved buffets based on pre-portioned items accompanied by salads and vegetables are usually staffed by the restaurant staff, with perhaps a chef to stand behind the buffet table whose job it is to replenish items from the kitchen and assist the customer in his or her selection. The restaurant staff assist in the serving of such items as desserts and cheese, the offering of sauces and accompaniments and the service of beverages, for example punch, wine, juice, coffee and petit fours.

The decorated carved buffet is when the chef is really needed. On such occasions, it is important that the chef presents a good appearance; too often the glory of a decorated buffet is marred by a lack of care by the chef in his or her appearance. An experienced chef du froid or larder chef will have a dress uniform for such occasions, but this is not always the case when commis are employed for this task. As well as looking professional, the chef(s) must be able to describe the items with confidence and have experience in dealing with the public. This is also an ideal time for more senior chefs to wear or display any medals or ribbons which they have won.

Buffet styles

Finger buffets

This is the most common type of buffet and is otherwise known as a cocktail buffet. An almost limitless range of items may be included in this style of buffet, and it is usually the job of the chef to compile a menu which takes into account the customer's budget. The price, of course, will reflect the cost of commodities, the amount of preparation which is involved, and whether the customer requires a snack to accompany drinks or a more substantial offering.

Some examples of items that may be included in a finger buffet include:

- All items suitable for hors-d'œuvre Moscovite (see hors-d'œuvre, p. 204)
- Bouchées, (small puff pastry cases) filled with chicken, prawns, seafood, curried vegetables, ham, mushrooms, etc.
- Sausage rolls
- Individual portions of quiches
- Barquettes and tartlettes
- Scotch eggs
- Pizza portions
- Small spare ribs
- Samosas
- Deep-fried fish (goujons) and shellfish (e.g. scampi)

- Sandwiches (closed and open)
- Canapés (glazed and unglazed)
- Items on sticks such as chipolatas, chicken livers wrapped in bacon, chicken tikka
- Various pies cut into portions, e.g. pork pie, game pie, chicken pie, gala pie
- Baked potato portions
- Crudités and dips
- Deep-fried breaded mushrooms
- Vegetarian alternatives should also be offered.

For the sweet course a few suggestions include: fresh fruit salad, trifle, fruit pies, fresh soft fruits (strawberries, raspberries, etc.) gateaux, pastries (eclairs, profiteroles, Danish, etc.), charlottes, rum babas and ice creams.

Fork or carved buffets

Fork or carved buffets are based on a selection of meats, poultry, continental sausages (salami, liver sausage, mortadella, garlic sausage, etc.) fish and shellfish; vegetarian alternatives should also be offered.

Portions should be of convenient size so that they may be eaten with just a fork. A selection of salads, usually of the single type variety such as potato salad, vegetable salad, mixed salad, coleslaw, etc., should also be included. Other suitable dishes for this type of buffet include mousses of fish or shellfish, ballotines, galantines, vegetable or meat terrines, pâtés and rillettes. For the sweet course, the same options as for a finger buffet can be served.

Fully-decorated buffets

A fully-decorated buffet allows the chef the opportunity to display his or her skill. The choice of items will be influenced partly by tradition and partly by the customer's requirements. There are certain items, however, that are associated with this style of buffet, in particular the centrepiece which can be a decorated ham, a decorated whole salmon or a boar's head. Other items on offer tend towards the more traditional form of menu, such as egg dishes, shellfish, meat, poultry, game, salad, vegetables and potatoes, pasta or rice, fruit, dessert and cheeses. As with all buffets, vegetarian alternatives should be offered.

Flowers, foliage, fruit and vegetable baskets

Foliage and flowers are often used to enhance the appearance of buffets: the thoroughly washed green foliage should be placed between the items on display and small, delicate flowers placed on top. Dishes of food that have been placed on under-flats can also be enhanced by the addition of decorative flower arrangements.

Baskets of fruit or vegetables perform several functions on a buffet table: first, it conveys to the customer a sense of freshness and quality to do with the food they are about to eat – it therefore goes without saying that only the freshest, first-grade items should be displayed; second, it provides colour and height to the display; and finally, with regard to the fruit basket, it can be offered as a healthy alternative to dessert (not to mention providing the chef with a cost effective provision). All serving staff must be briefed with regard to what to do if the customer requests an item from the display: the fruit of choice should be removed to the kitchen, prepared and then served to the customer. If the demand for fruit is great, the basket will need to be restocked.

Costing and menu planning

Cost is a major consideration when compiling a fully-decorated buffet menu, and it is not acceptable to present the customer with a fait accompli of just one menu; instead, it is far better to provide a selection of choices, each priced according to the amount of covers (i.e. people to be served), for example:

Decorated salmon for 20 covers	= 'x' amount
Decorated salmon for 40 covers	= 'x' amount
Decorated roast sirloin of beef for 20 covers	= 'x' amount
Decorated roast sirloin of beef for 40 covers	= 'x' amount
Choice of six salads	= 'x' amount
Choice of eight salads	= 'x' amount

This allows the customer, in collaboration with the chef, to choose a range of dishes, and perhaps some cheaper alternatives, for example forerib of beef in place of sirloin, crab in place of lobster, and so on. Once the range and quality of choices has been decided, then the total cost is divided by the number of covers to give a price per head.

An alternative method is to compile a range of menus which vary in price and quality, but which offer a set price per menu, for example:

Menu A (40 covers) @ 'x' amount per head.

For a more professional presentation and to make the customer's choice easier, it is advisable to produce a range of well-presented photographs which display examples of the choices on offer.

Buffet centrepieces

Ham

Raw hams, such as Parma, are not decorated, but are garnished with salad. Cooked ham, once cooled, is prepared for decorating as follows:

1. The rind is carefully and evenly removed; the soft fat is then shaped by scraping with a knife until a smooth, even covering is achieved.
2. The knucklebone is cleaned and the meat around it trimmed.

The ham is then decorated in one of four ways. The simplest method is to place the ham in a roasting dish, cover the surface with clear honey and place in a hot oven gas mark 6/200°C/400°F until glazed, basting every few minutes. This will give a clear golden glaze to the surface of the ham. The ham is often studded with cloves prior to the glazing. For presentation, the ham is garnished with pineapple or peaches, glacé cherries and salad.

The traditional English method of presenting a ham is to brush the prepared surface with English mustard, then sprinkle the surface with a covering of breadcrumbs which have been lightly browned under the salamander (artificially-coloured crumbs do not give as pleasing an appearance). A paper-frill placed around the knucklebone completes the presentation.

The third method of decoration is to prepare thoroughly the surface of the soft white fat until smooth and very even. Place the ham on a ham stand or wire cooling racks, and then leave in the refrigerator to become cold; once cold, coat the surface with two to three layers of aspic (see Hors-d'œuvre, p. 210) returning the ham to the fridge between coats. The surface is then decorated (see buffet decorating, p. 266). Once the decoration is complete, the ham is returned to the fridge, and when cold, given a few coats of aspic to seal the decoration (the decoration has a tendency to dry out and curl if not sealed).

The final method is the most complicated one but gives the most impressive finish. The ham is cooked and prepared as before but is coated with chaud-froid sauce (see Preparations, p. 198). This is done by placing the ham on a wire cooling rack over a tray with 3 cm (1 in) sides; place in a refrigerator to become very cold. Check the consistency of the chaud-froid sauce: if the sauce is warm or liquid place the pan containing the sauce in a bowl of ice and water until just on the point of setting; if cold or set, melt by placing the pan containing the sauce in a *bain-marie* of hot water, then cool in the bowl of ice and water as before. The consistency of the sauce is very important: too thin and it will run off the ham's surface, too thick and it will leave 'curtains', i.e. runs of sauce. The ham will require two to three coats, returning the ham to the fridge after each coating to become cold. Once an even surface has been achieved, the decoration may be applied directly to the surface or it may be given a coat of aspic to protect it from any colour leakage from the decoration.

Roast butcher's meats

Red meats such as beef, lamb and venison are roasted until just done (medium rare) and allowed to cool thoroughly in the refrigerator overnight. The colour of the meat can be enhanced by brushing the surface with melted meat glaze. The joint is then placed on a cooling rack over a tray, as for ham, and glazed with aspic. The fat can be decorated, the most popular is a trellis pattern, and glazed once more with aspic. Whether decorated or not, roast butcher's meats are usually garnished with artichoke bottoms filled with turned vegetables, such as carrots, turnips, peas or lozenges of French beans. The cooked vegetables are arranged neatly in the artichoke bottoms and then glazed with aspic. Pastry tartlettes may be used in place of artichoke bottoms.

The presentation of roast meats can be enhanced by carefully carving a few slices; these can be removed and glazed, as in the case of a best-end of lamb, or they can be curled over each other and glazed with the rest of the joint. This exposes the colour of the inside of the meat, which should be reddish-pink. The meat is presented on a silver flat which has previously been given a coat of light brown-coloured aspic. The bouquets of vegetables are arranged around the joint, with bunches of watercress to complete the presentation. Items suitable for this manner of presentation include: saddle of venison or lamb, forerib/sirloin of beef, loin of pork, best-end of lamb. The meat should be accompanied by an appropriate cold sauce, e.g. horseradish sauce for beef or cumberland sauce for venison.

Decorated whole fish

Salmon, trout and turbot are the main types of fish used in this style of presentation. On how to prepare the fish, see Chapter 4, p. 62; salmon, however, can be cooked in such a way as to give the impression that it is 'swimming'. Prepare the salmon in the normal way up until the point when it is to be placed in the fish kettle. Instead of placing the fish on its side, wedge it into an upright position by using round cans or moulds; curl the salmon around the cans/mould so that it forms a loose 'S' shape. Allow the fish to cool in its cooking liquor. Once cold, it will retain the 'S' shape – as if it was moving.

Trout may be presented in an upright position, but is not shaped during cooking. When cool, but not cold, split the fish along the back and remove the backbone; the head is then pushed towards the tail, causing the sides to bow out. This space can be filled with Russian salad covered with aspic; the whole presentation is then glazed with aspic.

To decorate a whole fish gently place the cooked fish on a board, and with a small knife barely cut through the skin, along the backbone and around the head behind the gills. The skin is then gently peeled back and removed. Underneath the skin, and along the back and sides, are patches of soft brown or white flesh; this is removed by gently scraping with the tip of a small knife, taking great care not to damage the surface of the flesh underneath. The eyes are also removed at this stage, if they have not already been done so before cooking. The fish is then carefully turned over and the process repeated until the space between the head and tail is smooth and clean, ready for the decoration.

The fish is now placed onto a wire cooling rack over a tray with raised sides and refrigerated prior to glazing. Once cold, the fish is given a layer of aspic and placed back in the refrigerator to set.

Meanwhile, the decoration can be prepared. In most cases the decoration will start with a fine border; this can be made from blanched and refreshed split leek leaves, lemon zest, red pimentos, truffle or garnishing paste, royale of egg, blanched and refreshed carrot, etc. The shapes should be small in size – $1/2$ – 1 mm – and even in both size and shape. The shapes are usually cut with a very sharp knife or scalpel, though dots are cut with the end of a very fine piping tube. Almost any shape may be used, but the most common are half moons, squares, diamonds, dots, triangles and rectangles. The shapes can be all the same colour or alternating colours, for example the white and green of a leek. To ensure an even border, it is a good idea to check it beforehand. The best way to do this is to lay it out on a white plate or along the edge of a white board. The chef should stand back slightly and look for any unevenness of shape or size – checking from above and to the side. It is important that the shapes are exactly the same size and are spaced equidistant from each other, otherwise the effect will be ruined.

When satisfied with the border pattern, it is time to prepare the main decoration. This is often in the form of a flower pattern, with the stems and leaves made from thin strips of blanched, refreshed and split leek leaves. The flowers are made out of bright-coloured ingredients, such as blanched, refreshed and sliced carrot, lemon peel, white of leek, red pimento, green pepper, etc. The shapes for the flower petals are usually cut with 'aspic cutters' and arranged around a centre dot or circle. It is best to arrange the design onto a plate or tray as this will allow time to perfect the arrangement. All the bits that make up the pattern must be moistened with melted aspic so that they stick to the surface of the fish. The design is transferred piece by piece from the plate to the surface of the fish. This is done by using the tip of a small sharp knife or preferably two cocktail sticks, one to pierce and move the shapes and the other to slide and hold them into position. A clean dry cloth is also needed to gently dab away any surplus aspic as the shapes are applied.

Once the design has been applied, the fish must be returned to the refrigerator to cool: this will set the aspic and attach the pattern to the fish. This is very important, as a decoration that has perhaps taken hours, will be washed away in seconds when it comes to glazing with more coats of aspic to finish and seal the pattern. This may also happen if the coating aspic is too warm and not on the point of setting.

Once the fish has been given its final coat of aspic, and been set in the fridge, it is transferred to the base or flat that it will be presented on; this may be a mirror, a silver flat, a porcelain fish plate, a block of ice or a decorated and glazed socle. The fish must have any loose or hanging aspic removed from around its edges with the tip of a small knife dipped in hot water. It is then garnished; for instance, if offering the fish as 'Bellevue' it should be surrounded with glazed stuffed eggs, and tomatoes filled with russian salad and then glazed. It is common practice either to surround the main item with portions, decorated as for the centrepiece, or to present them on a separate flat. This allows the *piece de résistance* to remain untouched until near the end of the service; it also greatly speeds up the service.

The above method is the most effective way to decorate a whole fish; however, it is also the most time consuming. An alternative method is to overlap thin slices or half circles of cucumber along the length of the fish; these are stuck in place by being passed through aspic and then glazed. Smaller fish such as trout may be piped with cold butter, natural or lightly coloured, or decorated with a simple pattern design. Certain fish such as trout, red mullet and sea bass can be stuffed, in which case the backbone is removed, and the fish is filled with a suitable stuffing. It is then lightly poached in fish stock or fish stock and wine, and presented garnished, decorated or glazed with aspic.

Boar's head

The boar's head is probably the most well-known and traditional buffet centrepiece: this is usually a pig's head made up to resemble the head of a wild boar. The head may be boned, rubbed with a mixture of salt, saltpetre, mace, cloves and juniper berries (pounded to a paste), stuffed with forcemeat as for a galantine, sewn up and cooked; but in the UK it is rarely prepared in this manner, as very few customers are prepared to eat it. It is more common for the head to be lightly cooked, decorated and presented purely as a display piece. Decorated individual portions of brawn may be offered as an alternative to consuming the head.

Lightly cook the head by poaching gently in white stock for approximately one hour, taking care to keep the ears, and other parts of the head in shape. Remove from the liquid, and if required place an item such as a carrot or potato in the mouth to keep it open (this can later be replaced by an apple); otherwise, place the head right side up on a wire cooling rack and allow to cool and drain thoroughly (preferably overnight). Once cold the head may be glazed in one of two ways: the simplest method is to mix gravy browning (blackjack) with a little melted aspic and brush over the head, building up the depth of the coating until black and shiny. The tusks can be made from apple or potato – as they need to be white; they should be soaked in sodium metabysulphate. The eyes are replaced with olives, an apple is placed in the mouth, and the muzzle, eyes and ears are given a contrasting outline of fine butter piping. The second method is to colour some aspic a deep reddish-brown, and coat the head. Proceed as for the first method, and present on a glazed and decorated socle or on a round silver flat with chopped brown aspic around the 'neck'.

It is not as easy as it once was to obtain a complete pig's head as they are often band sawed in half with the rest of the carcass, so it is wise to give your butcher warning well in advance.

Suckling pig

Prepare the suckling pig by removing the heart, liver and kidney; dice finely and fry in butter with a little diced onion. When cooked, allow to cool then mix with sausage meat, breadcrumbs, sage and diced apple, season with nutmeg, cinnamon, salt and pepper and bind with two to three eggs. Stuff the inside of the suckling pig with this mixture and sew up with a trussing needle and string. Score the rind at an angle on each side of the pig; season with salt and mignonette pepper; place in a roasting tray large enough to allow the legs, front and rear to be stretched out. Brush with oil or dripping and roast in a moderate oven gas mark 4/180°C/350°F for 20 minutes per ½ kg (1 lb), basting frequently. The skin of the pig should be light brown and crisp. Care should be taken to ensure that the extremities (ears, feet, tail, etc.) do not burn. Once cooked, allow to cool thoroughly; place on a cooling rack over a tray and glaze with light-brown coloured aspic. Present on a sloping crouton of fried bread, accompanied with bouquets of watercress and glazed apple quarters.

Decorated lobster

1 large (1 kg/2 lb) or 2 medium fresh lobsters (or you can use crawfish)	500 g (1 lb) vegetable salad 20 artichoke bottoms 1 litre (2 pints) fish aspic

1. Tie/truss the fresh lobster (frozen is not suitable) to a thin wooden board which is just larger than the lobster, stretching the tail out flat.
2. Cook in a *court bouillon* (see Chapter 4, Shellfish, p. 71). Allow to cool then remove from the cooking liquor.
3. Wipe with a cloth to remove any scum. Remove the claws and reserve.
4. Turn the lobster over on to its back and cut along the length of the tail with a pair of scissors or secateurs until the whole of the tail can be removed in one piece.
5. Place the tail and claw meat on a board and cut at an angle into collops, (½ cm

slices). Place the collops of meat on a wire rack and refrigerate until cold. Glaze the collops with aspic, then decorate each one with an identical pattern; glaze once more with aspic.

6. Mix the vegetable salad with a little melted aspic, the creamy parts of lobster flesh and trimmings, and fill the artichoke bottoms. Place a decorated collop of claw meat on top of the salad.

7. Brush the top of the shell with a little melted aspic, then lay the collops along the back, starting at the head with the largest first, eventually tapering down to the smallest collop.

8. Place the lobster shell onto a decorated socle or silver flat glazed with aspic. Surround with the artichoke bottoms.

Poultry and game

The most frequently used poultry centrepiece is a decorated galantine of chicken or duck (see Chapter 6, p. 156). This are often presented rolled but can also be presented whole, as is often the case with chicken.

Whole poached decorated chicken

1½–2 kg (3–4 lb) or more, fresh chicken	1 litre (2 pints) white chaud-froid decoration

1. Truss the chicken for poaching and gently cook in chicken stock for 15 minutes per ½ kg (1 lb). Allow to cool in the cooking liquor, drain and carefully remove the skin.

2. Place the chicken on a wire rack over a tray with sides; cool thoroughly in the fridge, then coat with white chaud-froid. Give one or two more coats, refrigerating after each application.

3. Once the chicken has been glazed with chaud-froid, the decoration may be applied directly to the surface of the bird or it may be given a coat of clear aspic and the decoration applied to the aspic (this helps prevent any discoloration of the sauce due to colour leaking from the decoration.

4. The chicken is cooled once more prior to being given its final coat of aspic, sealing in the decoration.

Unless the whole chicken has been prepared as a galantine, it is not normally served to the customer; the preferred option is to recreate the design of the bird on suprêmes or ballotines of chicken and to display these around the whole bird and serve to the customer.

Roast poultry and game

Choose fresh even-shaped birds. Truss and roast and allow to cool. Cut down each side of the breastbone and around the sides to remove the breasts – try and keep them intact. Fill the space left by removing the bones with pâté (for chicken, duck, etc.) or game farce (for game birds). Place the breasts on a board and slice them at an angle into ½ cm (¼ in) slices. Then carefully lay them on top of the pâté/farce to reform the breasts in a step pattern. Refrigerate, glaze with the appropriate aspic (for game birds use melted game aspic or aspic with the addition of meat glaze) and allow to set in the fridge. If desired, decorate and glaze with a final coat of aspic.

Chicken can be decorated any way you wish, but ducks and ducklings are usually decorated with orange slices, segments and zest and garnished with glazed orange quarters. Present game birds such as pheasant, partridge and grouse on a crouton that has been spread with game farce and garnish with game chips and watercress.

Carving

Buffet centrepieces such as roast butcher's meats, roast poultry and game birds may have a few slices carved and decorated, but it is not good practice to spoil the presentation by serving these to the customer, at least initially; once the majority of people have been served, and the display has been fully enjoyed, then the centrepiece can be removed to the kitchen and carved if required. In the meantime, serve decorated individual breasts or portions (these should surround the centrepiece) or provide a tray of ready-carved meat adjacent to the display piece.

Only when there is a limited number of customers or a very high staff to customer ratio is it possible to carve for each individual customer. It is important that carving is taken into consideration when preparing the centrepiece; any bones that may hinder carving should be removed, along with string, skewers, etc; some items may be boned entirely after cooking.

Presentation of pies, pâtés and terrines

Pâtés are usually presented simply: the surface of a whole pâté is decorated with fresh herbs, fruits and/or vegetables and glazed with a light brown aspic. Pâté may be sliced to order or glazed slices may be pre-prepared and placed around the main display. Terrines are often pre-sliced, leaving approximately one-third still intact; the slices are arranged so that they overlap one another. The intact piece of terrine and the slices are given a coat of light brown aspic. Whole pies are not normally glazed with aspic, but they can be brushed with a combination of meat glaze and aspic to enhance their presentation. Pies may be sliced and glazed so as to display the delights inside.

Presentation of smaller cuts and entrées

Fish fillets

There are several ways to present a fillet of fish, depending on the type of fish. For instance, white fish fillets like plaice or sole may be either folded into delices or rolled into paupiettes, then placed on wire cooling racks above trays with sides and given a coat of white or pink fish chaud-froid which is then decorated and glazed with fish aspic. Smoked fish fillets such as trout and mackerel are prepared and decorated flat then glazed with fish aspic. Darnes and suprêmes are given a clear coat of fish aspic, decorated and then glazed.

Chicken suprêmes

Chicken suprêmes are one of the most popular decorated buffet items. Poach gently in chicken stock, cool and trim to an even shape. Place on a wire cooling rack over a tray and coat with white chaud-froid; decorate and glaze with aspic.

Duck breasts

These may be gently roasted, shaped and coated with brown chaud-froid. To finish decorate and glaze with aspic.

Lamb cutlets

A French-trimmed best end or rack is gently roasted, then cut into even-sized cutlets. These are given a coat of brown chaud-froid, decorated and glazed with aspic.

Guidelines for the decoration of cold buffets

1. All decoration must be edible.
2. Never use blue as a decoration colour: one of the most common mistakes is to try and represent the sea by using blue-coloured aspic. This looks artificial, particularly in comparison against the natural colours used in decoration.
3. Take care that colours do not leak and spread on to the item to be decorated.
4. The use of feathers and plumage for decoration, once popular, is now discouraged as unsterilized feathers are a health hazard and could contain bacteria and parasites. Sterile feathers can be used, but these are usually mounted on a wooden block and must not come in contact with the food.
5. All items of decoration should be passed through liquid aspic to ensure that they stick to the surface of the food; if this is not done, the decoration will be washed off when the next coat of aspic is applied.
6. The base of a flat is usually given a coat of aspic: $1/2$ cm ($1/4$ in) of liquid aspic is placed on the base of the flat which is then placed in the fridge to set. Chaud-froid sauce may also be used to line the base of a flat, this is often sealed with a thin layer of aspic.
7. The correct shape of flat will help the presentation, i.e. a long thin flat for whole salmon, round flats for circular items, etc. Mirrors are often used instead of flats as they reflect the items on display, making an excellent presentation.

Guidelines for glazing with aspic jelly

1. The item to be glazed *must* be cold.
2. The aspic must be of the correct type and consistency.
3. The aspic must be on the point of setting: this is done by allowing the aspic to cool naturally, then immersing the pan containing the aspic in a bowl of iced water.

4. The aspic must be stirred gently but constantly to prevent it setting on the sides of the pan and becoming lumpy.
5. The aspic must not be stirred too vigorously as this will cause air bubbles, and will spoil the appearance of the finished product.
6. The aspic will become thicker as it nears setting point, the pan must then be removed from the iced water and used immediately and quickly; if it begins to set, glazing must stop and the aspic remelted by the application of gentle heat. The aspic is then once more cooled to the point of setting.
7. The item to be glazed should be supported by a wire cooling rack with a tray placed underneath. After a coat of aspic has been applied, the wire rack and items must be placed over a clean tray.
8. Any aspic that remains in the base of the original tray should be melted and strained into a clean pan, cooled and used again. Discard the aspic if it becomes discoloured or clouded: it must be kept crystal clear at all times, otherwise the finished product will be spoilt.
9. Any air bubbles can be removed by pricking with the point of a warm pin.

Hygiene and buffet decoration

Aspic and gelatine are classed as high risk foods as they are the perfect medium for the growth of bacteria. As a result, great care must be taken when using either item. They should be prepared as fresh as possible, cooled rapidly and used or refrigerated immediately. The amount that is prepared should be kept to a minimum and used only on a specific item to prevent cross-contamination. There should be no need to store aspics and sauces containing gelatine, but if absolutely necessary these items can be boiled again, cooled and stored under refrigeration, but for no more than 24 hours. Items which have been stored should be re-boiled for several minutes before use.

Areas used for decoration should ideally be chilled to approximately 5°C; if this is not possible, the item should be refrigerated for a period of time and then it should not be kept out of the fridge for more than two hours. Raw and cooked food should be covered and stored separately. (See also Chapter 2, Health and Safety, p. 14.)

Socles

Socles are decorated bases that support the food and give it height, a bit like a base for a sculpture or statue, except that they are moulded, carved or shaped from edible produce. They are glazed or coated with chaud-froid and decorated to complement the item of food on display. Socles are normally prepared from rice or semolina, or in the case of game birds, a large, carved, deep-fried crouton of bread is often used. Socles are not meant to be served to the customer, and should not be overelaborate; indeed, their use in salon culiniares is frowned upon as contestants tend to concentrate too much on the socle and not enough on the actual decoration of the food.

Ice, though not technically a socle, makes a very effective base for fish and shellfish: ice can be carved or moulded. Special moulds can be purchased, but these tend to come in a limited range and design. Different sized pans or flat-bottomed bowls may be used to create a round, tiered effect; salt sprinkled between the layers will seal the layers in place. Glazed fish or shellfish is then presented either on one base, as is usual for fish, or on various levels, which is the usual way to display shellfish. A spotlight will greatly enhance the presentation. Crushed ice may also be used around a tiered display to mount shellfish. A subtle hint of colour can be added to the ice to enhance a fish or shellfish display; this should never be blue as it will look unnatural – a slight tint of green is far more effective and acceptable to the eye.

Rice socle

Wash 1 kg (2 lb) of patna rice, place in boiling salted water for 5 minutes, drain and refresh under cold running water. Return to a thick-bottomed saucepan and add enough water to come approximately halfway up the rice; cover with a tight fitting lid and cook very gently for about 45 minutes, until dry and hard. Pass through a fine mincer or process in a food processor, then beat or knead on a moistened surface until very smooth.

Mould to the required shape with moist hands, or place in a mould that has been greased with white fat, and allow to set in the refrigerator. Once set, remove from the mould and trim to shape, for example a shallow boat which will hold a whole salmon in an upright position. Rice socles have a tendency to turn black on contact with air, they should therefore be wrapped in plastic film or a damp cloth and kept cool. Glazing with aspic or chaud-froid will also help prevent discolouration.

Semolina socle

Place sufficient stock or milk on to boil; remove from the heat and quickly rain in enough semolina to make a firm mixture, whisking continuously. Return to the heat and cook for a few minutes. Wet the inside of the moulds with water, pour in the mixture and allow to cool thoroughly (preferably overnight). Remove from the mould, trim and coat with chaud-froid and glaze with aspic. Once the socle has been given its base of aspic or chaud-froid, it is ready for decoration.

Decorating cold buffets items

The decorating of cold buffet items is a skill that is learnt, but with practice it can be elevated to an art form: an experienced chef will have an understanding of colour combinations, size and perspective, and design, all of which serve to complement the food on offer. The best designs are often the simplest, and practicality and neatness should be the main concerns.

The decoration is applied directly to the food as opposed to the garnish which is distributed around the food. Suitable items for decoration should have a natural, bright colour. Most items are blanched to make them pliable. Green-coloured items include blanched leek leaf, green beans, cucumber rind, watercress, asparagus and blanched and peeled green pepper. Leek leaves are blanched, refreshed and split into two halves; this is done by rubbing the blanched and refreshed leaves between the palms of the hands. The soft pulpy inside is removed by placing the leaf on a board and with a small knife scraping away the inside, finish with a clean cloth. Green-coloured items are used mainly for the stems and leaves of flower decoration. The stems are cut from thin strips and curled over at the top to give the impression of being weighed down by the flower head. (A common mistake in flower decoration is to place the flower head on top of a straight stalk – this does not look 'natural'.)

Red colours for decoration can come from blanched and peeled red peppers, blanched and peeled tomatoes, tinned red pimentos and carrots; coloured royale may also be used. Red is mainly used for flower petals as a contrast against the green stalks and leaves.

Designs for the decoration should be decided on in advance and the *mis en place* completed prior to the decoration being applied. This means that the shapes should be cut and the main design arranged on a plate or tray, ready for transferring onto the items to be decorated. The aspic should be ready for the decoration to be passed through it when applying to the prepared surface of the food. The shapes are lifted out of the liquid aspic with the tip of a small knife or picked up and held with one cocktail stick, another cocktail stick is used to slide and hold the shape in place. When preparing a lengthy design it is a good idea to be seated on a stool high enough to place you above the item.

Colours and preparation

For red colours, carrots are peeled, blanched whole, refreshed, then sliced thinly; a potato peeler will make nice even thin slices. Red peppers should be cut at the stalk and base-ends then down one side; open out and remove the seeds and pith. Place under a hot salamander, skin side up, until the skin bubbles and turns black; remove and place on a cool tray. Allow to cool for a few minutes, then peel off the skin with the help of a small knife. The most vivid colour is located just under the skin of the pepper, however, as the flesh tends to be too thick for decoration, place the pepper on a board, skin side down, and cut away some of the flesh horizontally with a knife, this will leave you with thin red-coloured strips which are ideal. Tinned pimentos are already skinned and only need to be sliced as for fresh peppers to form strips. Tinned pimentos are usually canned in oil, this should be removed with a clean tea towel.

Black is a more difficult colour to achieve, but can be very effective when used against a white chaud-froid background. Black truffle is the main source of black colour. The truffle is sliced extremely thinly and then cut by hand or with aspic cutters to the required shape. Truffle is, of course, very expensive, and may be substituted by truffle paste: this is a combination of truffle and cereal. Truffle garnishing paste has two drawbacks: first, it cannot be sliced as thinly as truffle and tends to break up; second, it dries out very quickly and will curl if not kept moist, for this reason it must be kept wrapped in plastic film when not in use. Other sources of black colour include black olives and pickled walnuts.

White colour may be obtained from white of leek, turnip or blanched chicory leaves; cooked egg whites (royale) is another alternative (see below). Other colours can come from blanched orange or lemon zest.

Royale

Fresh egg whites are placed in a lightly buttered mould, allowed to stand for one or two hours, then the mould is placed in a *bain-marie* in a very low oven or hot-cupboard until the white is set. During the standing time, and at the start of cooking, any air bubbles should be burst with a pin. This is a preparation that cannot be rushed and slow cooking is vital: if the heat is too high, small bubbles will form leaving small holes in the royale and making it useless for decorating.

Coloured royale is made by colouring with natural juices and purees such as spinach juice, tomato puree or egg yellow. Once cooked and cooled, the royale can be sliced with a scalpel, craft knife or razor blade. Aspic cutters may also be used to cut shapes.

Butter

Butter which has been kneaded to a smooth paste may be used to decorate items; the butter can be coloured or plain. The butter is placed in a greaseproof paper piping bag with a small opening, this is then used to pipe designs on to buffet items or to emphasize the features on a whole fish or a boar's head – the butter is piped around the eyes on a fish and around the eyes and ears on a boar's head.

Aspic cutters

Aspic cutters come in various sizes but the smallest assorted shapes are the most useful for decorating. The shapes are used mainly for producing flower petals and leaves but they can also be used for borders and patterns. The size of the cutters mean that often they are too large for smaller buffet items, especially borders, and these tend to be cut by hand with a small sharp knife or scalpel.

The cutting of shapes for bordering decorated items is best carried out with a very sharp blade. The border should be as delicate as time and skill will allow. The most effective borders are produced by cutting the leek leaf, fruit zest, carrot, etc. into strips then into small even shapes; a variety of shapes can made such as squares, rectangles, diamonds or triangles. It is important that the size and shape of the pieces are exactly the same or the appearance will not be as effective. Dots can be made by using a small plain piping nozzle, half moons by a larger plain piping nozzle. The best result is achieved by placing the squares, triangles, etc. in line, but not quite touching. The main decoration can be applied once the border is finished. Finally, the entire decoration is sealed with a final coat of crystal-clear aspic.

Hatelet / attelet pins

These are highly ornamental silver skewers which are usually placed into the top of larger buffet items. They should be decorated in such a way as to suit the food to be garnished, for example apples for pork.

Fresh flowers

Edible flowers such as courgette flowers, nasturtiums and flowers from fresh herbs, for example borage, provide colour and freshness to a presentation.

Chemising of moulds with aspic jelly

This method produces a thin layer of aspic on the inside of a dariole or similar mould. Aspic jelly which is on the point of setting is used to fill the mould; the mould is then placed into a container of iced water or crushed ice. The aspic will start to set on the sides and base of the mould. The thickness of the layer of aspic will depend on the size of the mould, and can range from 2 – 4 mm ($^1/8$ – $^1/4$ in). Once the required thickness of aspic has set, the remaining aspic is gently drained out. The mould is then placed in the fridge to completely set. The base inside the mould may now be decorated, so that when turned out the design is visible through the clear aspic. The mould is filled with mousses, forcemeats or diced items such as fish, poultry, etc. All fillings should be lightly set with gelatine or aspic to retain their shape when turned out.

The top of the mould is given a coat of aspic to seal in the contents, then placed back in the fridge to set before turning out. To turn out the contents of the mould, place the mould in a bowl of hot water until the aspic is at the point of just melting – this will only take a few seconds. Invert the mould on to a flat or plate, or, as most chefs prefer, on to the palm of the hand; gentle shaking will allow the contents to gently slide out of the mould.

Vegetarian buffet items

The following is a selection of recipes which are suitable for vegetarians.

Leek and cheese flamiche (6 – 8 portions)

250 g (8 oz) flaky pastry	60 ml ($^1/8$ pint) vegetable stock
50 g (2 oz) butter or vegetarian margarine	2 tbsp soya flour
	salt and black pepper
1 kg (2 lb) diced leeks	1 egg and 2 egg yolks
3 cloves of garlic (crushed)	sesame seeds
100 g (4 oz) vegetarian cheddar cheese	

1. Line a flan ring (20–24 cm / 8–9 in) with the pastry, reserving approximately a quarter for the top.
2. Melt the butter and sweat the leeks until tender.
3. Add the soya flour and cook out for a few minutes; remove from the heat and allow to cool slightly.
4. Return to the heat and gradually add the hot stock and bring to the boil.
5. Remove from the heat; add the grated cheese and season.
6. Fill the flan with the mixture. Roll out the remaining pastry, cut into 1 cm ($^1/2$ in)

strips and lattice the top of the flan. Brush with the beaten egg and yolks, and sprinkle with the sesame seeds.
7. Decorate the top of the flan by rolling out the remaining pastry.
8. Place in a pre-heated oven at gas mark 7/210°C/425°F for 25 – 30 minutes. This recipe may also be used to prepare individual flans.

Layered pancake galette (6 – 8 portions)

For the pancake mix:

100 g (4 oz) wholemeal flour
1 egg
250 ml (1/2 pint) milk
1 tsp of oil

salt
50 g (2 oz) vegetarian cheddar
   cheese for the topping

1. Place the egg, milk and oil in a blender and blend until smooth.
2. Add the flour and blend again.
3. Allow to stand for a minimum of 20 minutes (this allows the bran in the flour to absorb the liquid). Adjust the consistency with extra milk if required.

Spinach filling:

500 g (1 lb) spinach
25 g (1 oz) butter

1/2 tsp nutmeg
salt and mignonette pepper

Cook, drain and chop the spinach; add the melted butter, nutmeg and seasoning.

Fennel filling:

350 g (12 oz) fennel or 150 g (6 oz)
   fennel and 150 g (6 oz) finely
   diced leeks

25 g (1 oz) butter or vegetarian margarine
50 g (2 oz) vegetarian cheddar cheese
salt and mignonette pepper

Chop the fennel (or fennel and leeks) and sweat in the melted butter for 10 minutes. Liquidize until fairly smooth and add the cheese and season.

Tomato filling:

1 tbsp olive oil
1 finely-diced onion
1 clove of garlic (crushed)
350 g (12 oz) fresh tomato concasse
or 1 × a 21/2 tin of plum tomatoes,
   well drained and chopped

25 g (1 oz) tomato puree
1/2 tsp aniseed
vegetable stock or juice of tinned
   tomatoes to moisten (strained)

Heat the oil and add the onions and garlic, fry gently without colour. Add the aniseed, cook for 1 minute, and then add the tomato puree, cook a further 1 – 2 minutes. Add the tomatoes and moisten with the stock, and season.

To assemble:

1. Grease the base of a 13 cm (7 in) sprung-sided cake tin.

2. Place a pancake over the base; add half the spinach mixture and top with a pancake.
3. Add half the fennel mix and top with a pancake.
4. Add half the tomato mix and top with a pancake.
5. Repeat the above process, finishing with a pancake.
6. Top with the reserved grated cheese.
7. Cover with tinfoil and place in a preheated oven at gas mark 4/180°C/350°F for 20–30 minutes, until heated through.

Allow to relax in the tin for 20–30 minutes if to be served hot, or one hour if to be served cold, before portioning. Serve accompanied with a green salad and fennel and red pepper sauce (see recipe below).

Fennel and red pepper sauce (accompaniment for galettte)

2 deep-red peppers or 1 tin of red pimentos	1 tsp vegetable stock powder
¹/₂ tsp fennel seeds	125 ml (¹/₄ pint) dry white wine
15 g (¹/₂ oz) butter	dash of Pernod
75 g (3 oz) fennel	60 ml (¹/₈ pint) single cream
	salt and mignonette pepper

1. Place peppers on a baking sheet and bake at gas mark 5/190°C/375°F for 25–30 minutes, turning twice.
2. Remove the peppers from the oven and cover with a damp cloth for 10 minutes.
3. Peel and de-seed the peppers, then dice into large pieces (alternatively use one tin of drained red pimentos).
4. Fry the chopped fennel and fennel seeds without colour until soft.
5. Add the wine, stock powder and bring to the boil, simmer for 5 minutes.
6. Place in a blender and liquidize until smooth.
7. Strain and place in a clean pan; add the cream and Pernod and season to taste.
8. Reheat without boiling.

Vegetable samosas (10–16, depending on size)

250 g (8 oz) pastry (see Chapter 7, p. 180)	1 tsp grated root ginger
1 tbsp oil	juice of ¹/₂ lemon
1 tsp ground cumin	2 cloves of crushed garlic
1 tsp cumin seeds	250 g (8 oz) diced onion
3 tsp coriander seeds	250 g (8 oz) cooked diced potato
¹/₂ tsp turmeric	100 g (4 oz) cooked mung beans
¹/₄ tsp cayenne pepper	50 g (2 oz) raw frozen peas
1 tsp mustard seeds (yellow or black)	salt and pepper

1. Prepare pastry and allow it to relax; meanwhile, heat the oil in a saucepan and add the spices, fry gently until the seeds start to pop.
2. Add the onion, garlic and ginger and cook until soft.

3. Add the mung beans and potatoes and cook 5 minutes; add the lemon juice and seasoning, remove from the heat and allow to cool before use.
4. Work the pastry with your hands until soft and malleable, roll in one direction only giving one-eighth of a turn to each roll until you have a thickness of approximately 3 mm (1/8 in).
5. Cut to shape using a side plate, then cut across the middle of the circle of paste. Fold the edges into the centre to form a cornet shape, stick the edges with water, fill with the mixture, fold over the top and seal with water.
6. Deep-fry for 2 – 3 minutes.

To make meat samosas, substitute cooked minced lamb or mutton for the mung beans.

Vegetarian raised vegetable and hazelnut pie (ten portions)

350 g (12 oz) vegetarian hot water
   pastry (see Chapter 7, p. 179)
250 g (8 oz) diced courgettes
1 diced onion
25 g (1 oz) butter or oil
100 g (4 oz) ground hazelnuts
100 g (4 oz) wholemeal breadcrumbs

1 tsp shoyu
2 tsp fresh or 1 tsp dried rosemary
100 g (4 oz) ground brazil nuts
2 tsp fresh or 1 tsp dried marjoram
2 tbsp light tahini
250 ml (1/2 pint) vegetable stock
salt and black pepper

1. Pre heat oven to gas mark 7/210°C/425°F.
2. Fry onions until soft, add courgettes and cook for 4 – 5 minutes.
3. In a separate bowl, mix the breadcrumbs, nuts, herbs and seasoning.
4. Add the onions and courgette mixture to the breadcrumbs, add the shoyu.
5. Mix the tahini with a little stock and add to the filling; bind with the stock until the mixture just holds together in the hand. Line the tin with two-thirds of the paste, pack in the filling raising up towards the middle.
6. Dampen the edges with water and cover the top with the remaining pastry; decorate with pastry leaves and glaze with eggwash (or for a vegan version, egg substitute).
7. Cook at gas mark 7/210°C/425°F for 20 minutes, then at gas mark 5/190°C/375°F for 50 minutes.

If preparing the pie in advance, cook for 20 minutes at 210°C and then freeze; to complete the cooking, thaw overnight in the fridge then cook at 190°C for 50 minutes. To finish with jelly, add 1/2 tsp of agar-agar to 125 ml (1/4 pint) boiling vegetable stock.

Tortillas (8 – 10)

Tortillas (see Chapter 7, p. 188)
Mexican tomato sauce (see Chapter 7,
   p. 189)

Refritos (see Chapter 7, p. 189)
Green salad

To assemble: place tomato sauce on the base of a tortilla and add the bean mix (refrito), top with fresh green salad.

Index